ZION
Seeking the City of Enoch

Larry Barkdull
Lance Richardson · Ron McMillan

KenningHouse
Orem, Utah

KenningHouse is a publishing imprint of Barkdull Marketing, Inc.

Designed by Douglass Cole
Edited by Lyle Fletcher
Typography by SunRise Publishing

Manufactured in the United States of America
10 9 8 7 6 5 4 3 2 1

Library of Congress Catalog Card Number: 98-88267
ISBN 1-889025-01-1

To Elizabeth, Jozet, Bonnie

Especially inscribed to Robert and Helene Manookin

ଓ

Special thanks are extended to Bruce and Janiel Miller, Ted Gibbons, Eileen Kump, Lyle Fletcher, Larry Johnston, and Origin Book Sales.

people and places

Abiah   Wife of Ebanel. Rabunel's mother who died in the drought when Rabunel was a child. (Ăb ī′ äh)

Aramites   A people conquered by Mahijah at the beginning of his reign. (Ăr′ ä mītz)

Asher   A Watcher from the land of Nod.

Baruch   Rabunel's competitor. Husband of Leah. Father of Joshua and Rachel. (Bäh rook′)

Benjamin   Rabunel's oldest child. Married to Sarah. Father to Nathaniel.

Cain   The son of Adam and Eve who killed his brother Abel. Founder of the land of Nod.

Cainan   Not to be confused with Canaan. A land by the east sea founded by Enos, Adam's grandson, who named it for his son Cainan. There the patriarchs Enos, Cainan, Mahalaleel, and Jared lived and reared families for many generations. Enoch called it "a righteous land to this day." The birthplace of Enoch, Simeon, and Ebanel. (Kān′ ăn)

Chaz   The prince of Shum. Mahijah's son. (Chăz)

Council   The governing body of Shum.

Danbenihah   A former judge from the land of Abel. (Dăn běn ī′ häh)

Ebanel   Father of Rabunel. Son of Simeon. A shepherd who as a youth came to the valley of Shum from the land of Cainan. (Ěb ăn ěl′)

Enoch   Born to Jared in the land of Cainan. The "seventh from Adam," having the direct birthright. The great-grandfather of Noah. At twenty-five years of age, he was called by God and ordained by Adam to call the world to repentance. He established a city called ZION when he was sixty-five.

Enos   Rabunel's son and third child.

Eve   Rabunel's daughter and youngest child.

Gad   The captain of the Rahaj.

Grove	A secret place where the Watchers and the Rahaj took oaths and practiced acts of debauchery.
Hanannihah	The land where Micah managed mines. (Hăn ăn ī′ häh)
Haner	The destination of Rabunel's trading journey. (Hā nûr)
Jared	Brother to Rabunel. Father to Miriam.
Jerel	Second son of Rabunel. (Jĕr ĕl′)
Joshua	Son of Baruch and Leah.
Leah	Wife of Baruch.
Mahijah	The king of Shum. (Mäh hī′ jäh)
Micah	A former overseer of the mines of Hanannihah.
Miriam	Rabunel's niece. Daughter of Jared.
Moriah	Wife of Rabunel. (Mōr ī′ äh)
Nathaniel	Rabunel's infant grandson. Son of Benjamin and Sarah.
Nod	A land settled by Cain, son of Adam and Eve. A militant people.
Omner	A neighboring community to the land of Sharon. Place where Baruch traded. (Ŏm′ nûr)
Rabunel	Main character. Son of Ebanel. Grandson of Simeon. (Räh boo nĕl′)
Rachel	Daughter of Baruch and Leah. Love interest of Jerel.
Rahaj	The military of Shum. (Räh häj′)
Ramurah	The first king of the land of Shum. Son of Shum. Father of Mahijah. (Ră mūr′ äh)
Sarah	Wife of Rabunel's oldest son, Benjamin. Mother to Nathaniel.
Sharon	A land adjacent to Shum whose people Shum considered to be enemies. It became the envy of Mahijah for its incredible wealth.
Shum	A land founded, after a global drought, by a man named Shum. It became a prosperous tent city under Shum's son Ramurah and Shum's grandson Mahijah. (Shŭm)
Simeon	Grandfather of Rabunel. Father of Ebanel. The leader of the Watchers.
Watchers	False priests.

For I do know the mysteries of the holy ones; for he, the Lord, has revealed (them) to me and made me know—and I have read (them) in the heavenly tablets. Then I beheld the writing upon them that one generation shall be more wicked than the other, until a generation of righteous ones shall arise, wickedness shall perish, sin shall disappear from upon the earth, and every good thing shall come upon her.

—1 Enoch 106:19–107:1. Also found on a Dead Sea Scrolls fragment in Cave 4 near Qumran. See note 1 in references.

In the year 647, calculated from the time Adam and Eve left the Garden, a thousand-year effort was begun to prevent the earth's inhabitants from being annihilated by flood. A young prophet named Enoch was the key messenger of the warning. In a world where the people were almost wholly given over to perversions and wickedness, Enoch raised a city of holiness, a place of consummate peace, a society that subsequent generations would long for and attempt to duplicate. During the millennia of the earth's existence, the desire for that kind of society would permeate literature and occupy the thought of great people. Some in ancient times called it the City of Enoch, but Enoch called it ZION. It existed on the earth over 300 years before it was wholly "taken up into heaven" by God. Tradition and prophecy abound that in the seventh millennium, Zion will again be established on the earth and bring peace to a troubled world.

living among wolves

CB

I am Rabunel. This story is mine. I lived it, every part.

I first saw the she-bear out of the corner of my eye, a black flash bursting from the shadows of the hollow, crushing everything in her path. My son, Jerel, and I may have disturbed her den. I do not know. On this autumn afternoon near the first snap of winter, we had crossed over the mountain pass and entered the hollow through a narrow gully. We had made excellent time, but we knew we must get off the mountain before the snows came. The hollow was to be our camp that night. We would climb out the next morning, traversing a short but steep ascent, then follow the gentle descent to the foothills and into the warm valley where we lived. I wanted to hurry home with the satchel of gems I carried—a fortune beyond the comprehension of anyone in Shum. Jerel had a reason to hurry home too—a young woman named Rachel, whom he hoped to marry.

The bear charged us. Jerel dodged, but her giant paw caught him at the shoulder and sent him sprawling. The horse I was riding panicked and bolted into scrub oak by the high wall of the hollow, the tree limbs pounding into me. I felt as though my lungs would burst. The bear rushed me, her mouth open, showing her teeth. I drove my heels into the horse's flanks and tried to turn it, but the horse reared up, wild-eyed, flailing its forelegs as if galloping in the air. A hoof caught the she-bear on the chin as the bear swiped at the horse's

1

exposed chest and belly. I was thrown back into the shadows near the rocky wall of the hollow. The horse collapsed on top of the bear and pinned the beast to the ground. Razor-sharp claws had rent the horse's belly, and it lay heaving in its own gore.

I scrambled into the scrub oak as the bear thrashed to break free from the horse's weight. She struggled to stand, favoring a foreleg. When she turned and saw me, she roared and shook her head like a rabid dog. Hobbling on three legs, she started toward me. Jerel stood and heaved a large stone at the bear. It hit the bear with a dull thud and fell to the ground. The blow maddened the beast. She spun to face Jerel and bellowed as she raised herself to her full stature. Jerel faltered for a moment from fear. Then, picking up a stout branch and waving it with both hands, he cried, Father, flee to safety!

—Save yourself! I shouted. Run!

As I pulled my long knife out of its sheath, the she-bear swatted away Jerel's stick. Bolting to the far side of the hollow, Jerel scrambled into the cleft between two great boulders and wedged himself as far back as he could crawl. The bear lumbered after him and reached between the boulders, clawing at my son with her one good paw.

—Father! he screamed.

As the bear struggled to get at Jerel, she moved the boulders with her great weight, and once more Jerel cried out. I raced toward the beast with my knife ready, then leaped upon her back and thrust the blade with both hands into the base of her neck. I pushed the blade deeper as she reared back and careened. As I started to fall, I pulled the knife down with all my strength. I felt a sinewy snap like the breaking of a willow. The bear straightened as if she were surprised. I hit the ground. She made an attempt to turn, then collapsed on top of my leg, dead.

—Jerel! I cried.

I received no response.

—O God, don't let him die!

I tried to free myself from the weight of the bear.

—I'm coming, Jerel!

Stretching my body to its full length, I was able to grab Jerel's stick. I shoved it under the bear and pried up her immense body to free my leg. As I did so, fierce pain shot through me, and I cried out. I could see from the angle of my shinbone that it had snapped.

Jerel's stick became my staff. As I pulled myself up with it, my leg dangling in midair, I staggered over to Jerel.

—Oh, my son! No!

I carefully dragged his body from between the boulders. As I cradled his body, touching the deep gashes at his chest and leg, his skin was already turning sallow and cold. I thought we were safe. I thought I had calculated every risk of our journey. I thought I could cheat danger, that my life was blessed and beyond the hazards of an uncertain world. I had not pled with God to protect us on our journey. I had not even raised my eyes to heaven. Now, looking into the face of my dead son, I began to tremble. I buried my face in his shoulder and rocked him and wept.

છ

When no more tears would fall, I continued to rock my son and just stared, numb in all my senses. Long shadows settled in the hollow like damp fog, bringing with them a quick chill. I still had not tended to my leg.

The distant howl of wolves jolted me from my daze. The smell of fresh blood would not go unnoticed by them. After I laid Jerel's body down, I dragged myself across the hollow, carefully taking in my surroundings. To my right, as I faced the upper part of the mountain, I located the narrow gully Jerel and I had descended into the hollow. Except for some stubborn trees and bushes rooted in its craggy face, the hollow was a rocky pit with a few stands of pines and scrub oak at its edges. Spherical in shape, it measured thirty paces across, in my estimation. To my left was a steep trail leading up and out of the hollow. High walled on three sides, the hollow was open on the downhill side. I peered over the edge of the sheer cliff. The drop-off leading to a river below was impossible to descend. To get off the mountain, if I were to survive, I would have to attempt the steep trail—broken leg or not.

The sun finally dipped behind the mountain peaks above me. My leg pulsed, and I tried to put the pain out of my mind. Standing at the cliff that led to the river, I gazed across the hollow at Jerel's motionless form.

Parents should die first, I thought.

I didn't want to return to him, for there was only one reason to go and that was to make a grave before the scavengers arrived. Here. In the hollow.

Dusk brought a gray sky and clouds. I set about the sad task of making a grave for my son. With no other choice, I laid Jerel on the hollow's rocky foundation, stripped him of his clothes, which I would need, and began piling rocks on his body.

—I'm sorry, my son, I began to cry, There is no dignity in this.

My hands grew numb as the cold of the stones seeped into them. I thought, *What will I tell Moriah? How does a husband tell his wife that her child is dead?*

I went about the sad chore mechanically, placing a stone, crying, dragging myself to another stone, bringing it back, stacking. As I took a final rock in my hand, I paused before setting it on his face. I looked at his sunken eyes, once animated, once belonging to a little boy who held my finger as I walked. And I whispered, Good-bye, Jerel.

I stepped away and observed the miserable grave and heaved great sobs. I would try to make Jerel's grave more dignified tomorrow.

Three quarters of a moon rose in the cold sky, shedding a dim light on the hollow. As I looked off to the north, I took note of low-lying clouds moving east with the stiff wind. Snow was certain. In the moonlight, I began scavenging for my supplies. The water bags had burst. What little food we had carried was scattered on the ground. Of our two blankets, one was soaked with the horse's blood. My flints for fire had been lost in the rocky floor of the hollow. My clothing was inadequate for the cold, so I donned Jerel's clothing over mine, wrapped the other blanket about me, and sat and waited. The satchel of gems was yet bound to my waist and unharmed. As I shivered in the cold and watched the clouds reach across the moon like long, bony fingers, I began to fear I would freeze. A great heaviness settled in my head, weighty and ominous as death. I struggled to remain conscious, bundling myself in the blanket, curling into a ball, blowing into my hands. I lost the feeling in my toes and fingers, and my chin and nose went numb.

Then the sharp point of an idea stabbed my mind, and I dragged myself to the bear's carcass, estimating its length against my height. Convinced that my idea would work, I positioned my knife at the bear's belly, slit it open from groin to gullet, and let the entrails spill out. As the awful odor hit the frigid air, it made me stagger. I turned my head. Then, sensing the warmth, I held my hands near the opening and rubbed them. Ignoring my revulsion, I concentrated on the task at hand, pulling out organs and casting them aside. Then I lifted up the heavy rib cage, and, wrapping my cloak and blanket tightly about me, crawled into the cavity of the bear and let the rib cage down on top of me. As I curled up to fit, I drew in the satchel of gems and held them in my two hands. That night I would trust my life to the carcass of the beast that killed my son.

Night deepened. I was still in agony, and as I reached for my leg, I touched a hard lump at the break. Then the full gravity of what had happened pressed down on me.

—Jerel! I cried aloud. I have lost you in your youth! How I loved you!

ભ

When I heard the howling, I judged it as far away. Beyond the carcass of my horse stood a thicket where I detected rustling. Wolves! I lay still, hoping the bear's scent would frighten them. It did not. A sniffing at the bear's feet told me the area was being searched, and I hunkered down further into the bear's cavity, doing my best to become a part of it. Something tugged at the lower part of the carcass where some of the entrails were still attached, and I imagined an organ was being pulled away. Moving my hand to my hip, I touched my knife and tensed. A yelp was followed by the noise of an animal darting away. I heard distant growling and supposed that the horse had become a meal. I measured my breathing, trying to make it short and quiet. I listened and waited, on and on into the night, wondering when I would be discovered. Finally, the pack moved, and sounds of clawing and scuffling followed. A terrible realization shot through my mind, for I knew what was happening. The wolves were uncovering Jerel's grave. I clenched my knife, but I could do nothing!

As a last resort, I thought to pray.

The practice of petitioning God was one I had long before abandoned. That I was attempting it now would have delighted my father, Ebanel, and disgusted my grandfather, Simeon. But neither their approval nor disapproval could deter me now. My father had taught me about prayer as a boy. He taught me many things about God. But adolescence brought with it confusing opinions about Deity, mainly from my grandfather. As I tried to sort it all out, I appealed to others but was left unsatisfied. To some, God was an entity residing in carved stone. To others, God was a vague spirit or a kind of ether. Some claimed there were many gods, each responsible for this or that, often laden with traits of humanity, leaving them powerful but flawed—a dangerous combination, at least to my thinking. Gravitating to any of these notions seemed pointless, so I worshiped none of them and gave myself religiously to my work.

But tonight, I thought, *I will petition the God of my father, Ebanel, for protection.*

I prayed, O God, please help me!

൭

Perhaps I slept, maybe I fell unconscious. I stirred at the first nod of morning, as a glint of sunlight angled through a slit in the bear's carcass and awakened me. I marveled that I was not dead and offered a brief prayer of gratitude. Lifting the rib cage a bit, I saw that a spatter of snow had fallen, so I stuck a finger into the powder and found it knuckle deep. I brought a handful of snow to my lips and let it melt. When I tried to lift the rib cage further and get out, pain knifed through my leg, and I groaned out loud. Then, fearing I had been heard, I lay still, listening. Convinced I was alone, I made another attempt. I gritted my teeth, lifted the rib cage, and carefully rolled out.

As I lay in the snow, gasping, I raised my head and examined my leg. The skin was pink and swollen. Then I looked around. My blanket and clothing were stained the color of a turkey wattle. The stallion I had hoped would sire a noble line was now a skeleton. Except for the vitals, the bear's corpse was intact. Jerel's body was gone, with rocks scattered and strewn about where it had been.

My leg needed attention. I dragged myself to a tree and lay on my back. Then, using both arms, I lifted my broken leg and wedged my foot in where two limbs joined. I positioned myself to set the break. By pushing against the trunk with my good leg, I hoped to stretch the leg so that the broken bone would realign. My first attempt was timid, but, even so, I reeled and groaned. The leg had barely stretched, not nearly enough to set the bone, and the muscles of my leg began to spasm. I collapsed back in the snow and breathed quick, heavy breaths. I would need more courage. I would need more strength.

CЗ

Instead of praying for courage and strength, I cursed the same God I had begged to save me from the wolves.

—O God, you took my boy! Do you sit in yonder heavens watching our afflictions for amusement, detached from those who need you? If you are merciful, why do you allow misery? If you are just, why did you let my son die? If you are all powerful, restore him to me!

As I lay on my back, cold in the snow, with my broken leg wedged between two limbs and the foot of my good leg resting against the trunk, I shook my fist at an austere heaven and said, I will not give you the pleasure of my death!

Then, in anger, I repositioned the foot of my good leg against the trunk, reached behind my head with two hands, grasped the limb of an adjacent tree, and exerted all my strength to stretch my broken leg. I cried out, but continued to push and pull. The muscles that had tightened into a knot pulled back with greater force than I could exert. Again, as I pressed my foot against the trunk, the leg began to stretch. I clenched my teeth and strained hard with my arms. Tears formed at the corners of my eyes as I pushed more with my foot. Finally, the bone realigned, and the muscles in my leg relaxed. Relief surged through me as though water from a dam had been loosed.

Then I succumbed to unconsciousness. The next thing I remember was the sun standing straight above me. I groaned as I made an effort to lift my leg from the joint of the tree. But I failed and lay back panting. Another attempt rendered me unconscious again, for I next recall looking up at a gray afternoon sky. That I had lain in the bed of snow perspiring was evident, for I could see about me the outline of my shape melted down to the rocky floor of the hollow. Making a loop with my cloak, I leaned forward, hooked my foot, and lifted my leg from the tree. I waited until the aching subsided. Then, taking two sturdy sticks and positioning them on either side of the break, I tied them with strips of cloth I cut from my clothing.

A quick breeze stirred the powdery snow where I sat. As I looked heavenward, I made note of more clouds gathering at the jagged horizon, dark and heavy. Having been reared as the son of a shepherd on the grassy mountain slopes of Shum, I knew the signs of a coming storm.

I recalled a similar sight when, as a young man, I challenged my father on his beliefs.

—There is reality, I said, pointing at a distant, dark mass in the sky. I can see it, smell the moisture in the air, hear the thunder, feel the wind on my face.

—Then reality is only what can be perceived by the senses? asked my father. What about truth?

I often debated my father on his dogged beliefs. Our contests were mostly friendly, and we bantered over various issues. As I grew older, my questioning became more serious. My grandfather's views differed starkly from my father's, and Grandfather Simeon's persuasiveness drew me toward Shum for answers to life's questions.

—Your belief in an unseen power that controls the destiny of man borders on preposterous, I said to my father.

—Untrue! he answered. Beware that you do not fall prey to deception! If you believe that God does not exist, you distance yourself from law and accountability. And if you believe that the Adversary does not exist, you won't be wary, leaving him free to roam about undetected. It's the storm you do *not* see that will destroy you.

೦ಽ

After I finished putting a brace on my leg, I felt ashamed for my previous outburst of anger directed at heaven, and I whispered a penitent, I'm sorry. If you are there, please forgive my foolishness.

Then, pulling myself up with Jerel's stick for a crutch, I set out to find food. A brief tour of the hollow showed me the wolves had eaten everything. With no other option, I returned to the bear's carcass, smelled it for spoilage, and cut into the flank. The sight of it made my stomach turn. But after taking a deep breath, I held my nose and brought a bloody portion of raw flesh to my mouth and ate it.

I discovered I could tolerate it, hungry as I was, though it was tough and chewy and lacked the mild, sweet tastes I savored of domesticated animals—sheep, cattle, rabbit. With my hands covered with blood from cutting the meat, I felt as though I had regressed to the lowest form of humanity, more animal than man, more wild than civilized.

I judged it would soon be nightfall. To survive the cold, I would need shelter and warmth. The bear's hide would provide both. If I worked fast, I could scrape the bear's hide for a coat. Using my knife, I cut away the hide, setting aside the claws and teeth to later make needles, snare triggers, and arrow points.

When the snow fell that night, I bundled myself in the bearskin and ate more bear meat. As I did, I searched my mind, trying to determine if anything in the satchel of gems would be useful, especially something to make fire. Diamonds could shape a flint or chip obsidian into an arrowhead, but gems alone were of little use to me. That second night I sat in the hollow, wrapped in my bearskin, hoping I would not freeze.

For now, the hollow was my home.

For now, I had to live among wolves.

people as chattel

⋘

Jerel and I entered the mountain hollow thirty-three days from the time we left Shum. To arrive home as soon as possible was now our goal. The unseasonable warmth of a long autumn had begun to yield to winter's chill as we ascended the mountain pass. The leaves would soon turn color. I cherished the sunlight that was now growing shorter each day, remembering more keenly how I loathed the cold weather that vexed my aging body. My son reminded me that these mountains were known for attracting early winter storms. His remark would prove prophetic.

When Jerel and I had commenced our journey, we rode two horses bred to race. By applying my carefully honed trading skills—a calm voice, an expressionless face, and an aggravating patience—I had bartered the sleek animals for a treasure beyond my expectation—the satchel of gems. We now shared one horse between us—a chestnut stallion I also had acquired in the best trade of our expedition.

My twenty-five-year-old son Jerel held no passion for trade, but a foreboding urged him to accompany me. He had said detouring to Omner at this late season was a fool's errand. Shrugging off his notion of impending danger, I encouraged him to remain with his mother, Moriah, and his younger siblings, Enos and Eve. But he persisted, and, in the end, I conceded that Jerel's company would be welcomed.

Jerel was plain-looking like me. We both stood average height with olive skin and dark hair. Our most peculiar trait was a long snipe nose—an attribute Eve seldom let us forget. Jerel inherited my small-boned frame, a characteristic I loathed as a boy but was grateful for as an adult. Had I been burly, I might have followed professions that demanded physical labor. But my modest build pointed me toward mental labors, and I had gravitated to trading. Jerel, on the other hand, was enamored with the law.

cs

—The old woman looked delirious, said Jerel. We shouldn't have believed her. This path she set us on leads nowhere.

We had earlier encountered an old couple living at the base of a mountain range adjacent to the land of Haner. An ancient, toothless woman sat with feet to a fire, legs bare to the knees, as yellow and scaly as a chicken's—all the while leaning back on two arms that sagged flesh at the upper parts like a sow's thigh. She gummed advice about an alternative route to Shum, speaking as she did with her mouth full of something brown. I had made the mistake of asking if she knew one.

Her husband said, Listen to her if you want. I don't.

He kept watching the sky and said that, if it were him, he would winter in Haner rather than cross the mountains at this time of year.

—Two days in the mountains, two weeks to go around, said the old woman.

The old man threw his hands in the air, shook his head, and walked off mumbling, Black sky, bad omen.

—Two days? I asked the woman as I surveyed the sky.

—Let's not chance it, Father, said Jerel.

—Maybe a day and a half. Got a map? said the woman.

—No, I answered.

—Draw you one for a price. Give you boots too.

—We need food, I said. We can pay.

—Got beans, she said.

—How much?

—Two days' worth for a blanket.

—We'll need them. How about wool from Shum?

—Deal.

—Two days' worth of beans isn't very much, said Jerel.

—Get some more on the other side of the mountain, she said. You want the map?

—Yes, I said.

The old woman coaxed a charred stick from the edge of the fire, blew it cold, and scratched spidery marks on a flat stone.

—A bad idea, said Jerel. Who knows what danger is up there? And that storm is coming fast.

—Been here thirty years and haven't known any danger, said the woman. Might snow, but not deep this time of year.

—Which way? I asked.

She stood by putting a hand to her hip and groaning, took three steps toward the mountain, and pointed a fat finger at a shadowy dent in the mountainside. There, she said. Then she began to cackle like a hen, spit the wad into the dirt, and stood over it laughing, as though its shape had some humorous significance.

—Get the leftover wool, I told Jerel.

He began to protest, but I waved him off, saying, It will be all right if we make good time.

We left the old woman laughing at her spit and trekked into the mountains, wearing warm doeskin boots that her husband had made. I handed the chestnut stallion's reins to Jerel and said, Ride him if you want.

—I'll walk for now.

—Then I'll ride. When we return to Shum, I'll breed him into my stock. He'll sire a fine line.

My mind turned to Shum. I'd seen many place in my travels, but Shum's existence was remarkable. Cities were scattered here and there, but uncommon. The fact that people of diverse backgrounds had banded together, agreed upon laws, and accepted a form of government led by a king was marvelous. Shum, nestled in a broad, gentle valley, was a tent city where over five thousand families lived. But, instead of living in portable lightweight tents, many of the people built dwellings of permanent wooden frames, with heavily layered, finely woven mats draped over them. Their homes were dry, warm, and comfortable.

—Mahijah won't make you give him the horse?

Jerel spoke of the king of Shum, my occasional partner in trade. At my departure, Mahijah had pressed me to alter my journey to Haner and travel first to the land of Omner. The king gave me two mounts from his stables and had said to give them as a gift to the merchant of Omner. I'd asked why, after so many years of hostility with neighboring Omner, he wanted to enter into a trading pact with them now. He reminded me that my competitor, Baruch, had traded with Omner for some time and was becoming wealthy. Mahijah and I had discussed this before. For months, he had coveted the goods that Baruch had brought from Omner and sought an opportunity to seize control of the trade route there.

—It will destroy Baruch, I said.

—Since when are you sentimental when it comes to Baruch? I've never known you to hold any affection for the man.

—I don't.

—Then it's settled. We'll open a new trade route, and you'll increase your wealth with only time as an investment.

Twenty-nine days after that conversation, Jerel and I departed Haner with the treasure in tow and pointed ourselves back to Shum. The chestnut stallion was my prize, and my new alliance with Baruch's supplier in Omner would tip the scales of competition in my favor. Baruch possessed an aggravating tenacity, having managed to nibble away at my business until he had garnered a full third of Shum's gem trade. Now, that would change. Baruch would have to scramble or find another occupation.

Omner was a land rich in cattle and grazing lands. Between

Omner and Sharon lay a mountain range boasting an abundance of precious blue stones. Moreover, Sharon was an important trade center at the strategic crossroads of merchants' trade routes. Northwest of Sharon was Haner, our ultimate destination. It was also rumored to be rich in gems. But the country lay near Nod, a frightening land, said to support a terrible army, a place first settled by Cain and now home to his descendants and followers, a fierce people in appearance, shrewd in trade.

Before Mahijah had commissioned me to travel to Omner, I had convinced him to provide me an assortment of Shum's wool, tapestries, blankets, and cloth to trade with Haner. I promised to find a safe route so that we might trade for Haner's precious gems on a continual basis. Haner's proximity to Nod did not daunt me. A brave few had traveled to Haner using the mountain passes, thus avoiding the more direct route that passed Nod. They had returned with reports of incredible wealth, and I was intrigued. Taking into account both the potential and the risk, I calculated that a single trip would yield five years' profit. I was rich. I would become richer still.

Convincing Mahijah that opening a trade route to Haner would be profitable was no great feat. The suggestion of added wealth titillated his fancy. He had said more than once to me: Rabunel, you're the master of trade. Make me an offer, and I'll support you. And I had done just that. I had persuaded Mahijah to finance my expedition to Haner for half the profits. I estimated that my share would increase my wealth tenfold. In Shum, only Mahijah's holdings would be greater. Yet I would not be miserly with my wealth. I had recently taken notice of the poor in Shum, and upon my return, I would give them something.

—We've been fortunate, I told Jerel as we scaled the mountain. We've opened Omner by trading the king's two horses to the merchant there. He gave me the chestnut stallion. And, from Haner, we now carry a satchel filled with rare stones—twice the price I had expected.

Jerel yet watched the sky and seemed to ignore my boasting.

—I'll share the profits with you, I said. You can marry, if you want.

He shot a look at me and said, I'm too young for the responsibility. Maybe in a few years when I'm established in a trade.

—You're twenty-four! And I've always offered to make you a part of my enterprise. Neither your brothers nor your sister is interested.

—I don't think trading is for me, he said. You must be willing to hurt people to succeed.

—Competition is the way this world works, I said. People get hurt, but they go on and get stronger.

Jerel nodded and looked down. He said he supposed I was right but wished there were another way.

—None that I know, I said. It's like the animal kingdom—eat or be eaten.

—Are we animals?

—You've always been an idealist, I said.

—I'd like to study the law, he said. Maybe become a judge.

—Now there's a profession that doesn't hurt anyone, I remarked sarcastically.

—I think I could make a difference. Isn't there a desire in man to make a difference?

—Maybe. But when a family comes, *causes* are replaced by *survival*. I had all sorts of splendid plans before I met your mother. Over time, I discarded them one by one, and I was fortunate to discover I had a talent for trade.

—If I could find someone like Mother, I would consider marrying, said Jerel.

—What about Rachel?

At my question, Jerel smiled and turned his head away.

—You have feelings? I asked.

—Some.

—Deep feelings?

—I think about her a lot. I've found it hard to be away from her.

—She's a little young.

—Eighteen, like Eve.

He wouldn't look at me. To my thinking, Rachel was shy and plain, a little thin. But she had kind, brown eyes, a gentle way of speaking, and auburn hair. She was clean and organized, the youngest of two children, and the daughter of my competitor, Baruch. The idea of becoming family to Baruch grated on me, but I kept that sentiment to myself.

—Does she know your feelings? I asked.

—I have trouble expressing them, but I think she knows.

—How does *she* feel?

—I don't know. The same, I think.

—Perhaps you should ask her.

—Out loud?

I remembered how I'd felt when I'd first met my future wife, Moriah. Her father had come to Shum to trade. I loved her from that moment and begged my father to plead my case to her father. Like Jerel, I couldn't find the courage to speak for myself. So my father consented to help, and somehow I made a favorable impression, for I was allowed to court Moriah, and a marriage was arranged soon after. Over the years, Moriah had grown more beautiful, and I had never ceased being amazed that one so fair could love one as ordinary as me.

—I'll speak to her father, if you like, I said.

—You don't like him.

—I tolerate him.

—You would speak to Baruch for me?

—Yes. I did the same for Benjamin.

—Benjamin? You asked Sarah's father if Benjamin could court her?

Our laughter seemed to relieve Jerel, and he opened up. He'd never thought of his older brother as having a problem with timidity.

Whereas Jerel was of average height, Benjamin was tall. Dark-haired and thin, Benjamin had the look of intellect. In a serious mood, he could fix his black eyes so that they seemed without pupils. When he was a child, Moriah and I had worried that his pale complexion meant he was sick. But, despite the countless concoctions we put into him, he remained pale and active, and we became accustomed to his white skin. Benjamin had inherited both my stubborn streak and my knack for trade. All my children possessed these two traits to one degree or another but none as much as Benjamin. He excelled in strategy and could perceive the values and dangers in alliances. Since his teenage years, Benjamin had been fascinated with the Watchers, the priests of Shum, and had taken as his model Simeon, his great-grandfather, who was leader of the Watchers. The Watchers' ability to command the people's adoration appealed to Benjamin, kindling his desire to learn the Watchers' secrets and mystical rites. He had married Sarah, and their union had produced my first and only grandson, Nathaniel.

—Helping Benjamin win Sarah was a pleasure, I said.

—But talking to him since has been a problem, said Jerel.

—Yes.

Benjamin's gravitation to Simeon and the Watchers had driven a wedge between us. That consuming goal had caused him to seek Simeon's approval, not mine. Although I had made the introductions, Benjamin had married Sarah with Simeon's blessing, not mine. Their son, Nathaniel, was more Simeon's grandchild than mine. I loved my grandfather, but Benjamin's devotion to him, and Simeon's encouraging it, had resulted in my jealousy and Benjamin's drifting away from me.

—Do you think Chaz will send his father, the king himself, to ask you for Eve's hand? asked Jerel.

—That's not something I would cherish, I said.

—Why not? Chaz is the prince of Shum. Can Eve find a better match?

—I don't like him. He's as pompous and incompetent as his father.

—But you and Mahijah are trading partners.

—That doesn't mean I like or trust him. For the right circumstance, he would betray me as surely as he would another. To Mahijah, people are chattel, valued only for their benefit to him.

—So Baruch is expendable? said Jerel.

—Mahijah doesn't care.

—It would seem you share the same sentiments, if you're willing to join Mahijah in taking Baruch's livelihood.

I gave Jerel a quick look and said, You're quick to judge! Have you lived so long that you think you understand the complexities of a competitive world?

—Commerce is something I shall never understand, said Jerel.

We walked silently some distance. I had dismounted my horse and was leading it up a narrow path. Jerel followed the horse. I still simmered from my son's veiled rebuke.

—Trading for gems and horses is one thing, I called out, But my relationship with Mahijah does not go so far as giving Eve to Chaz!

My youngest child and only daughter was the beauty of Shum. She had inherited her mother's soft complexion, fawn-like features, and golden hair. Except for their difference in age, Eve and Moriah resembled each other more than any two of our family. Some people could not distinguish between them when they spoke. That Moriah and I had been blessed with a daughter was a miracle. After three difficult pregnancies—all boys—we thought the possibility of our having a girl was remote. Benjamin was a twin whose younger brother lived only moments. They were born in the first year of our marriage, then Jerel came the following year. Moriah struggled to recover from Jerel's birth, and for five years she didn't conceive. Then Enos came, arriving late and large-headed, a birth as exacting as Jerel's. The midwives managed to deliver him, but Moriah suffered indescribable anguish, and I feared her death for days. Thereafter, we both assumed her womb had closed forever. But, one year later, Moriah conceived, carried Eve to full term, and delivered her without incident.

Eve had blossomed like the wildflowers of Shum. She stood the same height as her mother, a palm's length shorter than me. She loved people, and they felt it—her cheery smile drew them in and sent them away glowing. She could not imagine evil in anyone. Eighteen years had changed a frolicking child into a beautiful young woman.

—I'm sorry I mentioned Eve and Chaz, said Jerel, huffing as he climbed. But you needn't worry about Eve. Enos dislikes Chaz as much as you and seems bent on protecting her from every male in Shum.

—And Enos could do it, I said.

Enos had grown into a handsome young man, light-complexioned, broad through the shoulders, flaxen-haired, well-muscled, and taller than his parents and siblings. Shum's military, the Rahaj, intrigued him. From his youth, he had made war heroes his idols, particularly Gad, the captain of the Rahaj. Enos hoped to pursue that discipline. He demonstrated a flair for leadership, moving easily in powerful circles and enjoying the confidence of those in high rank. I was cautiously pleased, but concerned for him.

—I doubt you'll have to talk to some young woman's father in Enos's behalf, said Jerel.

—If he can ever decide on just one.

We laughed.

Then Jerel said, Too many young women to choose from has never been my curse.

I checked the sky. Many of the dark clouds had drifted on down the valley without depositing their load. In the distance, they became thin and wispy, and I felt relief that the worst of our journey was behind us.

—I see the summit up ahead, said Jerel. Then it's all downhill.

—Evening is coming, I said. After we move to the other side, we'll find a sheltered spot to make camp. Then, in the morning, we'll get off this mountain and count ourselves fortunate having saved two weeks. I'm anxious to see your mother.

—And I'm anxious to see Rachel.

a bud of hope

ॐ

My morning meal was the same as my evening meal—a tough piece of bear meat. As I gnawed it, I tried to pretend it was sweet and set my objective on escaping the cold hollow. As nearly as I could discern, the wolves had not returned. Last night's storm had deposited only a thin, frosty layer of snow. I shook it from my bearskin and located the sun—a hazy circle of orange gold, hanging dim in a gray sky. Moriah, my wife of twenty-six years, would not be missing me yet. There would be no attempted rescue. As far as she knew, Jerel and I were on schedule and would arrive home in a month.

I chewed the bear meat and carved a tree branch into a better crutch. The last remnants of the hide provided the arm padding. What was left of the bear's carcass was a shapeless bulk of red-streaked flesh, unrecognizable as the beast that had killed my son. Fearing that the hide I had cut away for a covering would become stiff, I scraped off flesh and fat from the nether side, hoping my effort would approximate tanning. Given my situation, I could do little more. By afternoon, I had scraped half the skin with my knife. My hand ached, and the muscles in my forearm burned. Two tight blisters had formed on the fleshy part of my palm. After opening and closing my hand, I achieved movement, whereas before it had felt stiff.

As the moon rose and washed the hollow in orange light, I

scraped away the last of the flesh and observed the mound of dark scrapings. I sniffed my hands. They had taken on a rank, gamey smell, and I wondered if anything on earth could rid me of it. Gazing heavenward, I predicted a frigid night. I wrapped myself in the heavy skin of the bear, blew hot breath into cupped hands, and prepared to wait away my third night in the hollow.

ଓ

The sharp edge of dawn cut through the cold darkness, and a warm beacon of light burst over high peaks and tipped shadows westward. My first movements brought scolding from squirrels and mocking from jays. Peering out of the bearskin, I discovered that clouds heavy with moisture had deposited knee-high snow, white as lamb's fleece. That it appeared unblemished meant that the wolves had not returned.

I shook free of the snow, dragged myself to the bear, and carved chunks of meat from the partially frozen carcass. Digging deep into a flank where the tone of the flesh turned from pale to pink, I sawed a stiff piece away. From the look of it, the entire carcass would soon putrefy when the sun warmed it. It had lasted as long as it had because of the quick storm and its being packed in snow. The time had come to escape the hollow.

As a boy, I had watched my father construct snowshoes of pine branches. They were barely adequate, I remembered, but I fashioned one and latched it to my good foot. When I had packed a little meat, I draped the bearskin coat about me, bound the satchel of gems to my waist, and lifted myself on the crutch.

My first steps shot pain through my shin like an arrowhead piercing flesh. Each movement spoke impossibility, and with the addition of the snow, I feared I could not climb the outbound trail. But I had no other option but to try. I struggled all morning to climb the hill. At midday, I fell exhausted into the snow, rolled to my back, and saw that my former camp lay within a stone's throw. Heaving big white breaths into the frigid atmosphere, I felt as if an enemy had thrust a sword in my side. My leg had swollen tight again and smarted at the slightest touch. Since the splint made bending difficult, I devised another method for climbing uphill—stepping with my good leg, falling forward in the snow, then pulling my load and broken leg to me. Finally, when I had rested, I would lift myself on the crutch and repeat the process.

As I lay in the snow trying to summon strength, my despair led to another attempt at prayer. I first thought of Grandfather Simeon's god—one who favored the strong, the intelligent, and seemed especially partial to those who obeyed the Watchers. In my current situation, I did not think *that* god would be of much help. On the other hand, my father had taught me of a God who is not selective with his affections, who is our Father in heaven with whom one can converse as literally as a child talks to his parent, a Father perfect in the attributes of love, knowledge, mercy, power, who is recognizable as the Parent of the human family, having a purpose in creating his children. I needed *that* God to hear me now, for there was nothing I could think to do to save myself. I worried that my lack of practice would hamper the effort. Nevertheless, I tried, launching words heavenward as if having a conversation with One who I hoped knew me, with One who had an interest in me and who had the ability to answer.

I spoke the words aloud between my labored breaths.

—O God. My Father. Hear me!

I paused, feeling uncomfortable. I nervously looked around, as though someone might be watching, then felt foolish for my self-consciousness.

—If you are there—and my father says you are there—please hear me.

I paused again, tempted to propose some sort of bargain, then thought better of it and continued.

—I need your help. I cannot do this—survive—without you, without your help.

I could not think of what else to say. I closed my eyes and waited.

I felt a tiny bud of hope begin to grow within me, and as it did, the despair I'd felt gave way to calm.

Once more, the sunlight fell dark toward the eastern horizon, and the sky there became a foreboding gray. The white snow turned blue in the shadows, then dark as a puddle during a cloudburst. A climb that should have taken little time had taken the day. Under the boughs of a broad pine with gnarled roots that entwined deeply into the mountainside, I found shelter, rolled myself into the bearskin, and drew in the satchel of gems. Then, fetching the last piece of bear meat, I chewed it like cud and watched as huge flakes began to fall from a sky heavy with moisture.

learning to look up

ℭℨ

Several days before Jerel and I departed Shum, I visited my father, Ebanel. At midmorning, when the sun had burned away a hazy mist, I found him in his camp, hand-feeding a lamb with two canines called Dog and Teah waiting on him.

—I take my journey today, I said.

The lamb bleated and tried to bolt. My father caught it by its back leg, and Dog raised his ears.

—Hold this, my father said, handing me the milk-drenched cloth he had used to suckle the lamb. I received it, and, after wrestling the kid into a firm hold, he put a knee into the animal's shoulder and rubbed balm into a wound on its flank. He appeared old, his brown, leathery face weather-worn, with gray bristles on his chin and cheeks. Thin strands of silvering hair, made spidery in the wind, gave him a wild look. I hadn't inherited his height, but his age had bent him to my stature. His black eyes were alert and honest, and an active out-door life had given him a slim frame.

—Omner then Haner, I said, as though he had asked my destination.

Through squinted eyes, he gave me a quick, cold stare, then looked away.

—I thought you'd like to know, I said.

He worked the balm and grumbled.

—Now I know, he said.

—It's a courtesy. I didn't come for your permission.

Ebanel released the lamb and lifted himself with his staff.

—Dog. Teah, he called, Take her back to the flock. The two canines jumped at his voice and herded the lamb away.

—Perhaps you have some counsel, I said, summoning a civil tone.

—You don't want it.

I bristled, then said, Didn't I ask?

With his staff, my father scratched the earth and appeared to ponder the markings. The expression on his face conveyed what I was feeling: I had not sought his counsel in years.

—Mahijah is no fool, he said.

I was intrigued by his statement.

—How did you know my trip involved Mahijah?

—Who else? You play a dangerous game partnering with the king.

I became silent. Ebanel's disdain for Mahijah was evident. That such a man could be king was beyond his comprehension. My father called Mahijah "the rooster," because he crowed and strutted through the streets of Shum with a single shock of red hair protruding like a rooster comb from his otherwise bald head. He carried his father's sword, a broad, bronze blade crafted in the land of Nod. Said to have been damaged in battle when Mahijah relieved the Aramite king of his head, the tip of the sword was broken and never repaired—now a trophy that Mahijah paraded as a boy will flaunt his first black eye. Stirring gossip and beans over supper kettles, Shum's female population was divided over their opinion of the king. As he passed by, silly women tittered at Mahijah's attentions, some tattled about his extramarital trysts, others tallied how his female "partners" had risen in their social standing and otherwise profited by consorting with the king. Shum's men grumbled that Mahijah would never have arrived at his station had he not been born to it, but they supported him for fear of the Rahaj, Shum's army. Mahijah commanded no great love from the people, but I tolerated him because I had grown prosperous from our association. But now, Mahijah's son, Chaz, wanted to court my daughter, Eve. None of this sat well with my father. I had heard his objections; I would hear them again.

My father motioned me to follow him as he herded his sheep toward a lower meadow that favored thick grasses and wild orchids. The open pasture land was safer for his sheep, he said. He could sit on yonder bluff with a clear view of any danger.

As I followed him, I asked, Are you judging me because I affiliate with Mahijah?

—Cautioning you, he said. Then he yelled at an errant sheep, Get on back now!

Dog and Teah took note.

—Are you interested in hearing about my expedition? I asked.

—I suppose it has something to do with chasing wealth and leaving your family again. My father turned his attention to the sheep. Stay now! he called.

I summoned a proverb: *Offer a poor man wealth, and he will turn on his fellows as quickly as the rich.*

My father gave my words pause and commented, Well said, my son, but what of you?

—I support my family, I answered. Is there no virtue in being a good provider?

—Yes, but you have enough to last two lifetimes. Do you mean to get more? You seldom see your family now, and I fear you'll lose them.

A longtime rub over lifestyles revived a familiar resentment deep inside me. I knew my father to be a knowledgeable man, even a wise man, but to my thinking he simply did not grasp how life worked outside his little sheep camp. Others in Shum seemed to see me as an important person. I was a wealthy merchant; I was a member of the Council. From them, I received respect. My grandfather frequently told me he was proud of my status. But no matter how successful I became, it seemed that my own father couldn't bring himself to acknowledge my success or appreciate my accomplishments.

ॐ

Then we let silence speak with itself a long while. As we came to a high point of rock, my father sat and lay his staff near his side. Below, Dog and Teah had moved the sheep into the meadow and had taken up their watch under the shade of a tree. Moving to a spot near my father, I sat and watched the flock, their gentle grazing motions, the occasional raising of heads.

—Feels like a hot one, said my father, wiping the sweat from his face.

I shaded my eyes as I marked the sun's location—still overhead, though now westering. I said, Too warm for my liking.

—Could be deceptive, he said. We may be in for an early winter.

He pointed to an osprey hovering above the lake north of the meadow.

—Look, he said. His voice was a whisper. It's beautiful, don't you think?

—Yes.

—And lethal, he added.

I watched the osprey high in the heavens, open-winged, riding an air current effortlessly. Suddenly, it tucked its wings and dove like an arrow arching earthward. When it touched the surface of the lake, a spray of water rose, and the osprey flew off with a writhing fish in its talons.

—Amazing, I said. I've seen that hundreds of times, I suppose, and I still marvel at the osprey's ability.

—It waits for an opportunity to strike, my father said. The fish never learns. If it would learn to look up, it would live a much longer life.

I knew his meaning.

—I'll be careful, Father, I said. I know you love me.

—That I do, my son.

why do I stay?

ༀ

Within a short time of my retiring on the fourth night, new snow had filled the hollow, totally covering the bear carcass and the horse skeleton. I pulled my bearskin wrap around me and huddled under the boughs of the pine where the ground was dry and blanketed by a bed of brown needles. I looked up through the wispy branches and watched the top branches sway with a troubling wind. Shrouding the tree and entombing me within, gusts of icy air delivered drifts of snow from high peaks and piled it deep.

I gnawed at the underside of the bearskin, the hunger in my stomach competing with the throbbing in my leg. Like a mole tunneling, the cold burrowed into me, and once again I attempted to make fire. I tried to achieve a spark by striking a ruby against a diamond, a sapphire against an opal, a garnet against an emerald. Nothing. As I returned the cold gems to the satchel and curled up on the bed of pine needles, I heard the distant baying of a wolf and the answering howl of its companion. Perhaps I would die beneath the tree.

Between the boughs of the pine, I searched the heavens for signs of reprieve. For the first time that night, the skies had cleared, and I could now see glimpses of the moon and the stars. These welcome sights gave me hope. Perhaps the storm had ended. I noticed that the snow had buried the pine's lower branches and surrounded me. At sunup, I would try to dig out.

Sleep had fled from me. I bundled the bearskin about my body and shifted my leg, seeking relief. Night was the worst time—when pitiless cold clawed at my break, causing my leg to painfully throb and my breathing to become shallow. Moreover, hunger had become my cruel companion. With my knife, I dug pine roots to eat. When an acrid taste rose in my throat, I doubled over. Then my abdomen clenched, and I heaved yellow into the white snow and held my sides until the spasms ended. I tried to spew out the bitterness, but the slaver froze on my chin, and I hadn't the will to wipe it away.

—Let me die then! I cried out to heaven. What purpose can this suffering serve?

I found myself counseling a God I did not know. Slamming my fist into the trunk of the tree, I bloodied my knuckles, and pieces of bark broke loose. I clutched my hand and howled until the stinging stopped. Once more, as I lay down, I drew to me the satchel of gems, but embracing them gave me little relief. They had absorbed the wintry cold and were chilling against my body, and soon I had to distance them from me.

I shifted and reshifted my body, trying to achieve some comfort. If I died that night, I might as well die comfortably. Beneath the tree, I brushed an area clear of pine needles, bound myself in the bearskin, bunching it up at a corner, and laid my head on it. Only my eyes and nose were exposed. As I breathed, twin clouds of moisture formed at my nostrils and faded. Again, I looked up at the moon and judged it a fraction larger than last night's. Full now, I guessed. Perhaps brighter.

My thoughts turned to Jerel. A purer child there had never been. As a youth, Jerel demonstrated a gentility that had translated into myriad acts of thoughtfulness. Many times I imagined he would have made a good shepherd. My father would have loved that notion. I fought back the urge to weep. Tears and frigid weather are poor companions.

As I lay beneath the pine, I remembered an incident from my youth. My father loved to discover life's secrets by observing nature, and he often would invite me to join in his discoveries. As my father was stirring a supper kettle one night, a moth had been attracted by the firelight. My father then asked me this question.

—Rabunel, do you think the moth is beautiful?

—Yes, it's beautiful.

—Do you know its cycle of life?

I rehearsed the cycle in my mind. An egg hatches, which becomes a larva, which becomes a caterpillar, which spins a cocoon, which emerges as a moth, which lays other eggs.

—Yes, I know, I replied.

—Is the moth's cycle of life the same as a sheep's?

—Of course not.

—Two life-forms, two spheres of existence, he said. In its own kingdom, each is happy. That is the ultimate design of creation.

The idea that happiness was the purpose of creation had never occurred to me. I argued, A moth cannot be as happy as a sheep, nor can a sheep be as happy as a man.

—You judge happiness from your point of view, said my father. You think happiness is an outgrowth of intelligence. In its sphere, the moth is as happy as the sheep.

My father stirred the stew and brought a steaming ladle to his lips. A quick sip brought a smile to his face that said the stew met with his approval.

—The purpose of man's creation is happiness, he said. Everything you do should point to happiness.

I ate his stew and watched the moth flit in and out of the light. I knew that seeking for pleasures was not what he defined as happiness. I asked, Are you happy, Father?

He paused.

—When I married your mother, I thought there could be no greater happiness. Then you children came to us, and my happiness multiplied. Turning from his kettle, my father relaxed his ladle and looked at me. He said, Yes, my son, I'm happy.

Was I happy? I wondered. I was happy being Moriah's husband. I was happy being a father. I thought having a trade that challenged me and that supported my family made me happy. From that point, my list blurred. Good health and good friends were sources of happiness, I supposed. But I'd seen crippled and friendless people who were happy. I once had thought that my happiness would increase as my honor and property grew.

Was I happy? I considered where I lived. Much of the earth was populated by nomadic tribes, unlinked to civilized living. Shum, on the other hand, afforded its citizens protection and an opportunity for prosperity, and I had thought I was happy there. But I also knew Shum's leaders. I sat on their Council and had a voice. I knew the price of power and the penalty of challenging that power. I knew that what drove those who governed was domination and gain more than service and responsibility.

Was I happy? I had seen Shum's governmental and religious leaders define and redefine morality as though it ebbed and flowed like tidal waters, and their examples had widened the boundaries of decency, introducing a norm of expediency and privilege. As a youth, I once had been entrusted to watch the sheep, and my father had pointed at a distant knoll and said I should use it as the boundary for predators. Should I spot a predator crossing the knoll, he had instructed, I would be close enough to leap to action and save the flock. Then one sleepy afternoon, when the day was hot and the sun was high, I first spied coyotes at the fringe of the knoll, sitting on their haunches. I didn't chase them. A common sight was coyotes roaming, but driving them away seemed fruitless given the distance of the ones I saw. So I rested and watched. When they edged a bit closer, I was alarmed, but then relaxed when they stopped. With each advance, I continued to hesitate, constantly recalculating the span between the coyotes and the sheep, judging that I could sprint the distance easily. In the end, I was wrong.

My father had once asked me, If you know the evils and dangers of Shum, why do you stay?

—Few places could offer me the opportunities of Shum to support my family, I had said.

—If you lost all your possessions, would you still choose to live in Shum?

It was a question worth considering.

enoch the seer

ଓ

Whereas I held Baruch in low regard, a man named Micah drew my admiration.

Micah had migrated to Shum from the frontier of Hanannihah, where strapping men mined precious gems and ores. Leaders of such rugged sorts needed to be mighty in physical strength. Micah was such a man, as powerful in body as he was in character. He had managed the mines of Hanannihah for fifteen years. After losing his wife and children in the great drought, he came to Shum, seeking a new life. In the community, his leadership acumen soon became apparent among men of high position, and he was asked to speak his opinion on many subjects. That his background as a miner could spawn such a brilliant command of language had always intrigued me. His physical features were no less impressive. Square-jawed, standing a full head higher than me, and twice my width—not of corpulence but of brawn—Micah had an imposing presence. His dark hair was thinning, revealing a tanned scalp, most likely from days spent laboring beneath the hot sun. The black eyes that lay deep in his head could fix on a person without glancing away.

At the time Micah came to Shum, the earth was full of violence. Beyond the safety of the city, marauders prowled the wilderness and often preyed upon the weak or careless. Only those who knew the wild areas well dared travel them without the safety of a caravan. A long drought had taken the lives of a full third of the people throughout the land. Although the drought had now abated, its effects were still felt. Lack of food made for widespread violence. Murder was common, since no law existed in the wilderness except survival. One could travel in some areas and see hundreds of carcasses of cattle and sheep covering withered fields; broken plowshares abandoned on hard, dry ground; and parched riverbeds, cracked like the lips of a desert traveler begging for moisture. For these reasons, intense fear accompanied those who ventured from the cities, as many such travelers met their deaths.

Micah's influence among the people carried astounding weight. His ability to communicate and build strong relationships had gathered to him a fortune and the respect of the populace. Mahijah seemed to recognize the power that Micah wielded, for Mahijah sought counsel from him, although guardedly, on matters of state. Micah tolerated Mahijah but spoke his mind. Only Simeon dared say as much. The Watchers tolerated Micah, while Micah publicly ridiculed them. To anyone who cared to listen, Micah would declare the priests of Shum to be scoundrels and frauds, saying their incantations, potions, and secret ways were abominations before God. The Watchers winked at Micah's denunciations because he had the king's ear and the public's trust, but I felt he was treading a dangerous path. Still, if I could have been any other man, I would have been Micah.

Micah was the first to tell me of Enoch's coming. Before all the commotion that Enoch's preaching generated, Micah was commending him to all who would listen. And Micah spoke unchallenged. He called Enoch a *seer* because he claimed to *see* unseen things: the spirits of all men past and future, the extensive works of God. To most, Enoch was just an enigma. He lived in the mountains removed from people, emerged to teach them, then retreated into the hills. Some saw his behavior as essential to his mission; most saw it as marked insanity. Shum's leaders labeled him a wild man and claimed that

Enoch had formed alliances with Shum's enemies. They said he had come to cause insurrection, to declare himself king, to confuse the people with claims of divine commission. No one was as persuasive in speaking against Enoch as was Simeon, for he and Enoch had come from the same land of Cainan. When Simeon decried Cainan's people as ferocious, as a people who would bring Shum into captivity, as a people who worshiped strange gods, practiced a perverted religion, and were militant in nature, the people of Shum listened. Although that systematic discrediting of Enoch prejudiced most of Shum, many went out to hear him, if for no other reason than curiosity.

Enoch carried scrolls containing the genealogies and writings of the patriarchs, the fathers of the race. Being of that birthright, Enoch had, by lineage, rights of leadership under his fathers. Some were in awe that this great man had come among them; others denounced him as a fraud; while the rulers of Shum saw him as a threat.

A few days before I left for Omner, I met with Micah and questioned him about Enoch and his message. Micah amazed me by censuring Shum, though I could tell he was holding back and not revealing his innermost feelings. Had he been any other man, I would have dismissed his words, but Micah was a man not given to brash statements. His candor demanded my attention.

—You are of the Council, a devoted servant of Mahijah, he said to me. Why should I tell you what is in my heart that you may report it to the king?

—I'm my own man, I said.

—You're Mahijah's partner.

—Only on occasion. Today I'm more interested in what *you* have to say.

Micah turned his head to look in my eyes for a moment, then handed me a sack of shucked corn and another of wheat.

—I've known you to be a good man, Rabunel. If you want to know what I believe, then follow me, for I have work to do.

I shot him a puzzled look but then nodded and hefted the sacks. That a man of Micah's stature was so committed to Enoch made me reconsider my opinion. Since I respected Micah's views more than any other's and wanted his true feelings, I balanced the sacks of grain on either shoulder and stepped to the pace of Micah.

As he and I walked the paths between the tents at the center of Shum, I felt myself fortunate that Shum was my home. I knew the ways of travel and seldom faced danger when I ventured forth, but I was always grateful to return to the safety of the city. Still, Shum was an enigma. It lay sequestered in a fertile valley where dew and rain fed rich, black soil. Farmers cultivated crops that never failed. Herders pastured fat animals. It seldom snowed, and when it did, it quickly melted, never lasting more than a day. The people as a whole were prosperous, and Shum's fame had spread throughout the earth. Many herdsmen flocked there and paid enormous prices for a plot to pitch a tent and for pasture land to keep their livestock. The poor came too, for they were less poor in Shum than in other places and had greater safety. Shum's neighbors also prospered, for the valleys in that range of mountains boasted areas of wonderful fertility. But none were as prosperous as Shum.

When we were walking through the part of Shum where the wealthy of the city resided, Micah asked, Can you name those who live here?

I observed the brightly dyed tents staked at the middle of the city that marked the dwellings of the affluent and knew each of their owners well. Every tent varied in shape and size, and each was colorful, elegant, spacious, decorated ornately, and perfumed with incense. The spaces between the tents were dressed with soft grasses and flowers.

—Yes, I answered.

Of the inner tents of Shum, I knew every person. I loved this part of the city and rarely ventured from it except to trade or to visit my father. Evening was my favorite time of day. I knew it to be thick with activity: women preparing meals with tempting aromas wafting with each gentle breeze. Life had been good to me, and I thought I was as content as a man could be.

—For two generations, this part of Shum has known no want, said Micah. And we presume our prosperity will outlast us. That's a dangerous and arrogant attitude.

—You sound like an extremist, I said. Why are you so heavy-handed?

—Shum is much like Hanannihah before the drought. We were so rich that we thought we were safe. But you can't eat stones. We gathered fortunes around us and, in the end, left them all behind—those of us still alive—to find food.

—The granaries of Shum are full, I said. What's your point?

—The granaries are full, but the poor who live beside them are starving.

We walked on until we reached the extremities of Shum. Contrasting the grassy avenues at the center of the city, dusty paths lay between dwellings in Shum's outer areas, the grim pockets of poverty. Dirty water was thrown out to settle the dust. Dogs played with those who would later eat them. Naked children splashed in puddles and chewed potato skins and melon rinds. Small, earth-colored tents of animal skins were staked randomly and looked to be unable to keep out the weather. We passed sparsely toothed women who hung bunches of herbs, strings of peppers and roots. Some plants would later be ground into medicines or used in balms. The stench of Shum's dung heap lay just beyond us and festered in the hot sun. Poor men, hired for day labor, tied strips of material about their mouths and noses as they buried the fresh increase with dirt. Still, the fetid odor drifted in on occasional winds. I passed the old and withered, those who had the look of hopelessness, having worn themselves out labor-ing, never having enough, suffering lifelong hunger and defeat, with even a modicum of respectability just out of reach. I thought about how well equipped the Rahaj was and how minor adjustments in out-fitting the army could, for these poor people, make the difference, between despair and dignified living. The existence of the impover-ished looked to be hard, dirty, meager. The area they lived in smelled of foul food that would have been discarded by the rich people.

I heard the cries and croupy coughs of sick children. I heard the weary lullabies of those who tended them. I saw the implements of austere living, the sickles of field workers, the tools of day laborers, the earthen basins of overworked women. I pondered the inequality that can exist within such a short distance, how affluence and poverty can exist side by side yet not know each other. I felt ashamed that the people at the center of Shum lived well, while their neighbors sweated out a miserable existence below that of beasts of burden—for even animals labored less and were better fed. Whereas the beasts were cared for, I wondered what security the poor enjoyed. They toiled in a condition of despair, with only the expectation of indigence for their old age. What they were paid did not meet their needs, for those who employed them paid as little as possible for their labor. I mourned for the undernourished minds that might have blessed a generation and lamented for the latent genius and talent now plowed under in the same ground that was harrowed for a pittance. And the whole world was the poorer.

—This is Anna, said Micah, gesturing to a young woman who looked to be the age of my daughter Eve. She held a crying baby, while two toddlers hid in her well-worn skirt. I dropped the sacks and offered a slight bow. Micah asked if her husband had returned from the mines.

—In a month, I hope.

—Do you have enough to get by?

Anna looked away.

Micah bent down and took Anna's little boy on his knee.

—I've got something for you, he said.

The little boy's younger sister stuck her head out from behind her mother.

—You too, said Micah to the girl.

She draped her mother's skirt over her face. Micah handed the boy three sticks of cane and said, One for you, one for your sister, and one for the baby.

—You're too good to us, said Anna.

—I wish I could do more. Have you got a basket? We've brought some grain.

—We can't pay.

—It's not for sale.

Her eyes became moist, and she said she had a hard time accepting his charity.

—Things will turn for you, said Micah. Someday you'll have some extra and be on the giving end.

Into the afternoon, until the grain was gone, I followed Micah on his rounds. He introduced me to each of his friends, engaged them in caring conversation, filled their baskets, and left them with their dignity.

When we finally sat to rest, he asked, Can you remember the names of all those you met today?

—Yes.

—Did you meet any less worthy of your notice than those in the center of the city?

—No, in many ways they're more worthy.

—Then you truly are a good man, Rabunel. We, of Shum, think ourselves good because we only do a little bad—we tell *small* lies; we envy others just a *little*; we take *small* things but don't call it stealing, and we're just using our language nimbly if we employ it to trap or outwit others. What harm can these be? We pride ourselves since we have fewer poor people than do other lands. But do we hear our neighbors' cries? Do we know the names of the widows and orphans? Do we see the tears of those who are ignorant with no opportunity to learn and no hope of a better existence? Do we know the empty ache in the stomachs of children whose fathers cannot provide enough? We congratulate ourselves as being God-fearing, yet we persecute the meek by withholding our substance and by building monuments to our industry in their view. And there are other poor among us: the poor, abused women whose husbands make them slaves in their own homes, whose husbands require of them strict obedience and oppress them with condescending language. These women live, as do their children, in a world of fear, violence, and verbal assault, many with broken hearts from husbands committing adultery and making a mockery of sacred vows taken before God.

—You learned all this from Enoch? I asked.

—Not all. But his words have helped me consider life with greater care.

—It's a harsh view.

—Perhaps, but honest.

—I'm not interested in messages of doom. It is hope I savor.

—Enoch's message *is* one of hope. But honesty must precede hope. He speaks of the destiny of man, how God put into him a spark of divinity that, if he will be true to it, will help him rise above his current situation of depravity and inequity.

—So he seeks to reform society?

—The individual first, then the family, then society. The hope and the possibilities he preaches can be obtained in no other way.

I remembered how many people went to the hills to hear Enoch when he first came to the valley of Shum. I'd been amused with the reports that surrounded his coming but had remained in Shum with my son Enos to tend my business. But for some in my family, Enoch's words had piqued an interest. Moriah, along with Jerel and Eve, went with my father to hear the seer. They returned cheery-faced and animated, chattering all the while. My eldest son, Benjamin, had another reaction. Being a disciple of his great-grandfather Simeon— Enoch's most outspoken opponent—Benjamin refused to waste his time on what he called trivial matters, such as chasing soothsayers and wizards or listening to radicals.

—I'm going to hear him tonight, said Micah. Will you come with me?

—Me? Oh, no. In my position, I cannot.

—Your position is that important?

—There's some danger in becoming associated with Enoch. I would fear for my children if I went.

—As you wish, but the offer stands.

Micah stood, pulled me to my feet, and embraced me. He thanked me for helping him and listening. As he left for the hills, I wished I had not just accepted his thanks but had extended to him my own. That night, out of respect for Micah, I sneaked into the hills near my father's camp to hear Enoch. What I had witnessed that day gave me food for thought. When I arrived, I listened to the seer with greater attention.

Adjacent to my father's camp rose a hillside from the grasslands surrounding Shum. The pitch was gradual, allowing an easy ascent to a bowl-shaped glen bordered by pines. It was situated so that one standing at its brim could speak in a normal voice and be heard by all in its borders. That was where Enoch taught the people. At that first meeting, I wrapped myself in a cloak and hid beneath a tree within earshot to listen. Though full of curiosity and interest, I still expected to be disappointed at what I heard—at best, mildly entertained. As I surveyed the grassy area, I was amazed at the number of people—old, young, rich, poor—sprawling out to the edges of the glen, intent on hearing the seer. I felt full of anticipation like a boy on his first hunt, but I hoped it didn't show. I wished to remain unnoticed.

When I first saw Enoch, I perceived little that was intriguing or charming about him. He measured about the average height of a man, about as tall as me. He wore no head covering. His dark, wavy hair fell down to just above his shoulders. His eyes were not as dark as his hair and seemed gray at one time and green at another, depending on the light. Providing a rich complement to his hair, his skin was olive-hued, like mine. He was erect in posture, broadly built, denoting a body accustomed to physical labor. His clothes were plain-colored, simple, durable. That he was a young man in his mid-twenties surprised me, for he had the visage of maturity. His voice was mild, yet sure, halting at his first words, then leaning toward raspy with a hint of shyness, growing forceful and clear as he continued. I could detect he had little of worth except his walking staff and the set of scrolls, and I could account for no reason he should be labeled a wild man. From the Watchers' report, I had expected a wild-haired zealot spewing wrath, living hermit-like in the wilderness, emerging like a trap-door spider to snare unsuspecting prey. On the contrary, Enoch's comportment conveyed gentility.

I was impressed that Enoch walked among the people at first, speaking with them individually. I wondered what his motive could have been for choosing such a hard life. He sought no riches. In fact, he cautioned against seeking wealth as life's overriding goal. In nothing he said did I perceive any aspirations to honor, position, or dominion over his listeners. On the contrary, he said he was a servant on a servant's errand—and that errand was to make his God known to this people. He spoke easily to children, telling them stories of his homeland, faraway Cainan by the east sea. He spoke of Adam's grandson Enos, who established the land and named it after his own son, Cainan. He said all lands should know the peace of Cainan, for its government was patterned after Adam's.

I knew of that land. My father had lived in Cainan as a boy. Later, his widowed father, Simeon, rebelled against the teachings of the patriarchs in Cainan and removed to Shum because he had heard of its wealth. Although my father was obliged to yield to Simeon and relocate to Shum, he brought with him in his heart what he had been taught in Cainan. Then, when he was of age, my father left Simeon and that way of life and retreated to the mountains of Shum to raise sheep and children and to keep a finger on the pulse of the city. Beneath the hills that bordered Shum, he settled with his wife, Abiah, who died soon after my birth, so my father reared my brother and me by himself and tended his sheep to support us. As a lad, I sat with him many times under starry skies and heard him mourn for his wife and lament the corruption in the land. He said he preferred the company of his sheep to partaking of the evils of the city of Shum.

To this day, the land of Cainan was feared. Rumor declared a fierce people lived there. Simeon himself was the first to propound the notion, but Enoch said Cainan was a righteous land. According to my father, what Enoch said was true.

Then Enoch stepped to a high place and addressed the people.

He began by speaking of the God of heaven who had created our first parents in His own image.

—Why do you stumble on this subject? he asked.

He opened the scrolls and rehearsed his paternal ancestry: Adam, Seth, Enos, Cainan, Mahalaleel, and his own father Jared—how each had known and spoken with God, recognizing him as their Creator. The plainness and clarity that Enoch's words introduced to my mind astounded me. The Watchers had taken the same truths and skewed them with mysticism to the point that no one could clearly understand them.

—The existence of these great men is not in question, he said, For they all yet live on the earth. So why do you doubt the God who created our fathers and whom they declare that they know? We, each of us, are progeny of the patriarchs, and thus we are all brothers and sisters—and if brothers and sisters, then we're equally loved by our fathers and by the God who made them and us.

I found myself nodding at his words, accepting his declarations as true.

—I am a messenger from God with authority to speak in his name, said Enoch.

He paused then, and I sensed the eyes of the congregation focus on him.

—I am of the same lineage as you, he said. As our fathers know, so I know, and I have seen God, and he has sent me to this land to declare his name and turn you to the way of righteousness.

I felt something I had never felt before, a surge of energy, a brightness like the first rays of morning. His words entered my being as though they had weight, and my heart began to pound, my bosom seemed afire. I looked up but saw nothing. Still, my face felt flush, and a warmth stirred within me and began to fill me up, as though I were an empty vessel. I felt my eyes become moist, and I quickly pulled my cloak over my face.

He boldly delivered his message, one of warning yet of hope, and I was dismayed that some of the assembly were visibly offended by him. Denouncing the leaders of Shum was one of his persistent themes—their abominations and vile compacts of power brokering would lead the entire valley into ruin, he said; their examples should sicken the most callous of Shum; and all creation mourns the wickedness here.

I remembered hearing those same leaders complain that Enoch had come to Shum to remove them from their positions and establish himself as king so that he could then force the people into his religion.

—My message to you from God is this: repent or be destroyed. Shum is doomed. My warning is to get out.

I was not prepared for such an extreme admonition. Enoch's rebukes cut to my heart. I was of the leadership of Shum that he decried. To be reminded of indiscretions was one thing, but to leave? I began to doubt the good feelings that I had had about Enoch and his message and began to think I had wasted my time. Then I witnessed a remarkable thing: Micah stood before the gathering and declared with soberness that he knew Enoch to be a prophet of God.

At Micah's declaration, Enoch's message had substance, and once again the feeling flowed into me like a warm fluid. Still, it was hard to give myself over to such sensations. But I could not deny I had felt something.

For the remainder of the evening, I stayed hidden, and I wouldn't reveal myself until the day Micah and I saved Enoch's life.

a stranger and a sojourner

ೞ

Morning came quietly, like the pause after lightning before the clap of thunder. The stillness should have awakened a warning in me, but, had I known, I could have done nothing. I sensed a deep rumbling, more a feeling than a sound. I sat up, alert. Suddenly, the earth shifted beneath me, and a blast of wind bent the pine, the trunk taking the shape of a taut bow. I tried to brace myself. Then the mountain trembled as if it were a frightened child, and the urge to scream shot through me. When I felt the vibrations deepen, a storm of white burst upon me. The pine twisted, and its limbs tore away. Its roots were ripped from the ground, and I was thrown into the squall. Rocks and limbs caught in the wake of the white tempest tumbled about me as though weightless. Perhaps I was dragged under; maybe I rolled. I felt as though I had been clubbed by an enemy. Then everything went black.

How long I had lain unconscious I could not tell. When I awoke, I could neither move nor see. The darkness was as complete as the black hole of a grave. I thought I was lying on my back, but perspective had vanished with my sight. I perceived no feeling in my legs and wondered if they were frozen. My arms were pinned to my sides, but I discovered I had limited movement in one hand. Then I wondered how I was able to breathe. I could feel no snow on my face, so perhaps I lay in a pocket of air, or maybe an airway led into the cavity that held me. In either case, I would not suffocate. I should have been relieved that I was yet alive, but when I considered my situation, I knew I would have preferred a quick demise over dying by degrees.

The tips of my fingers touched the cold handle of my knife. With some exertion, I grasped it and began to dig near my waist with the blade. My efforts were pitiful, and I began to doubt I could free myself before I froze. I enlarged the cavity somewhat but still could not move either arm. Without warning, snow fell down onto my face. After several attempts to blow it aside, a slender shaft opened in the snow above me. I peered out with one eye and saw a lone star glinting in the night sky. Spellbound, I gazed in awe at the sole luminary for a time and took it as an omen of hope.

That night, my circumstances pressed me again to pray. But I was ashamed of my hypocrisy—feeling after God in times of trouble, ignoring him in seasons of prosperity. Perhaps I was not a good candidate to be heard by God. Then I reconsidered. Would a parent refuse to speak to a wayward child? I surprised myself by saying the word *child*. Enoch taught that humanity didn't spring into existence through some cosmic anomaly. He said mankind had been *parented* by design, and I remembered my father had said the same.

Now, buried between life and death, I changed the tenor of my prayer. I pled to my *heavenly Parent*, one who I could imagine rushing to me as much as I would hurry to one of my children. I prayed more out of hope than from worthiness. I cried for deliverance, for assurance. If I were to face challenges, I no longer wanted to face them alone.

Then, lying cold in the snow, I felt something warm—a confidence, something personal and reassuring—the same sensation I had experienced while listening to Enoch—something eager like the first motion of spring. Deep in the snow, I felt that someone had thrust in a hand of hope and was offering to lift me.

That my face was pointed eastward became apparent when I saw the sunrise. Again I tried to move my arms and legs without success.

Only my wrist had mobility, and I resumed the quick digging motions with my knife. My despair returned.

—O Jerel! I cried. Tears filled my eyes and froze to my cheeks as I was overwhelmed with a sudden rush of anguish. How I missed my son! He hadn't accompanied me for profit; he just wanted to do a simple act of kindness. I cried for Moriah, trying to summon her face to my mind. Oh, that I might see her once more before I died!

At my waist, I had hollowed a small nook in the snow and found that my hand could move with some freedom. As I touched the leather strap, I knew the satchel of gems was still bound to me, and I considered the cost. I would have given them all and more for the life of my son.

A sharp pressure on my chest startled me. It shifted from side to side, then settled over my abdomen. I tightened the grip on my knife. Suddenly, a black nose filled the opening and sniffed in my face. A quizzical whining came, followed by another. I knew my visitors: I had been discovered by wolves!

I felt digging at my feet, and the snow's weight at my feet became lighter. Then, as though I had stepped into the vise of a trap, I felt powerful jaws lock onto my boot and tug. I cried out when the splint on my leg was yanked, and I kicked with my good leg. I felt it connect with something, and I heard a yelp and the sound of the animal bounding away. Then, when it returned, I sensed another had joined it. One sniffed at the hole over my head, and the other began to dig at my feet. I clutched my knife and imagined myself as a meal.

A poor answer to a prayer, I thought.

As the wolves continued intensely pawing away at the snow, I prepared my next move. Only surprise would give me an advantage, so I prepared to explode from the snow. My heart pounded, and my breathing quickened as I tensed. Then a thought flashed through my brain: *What if my arms don't work? What if they're frozen? With my hurt leg, what can I do?*

The digging continued furiously. I felt clawing at my chest and arms. When I felt something yank on the bearskin, I burst up through the snow, screaming, flailing my arms, and flashing my knife. As the two wolves yelped and darted around me, I jabbed one with my knife, and it tore down the mountain. The other latched onto my arm, teeth bared, and fought with me as I rolled out of the snow pit. As I stuck it in the shoulder, the animal howled and backed away, then came at my neck. I fell back with the wolf on top of me. I grabbed its throat, trying with all my strength to hold the animal's gnashing teeth away. Then I thrust the blade into the wolf's chest, brought it out and stabbed again and again, until the wolf crumpled into the snow.

I began to weep, not from remorse, but from fear. Twice more I stabbed the dead body, and I pushed it from me as a swath of red seeped into the white snow. I rolled onto my back, heaving great breaths into the frigid air, my forearm covering my eyes. My heart pounded in my chest as though it would leap from my body.

—I can't take any more! Can you hear me!? I shouted at the heavens.

Silence was my answer, and I lay there and cried.

Then I pulled back my arm and looked into the sky, a singular question struck me: *Had my previous prayer been answered? I was alive. But at what price?*

I went to an elbow and considered the dead animal, hungry and trying to survive just as I was. I considered what might have been the outcome. Still trembling, taking in quick, shallow breaths, I looked heavenward and wondered whether or not I should offer thanks. Then a deep sadness enveloped me. I could see that the wolf was a female, likely the mate of the companion that had run off. That her belly was fat told me she was pregnant with cubs, which would have been born in the spring. I felt the enmity between us leave, and I was sorry for the wolf. For the moment, I withheld my thanks. I wondered if expressing gratitude for my being alive while another had lost its life would be insulting to God.

The pain had returned to my leg. The strips that had bound the splints needed replacing, and the pine snowshoe was broken. As I sank into a drift to repair the splint, I saw that the avalanche had thrown me back into the hollow, erasing everything on the mountainside and covering the hollow deep with snow and debris—rocks, timber, branches stretching up through a white sea like the desperate hands of drowning men.

I cut into the wolf and was grateful for the meat, such as it was. But what I would have given for Moriah's bread! I closed my eyes and imagined I could see her rushing about her daily chores. Maybe in quiet moments her thoughts would turn to me and she would yearn for my return. Each time I had departed on a trip, I had tried to convince her that it was for her and the children. I had said so for such a long time that I had come to believe it, but I doubt she ever did. Tears always accompanied good-byes.

My father said it was irresponsible of me to leave my family without good reason. I argued that their support was reason enough. He said I was married to my work more than my wife. It was a subject on which he and I clashed. Another was his challenging my competitive nature, saying it was evil to destroy people. He meant my competitor, Baruch, and accused me of trying to ruin him. I argued with my father that he had misjudged my intentions, but even if he were correct, that was the way of business. Baruch knew the risks when he chose the profession, and he would do the same to me, given the chance.

I raised myself with my staff and hobbled to the edge of the hollow. The cliff was as sheer and steep as I remembered. Standing knee-deep in the cold, I wondered, *Had my pride brought me to this? Had I exchanged the life of my son for the satchel of gems strapped to my waist?* I turned and scanned the complete circle of the hollow. I knew every detail. How many days had my stay lasted? I had lost count. I had come to the hollow as a wayfarer and was forced to make a home of it. But remaining was beyond question. I longed to be on my way…*home.*

The word acted on my senses like a soft kiss. But it was not Shum I wished for—Shum was a location, just as the hollow was a location. What I wished for were Moriah, Benjamin, Enos, Eve, my father— they were my home.

Like a whisper, I heard, *You're a stranger and sojourner here.*

My only desire now was to leave, and I was determined that I would rather die in the attempt to flee than remain in the hollow.

ॐ

The tree, once my shelter, had been carried over the cliff by the avalanche. Its roots had lodged between boulders at its edge, and the top hung down, pointing toward the river. The pine had been stripped of most of its limbs, and I climbed on it cautiously to see if it would move under my weight. It seemed to be wedged tight and didn't budge. Perhaps I could wrap myself around the trunk and shinny down, using the broken limbs to catch myself. Where the treetop ended was a drop-off the length of a man. From there, I could fall into a drift of snow that was piled up deep against the lower face of the cliff, and I could slide to level ground.

I carved more meat from the wolf and stuffed it in the satchel of gems. Because I would need to use my arms, I pitched my crutch and satchel to where I hoped to land. Shading my eyes, I examined the sun's position in the sky and realized that dusk would come soon. I must hurry. I would need time to establish a camp below.

As I mounted the log, I set my sights on the stub of a limb below my foot and slid down the trunk until I reached it. I adjusted my hold and marked my next goal: a broken branch. With some difficulty, I reached it as well. When I slid to the end, I stopped, reminding myself that I must land feetfirst, regardless of the pain, in order to control my fall.

Just take courage and drop, I said to myself. Then I repeated it with more force. *The anticipation has to be worse than the pain.*

I was wrong.

As I let go of the tree and fell into the snowy slope, I felt my body tighten, and I landed on my backside, tumbling out of control. I clawed at the snow and dug in with my heels, trying to stop before I slid into the river. I remember slamming into something hard—a rock, possibly—that brought me to an abrupt halt at the edge of the river. I grabbed for my leg. I had not felt such intense agony since it had snapped under the weight of the bear. As I waited for the pain to subside, I reached for the satchel. I judged myself lucky—on second thought, blessed.

I was still alive.

I was free of the hollow.

I let out a shout of elation.

staying with the sheep

ॐ

On the night before my departure for Sharon, I once more visited my father to bid him good-bye. The calm of our early morning talk was interrupted by my daughter, Eve.

—Mahijah will address the people tonight! she shouted from a distance.

I *heard* Eve before I *saw* her. Shading my eyes from the morning sun, I saw my daughter hurrying up the foothills, her hair flowing as the golden mane of a filly on a romp. Her sandals were saturated with dew. Mirroring the colors of wildflowers, her dress, caught by a gust of wind, billowed out in front like a basket hoop, and she pushed it down at her thighs.

—Raiders from Sharon were caught and killed in the borders of Shum, she said.

She breathed heavily, trying to catch her breath, her cheeks the color of apples. The breeze soon calmed, in the foothills where my father and I had spent the night guarding his sheep and talking of life. Near my father's camp was the place where Enoch taught. I had often stopped to visit my father during the week of my departure for Omner and Haner. When he and I heard Eve's news, we knew it concerned the melee that had recently stirred Shum into an uproar. A long-standing dispute had resurfaced with the people of Sharon, Shum's neighbors to the northwest. We knew the people of Sharon hated us, but never before had they been aggressive.

—Sharon is near Omner, my first destination, I said. How many raiders were killed?

—Leah says twenty, maybe thirty, giant men.

—Sounds like Leah, said my father.

Leah was the round, ruddy-complexioned wife of Baruch, my competitor. Their children, Joshua and Rachel, were now the ages of my Enos and Eve. Our children had grown up together and had become good friends, despite my competing with Baruch. Leah fancied herself as Moriah's dearest friend and made sure that Moriah was aware of all the news of the city. Moriah mostly didn't mind, for Leah had a genius for juicy tellings and made it her business to collect tidbits of Shum's goings-on. I could imagine her rushing through Shum, making the story of Sharon's raiders larger with each retelling.

—Do you think the news is true? I asked my father.

He shook his head and waved away my question as though he didn't have the energy to discuss the obvious.

—It's true, said Eve.

She had heard the runners heralding the news, banging drums, startling dogs. She had seen the Rahaj shouldering the poles on which the bodies of Sharon's raiders were carried. She had heard Simeon call for an assembly of all Shum and had heard Mahijah's call for the Council to declare war on Sharon.

Eve came close and took my hand. Kissing her on the cheek, I brushed the hair off her face and forced a reassuring smile. She returned it, though unenthusiastically. I glanced at my father, who had straightened at Simeon's name being mentioned. I tried to sidestep his obvious irritation.

—You saw twenty or thirty? I asked Eve.

—I couldn't see for the crowd, but Leah said so.

Eve said that she had heard the people gasp when they saw the ferocious appearance and the frightening war gear of the raiders.

—Enos would know, she said, starting to recall more details.

He was with the Rahaj when they placed the bodies on a scaffold for display. Mahijah stepped to the Seat of Justice then.

In my mind, I could see the place at the center of Shum—a tall, arched stone under which the king and his judges discharged their responsibilities. Spread before it was an inlaid wood floor of immense proportions constructed of intricately designed geometric patterns. There, high courts were held, and Mahijah assembled the people for pronouncements. Above the Seat of Justice, on an ornate scaffold, sealed in a beautifully carved teak vault, lay the mummified body of Ramurah, Mahijah's father. To its side lay a narrow, grassy field where punishments and executions were carried out. Judgments evoked at the Seat of Justice in view of Ramurah, the deceased king, took on an air of solemnity.

—What did Mahijah say? I asked.

Eve puffed up pompous-like, made her voice deep, and quoted the king, saying, So shall be the fate of all the enemies of Shum! Let every man prepare for battle. Sharon is in our hands.

—And the people? asked my father, not amused.

—They applauded Mahijah's words. Then Simeon stood.

—He loves an audience, said my father.

Eve made herself old and summoned a stern voice to imitate her great-grandfather. Then she wagged a mocking finger and recited, We have other enemies in our borders, those who would enslave us with their false ideas and their unfounded accusations of our godlessness.

—Simeon speaks of Enoch, said my father.

—Yes, said Eve, But his statement frightened many of the people. I heard them murmur about the prophet in the hills.

—Most have come out to hear him, said Ebanel. The seer is an enigma—a wild man to some, a man of God to others. What did Mahijah do when the people didn't rally to destroy Enoch?

—He became agitated at their lack of response, said Eve. He called for Shum to rid itself of its enemies—from the raiders of Sharon to Enoch, the seer. Tonight, everyone is required to assemble.

My father looked out at his sheep. He appeared more ancient in the dim light—the grizzly stubble on his chin and jowls was patchy and uneven, and the shadows at his eyes made them look sunken.

—Tell Mahijah and Simeon I stay with my sheep, my father replied, shifting his weight.

For years, I had given my father polite audience, though discounting much of what he said as the mutterings of a lonely shepherd far too removed from human company. But since Enoch had come, I had been willing to seek my father's counsel.

—Mark what I say now, he said to Eve. The bodies are not of people from Sharon but made to appear so. I expect they're nomads, perhaps poor shepherds as am I. The intrigue of Mahijah and Simeon is an evil one, and they're willing to murder to obtain their objective.

Eve shot me a startled look, and I returned it, signaling her to not respond.

—I suppose Chaz will speak too, said my father. He loves to hear himself talk.

My father was not known for his tact. Eve looked away and held her tongue. Chaz was the prince of Shum, Mahijah's son, the one who courted Eve, the one whom Eve loved. Then my father addressed me with a solemn look, Do not attach yourself to the king or to Grandfather Simeon; they're of the profession of Cain.

I didn't argue. Taking my daughter's arm, I steered her toward Shum, departing my father's company before either of us said something we couldn't take back.

As a boy, my father had been brought to the valley against his will by his father, Simeon. That, coupled with Simeon's abandoning the teachings of the patriarchs, caused a rift between the two, making them seem more like enemies than father and son.

As I walked with Eve back toward Shum, I tried to explain why some people are as they are. The valley, always beautiful, lay before us crescent-shaped, high-grassed, and green. Beneath the shadows of my father's wooded mountains, converging streams springing from rocks in high places had formed a river, and it meandered along the fringe of the valley.

The land of Shum was discovered by a man named Shum, a generous soul who had named the land after himself. In those early days, nomadic people living in family tribes came to dwell in the valley at the invitation of the man Shum. He encouraged the tribesmen to remain there rather than follow their wandering lifestyle. That the valley had water and fertile ground convinced many to settle there. My father said Shum was a righteous man who had separated himself from the wicked traditions of his fathers and had gone in search of a land where he could live in peace. When he found it, he settled and was determined to rear a family there. As others came, heads of the families developed rules of trade and mutual courtesy, though no formal laws. The man Shum settled in the center of the valley where a spring burst from the earth. There he hollowed out a cistern, and the pool supplied water to the valley's inhabitants for three generations. He allowed all men free access to his well.

—He received nothing for his labor? I once asked my father.

—If you mean, did he receive anything that would increase his wealth or standing, I would answer that he received nothing. He allowed everyone to drink from the well, and his sheep grazed alongside those of other shepherds.

—A different time, I observed.

—And a better one, my father concluded.

Mahijah, Shum's grandson, now owned the well and collected taxes for use of the water, which had made him wealthy. Ramurah, his father, had not done so. But Ramurah had built Shum into a great city, purported to be second only to Nod in military might. All nations feared the land of Shum, and it had many enemies whom Ramurah had conquered. Ramurah died while hunting, it was said, falling and breaking his skull, and the people mourned for him. Mahijah ruled in his father's stead. A poor substitute, the populace had murmured. But Mahijah expanded the military element of Shum through the Order of the Rahaj, and the people felt secure. He aligned the city to the Watchers' doctrines, supporting that system of priests because they sympathized with his enterprising goals and commercial interests.

Under Mahijah's rule, the people had prospered, in large part because the Rahaj intimidated foreign lands.

The sun had moved midway through morning when Eve and I drew close to Shum. At our easy pace, half a morning was what was needed to make the trip. Only wisps of clouds marred an otherwise blue sky. A certain coolness predicted the season's changing, and the air was charged with the smell of wheat and corn, meaning harvest was at hand. Green meadowlands that encompassed the city would turn to yellow within days, and geese would rise from the far marshlands and wing southward. All told, walking the meadows of Shum from the bordering highlands was a trek I always enjoyed. I loved watching the myriad shapes of the city become sharp as I neared it. But, even at a distance, Shum was an imposing sight, a circular tent city of some five thousand dwellings. I loved Shum, but I worried over what was happening within its borders.

As Eve and I strolled and talked, a solitary figure came running toward us.

—Who is it? I asked.

We shaded our eyes and strained to see. Suddenly Eve tightened her hold on my arm and stepped to my side.

—What? I asked.

I turned to see her blush and knew I should keep still.

—It's Chaz, she breathed.

I had not known Eve to become quiet for too many things. She was quite a conversationalist, a gift she could call forth even in the dullest situation. But as Chaz approached, I felt her tingle with emotion. His features were sculptured like a statue's. His smooth face suggested it was seldom in need of a razor. Tall and muscled, he made two of me. A wavy, black mane fell to his shoulders, contrasting sky-blue eyes and fair skin. In every way, Chaz appeared regal—a stunning specimen of manhood. Before he spoke, he bowed to me and asked my permission to speak. I bade him do so.

—My father has called together all Shum tonight, he said.

This message from Chaz implied that my presence was requested at the Council.

—I'm preparing to leave for Omner, I reminded him, glancing at the sky, trying to ascertain the time of morning. What of Sharon? I asked. Are the rumors correct?

—Dead, replied Chaz without emotion. The raiders of Sharon are dead.

Eve steadied herself on my arm. Then it's true? she said. They *were* raiders from Sharon?

Chaz looked into my daughter's face and nodded.

—Will you come tonight? he asked her, smiling. His tone became tender, and I began to feel like an uninvited guest.

I sensed my daughter stir and seek for composure.

—Yes, she said in a shy voice, I'll come with my family.

Chaz cleared his throat, turned from her, and spoke to me in a resonant tone that I supposed he reserved for addressing men. He said, My father would like to see you before you depart on your journey, Rabunel. I hope to see you on your return.

I offered a slight bow, and, as a father will, I tried to appear imposing. I found myself agreeing with my father: Chaz *was* the proud offspring of "the rooster." I disliked the boy but couldn't decide why. Perhaps I didn't appreciate the attention he paid my daughter or the fact that she seemed to enjoy it.

As I watched the prince of Shum depart, I considered my daughter's expression.

—A handsome boy, I said, But I wonder, for all his polish, can he stay true? I hope you're not making a decision that will someday hurt you.

Eve looked off. The moment was ill-chosen to counsel her. Still, I couldn't help it. I knew his character. Given the choice, Chaz would elect property over people and self-elevation over benevolence. I doubted that he had ever denied himself anything. I questioned if such a man would cherish my daughter. Would she receive his complete devotion, or did he see in her a prize to display and then discard, as would a child tiring of a toy? I feared that when Eve was entangled in the arms of emotion, she would not be able to break free and consider the danger.

—Go to the city, I told her. Tell your mother that I have gone to speak with my grandfather, Simeon. Then I will come to her.

Eve looked toward the sun.

—You haven't much time, she said.

I nodded and squeezed her hand. Then she, who was so precious to me, hurried back to Shum.

straddling the gulf

௸

Looking up past the hollow, I saw a hawk circling overhead, a dark silhouette against the welcome dawn. Seeing the bird, and feeling the pain in my leg, reminded me I was yet alive. The hawk hovered above the hollow, and I reminded myself that I was free. I watched the magnificent bird command the sky, hold its course with its flight feathers splayed wide like long fingers, and I wondered what meal it would find on a mountain of snow. Then suddenly the hawk tucked its wings, dove, hit a snowbank, and rose with a mouse in its talons. I remembered the osprey. Its fish had no more sense to look up than the hawk's mouse did. My father was correct in his observation long ago, and time had changed nothing.

—Beware of your enemies, he had told me.

—Which? I had asked.

—Poverty and ignorance, he said. They're the worst. Ignorance is a conqueror's doctrine because an ignorant people is an easily controlled people. The wicked use ignorance to enslave. Ignorance shackles people to poverty, and poverty deflates hope.

As I gazed back up the cliff I had descended, a sharp fear shot through me: I didn't know a safe way home. The old woman's map had indicated a route that led through the hollow. Now, separated from the route by the cliff, I would have to find another way. Across the river was a thick forest covering a gentle slope. I had no idea what lay beyond. Upriver was steep and impassable. Downriver, I could see a steep descent that appeared treacherous. I had to choose. I had to be right. My life depended on it.

I resolved to pray. Believing that only God knew the safe way home, I asked his help. Then, clearing my mind, I waited for an impression, a stroke of communication that would steer me right. As I stepped near the river where it dropped off the mountain and cascaded into the valley below, I felt a calm clarity of thought touch my mind, and I started down.

A piece of wolf meat would be my morning meal. As I reached into the satchel, I pulled out a handful of blood-stained gems and raw wolf flesh. I paused. Holding my treasure in my hands, I again contemplated the price.

As I ate the meat, I tried to rub the blood off the gems. The meager meal left me aching inside. *How many days had I subsisted on foul portions of little or nothing?* I wondered to myself.

I hobbled on my crutch, following the river's course down the mountain, until I fell exhausted into a snowbank at the water's edge. My leg pulsed with pain. Rolling to my stomach, I dipped a cupped hand into the freezing water and brought it to my mouth. I repeated the effort until my fingers became numb and blue.

Suddenly I heard an unfamiliar sound in the distance. I moved behind a rock. I patted the knife at my side, appreciating the dangers of the wilderness and knowing how swiftly a situation can change. As the sound grew closer, I leaned into it, straining to discern its source. Over the clamor of the river's flow, I detected the sound of a horse blowing and the even rhythm of a horse lifting its legs high in the snow, its hooves packing the icy flakes flat with each step. Then I hid as the rider came into view. He wore silken robes of robin egg blue. A wide, scarlet sash skirted him at the waist; a braided rope of gold strands adorned him at the shoulder. I had seen such attire many times among the Watchers of Shum. Although partly covered by a warm-looking, doeskin cloak, the similarity was enough to tell me the traveler was a priest. I sighed, and my heart filled with hope.

As I moved to step from behind the tree, a remarkable thing happened. I heard a soft voice—or rather I *felt* a voice. It seemed to say, *Be still. There is another way.* But when I saw a rabbit dangling from a whip of leather at one side of the traveler's saddle and the clutch of food tied to the other, I dismissed the warning, allowing my stomach to speak louder. I stepped into the traveler's path.

—I am Rabunel, son of Ebanel the shepherd, I said, raising my arms high in a sign of peaceful greeting. My grandfather, Simeon, is a priest of the Watchers of Shum.

The horse became startled, and the rider reached for his knife.

—I'm not an enemy! I'm just a sojourner like yourself, seeking a way home, I said, dropping to a knee.

Relaxing his hand, the priest set down the reins of his horse and leaned forward. He said, My name is Asher. I've just come from the way of Shum. The land of Nod is my home and destination.

—I've heard of Nod, but I've never visited the place, I said.

Then I stood, lifting myself with my staff, and Asher took note of my splinted leg.

—From a vicious bear attack, I said. Then I rehearsed how I'd lost my son and was trying to find my way to Shum.

Asher listened with apparent interest and astonishment. He wondered aloud how I was alive.

—By the grace of God, I answered.

He nodded, then continued looking me over.

—You could be of great service to me, I said.

—How?

—You can see my desperate state. A little food and a transport to Shum would save me.

Asher straightened, his eyes narrowing. Are you a fugitive? he asked.

—No, I replied, A merchant.

—I cannot detour, he said. My presence in Nod is urgent.

I felt a twinge of anxiety, and my mind raced. My skill as a communicator was failing me.

—I appeal to you by the God you serve, I said.

—It is God's service that makes my journey imperative, he answered, lifting the reins and coaxing the horse forward. Then he said, But I wish you Godspeed.

Stepping in front of him, I took the horse at the bridle and said, I can pay.

Asher sat back in his saddle.

—As I said, I'm a merchant, I said.

He paused and seemed to study me. As he did, I became conscious of my appearance—filthy, bearded, clad in ragged clothing, wounded, wrapped in a reeking bearskin. I was surprised when Asher said he would listen to me. Then he looked at my tight grip on the bridle and gestured toward my hand. I released my grip.

—It's hunger that drives me, I said.

Asher remained on his horse. His black eyes were hollow, reflecting no light, partially shaded by connected bushy eyebrows. He was a small, square man, ruddy-cheeked, with a bulbous nose. He had the guise of a small bull, but I judged I could take him in a fight, if not for my current condition.

—My home is Shum, I repeated. In my land, I'm a man of substance and influence. I'm a merchant and trade in gems, but a set of terrible circumstances has brought me to my present miserable state. Still, I have means to pay for what I ask. I beg you for food and a ride to Shum—or at least a ride off the mountain.

—Food perhaps, Asher said, But my supply is dwindling. A ride is impossible.

—Food and a flint for fire, I pled, Snares if you have them.

I pulled aside the bearskin and retrieved the satchel of gems and shook them.

—Precious stones, I said.

Asher became silent, eyed the bag, then slipped off the horse and came near. Measuring his words, he said, Priests have little use for gems.

—For your ministry, then, I replied as I opened the satchel and brought forth a handful of blood-smeared stones—rubies, diamonds, sapphires, emeralds.

He admired an emerald and asked if he might hold it. I cleaned the stone, then rubbed it to a lustrous green and placed it in his hand.

—For food and a flint? I asked.

Asher said nothing as he turned the emerald between his thumb and forefinger, letting it catch the sunlight and shoot lime-colored rays onto his palm. I polished a ruby and placed it in his other hand.

—Surely you can part with a little food, I said.

—Impressive, he said, still gazing at the red stone. What else do you have? For the right price, I'll give you what you want.

A feeling of hopelessness churned in my stomach. I recognized the sensation from former negotiations gone awry—a notion that my bargaining position was weakening and that there was no way to win.

—The emerald and the ruby for food, I said. Do we have a deal?

—Of course. What else do you have?

With no degree of pleasure, I dug into the satchel and retrieved more gems. Then, as I was pulling out my hand, Asher drew his sword.

—The price just went up, he said, nodding at the handful of gems I held.

—You want all of them?

—You're obviously a thief, so I'll relieve you of the stolen goods.

I took a step back and reached for my knife, and, as I did, Asher lunged at me and slashed me at the side, just above the left hip. I clutched my wound and dropped the satchel at my feet, collapsing, bleeding.

—You're fortunate we're not in Nod, he said. You would be beheaded, and your body would be scattered among the wild beasts.

—I'm not a thief! I cried. If you leave me like this, I'll die.

But by that time, Asher had picked up the satchel and mounted his horse.

As he rode by me, he said, You deserve to die.

Then he strapped the satchel to his waist, and, as he was leaving, I heard him thank his god.

I pulled back my clothing, now scarlet and saturated with blood, to expose the wound. I lifted the skin, revealing a slit as deep and red as a trout's gill. I could not quell a cry. Asher had cut me diagonally. The gash pulsated with the rhythm of my heart, seeping blood at its corners. I folded the flesh together, packing snow into the cut, then pressed it tight with the heel of my hand.

Again the soft voice came, reminding me of its warning, and a surge of disappointment in myself shot through me more painful than the wound. I remembered I had begged for divine intervention but had yielded to the urgency of the moment. I felt a heaviness in my heart, the kind one feels at the news of death. *Had recent events taught me nothing?* I inquired of myself. I feared that, by ignoring the voice, I had distanced myself from the Deity whom I had so earnestly entreated.

ognl

As I bled from the wound, I remembered how, after I had first listened to Enoch, I sneaked away from Shum each day for seven days to hear him. On the night of the eighth day, I spoke with him.

I recalled that swollen clouds had rolled into the mountains, obscuring peaks. Dusk had loosed fireflies, wide-eyed owls, hungry opossums. Evergreens had become as black as the night that swallowed them, charging the air with the welcome aromas of pine and resin. As summer had moved toward autumn, darkness and cool had begun to come quickly to the high, forested areas. On my way to hear Enoch, I trekked the foothills alone. I lit a torch and walked as quietly as I could.

I recalled Enoch's speaking of Cainan, his homeland. It was a land of peace, he had said, and the righteous people there had paid the necessary price for the harmony and unity they enjoyed—forsaking impure desires and seeking the benefit of all. He claimed that in Cainan there were no poor and that from the earliest days the people had sought to duplicate Adam's original society by abhorring selfishness and embracing godliness.

I wondered what change of heart would be needed for such an achievement. It seemed impossible. Still, I wanted to believe that life could hold more meaning than what little the endless struggle for sustenance offers. I asked myself, *Wasn't man created for something greater than this? Is life only about what we have? Isn't it also about who we become?*

Ahead, and up the mountain, I saw the flickering of torches and detected the distant voice of the seer. I neared. Extinguishing my flame, I once more secluded myself beneath a tree not far from Enoch and saw that I was one of a small group of truth-seekers that had traveled from Shum. Micah sat in front at the center.

An unseasonable chill settled on the mountainside. The clouds had ebbed, and stars now appeared in a clearing sky. A yellow moon rode the tide of night until it was full and high. Torches were doused, and their light yielded to dark, quiet peace. I wrapped myself in my cloak and reclined against the tree.

As was his custom, Enoch moved among the people, greeting them, exchanging pleasant conversation. Then he settled on an outcropping of rock and began to teach. He recounted his calling from God. It was a bold claim similar to the one I had heard the Watchers make. In my estimation, the Watchers' religion was so much pomp and pageantry, more show than substance, designed to capture the people's imagination, flatter them, prey on their fears, and confuse ignorant minds.

—Your priests and leaders are corrupt. They stand before the people, preaching family and morality, then go off to secret places and seduce foolish women. They walk the streets of Shum decrying violence, then, in private, they plan the murder of their opponents. They boast of liberty, then tax the public into slavery. They kiss orphans, then steal crumbs from their tables. Rhetoric is their language, and self-seeking defines their every thought and action. They build their fortunes on the backs of the poor. They cause the impoverished to suffer in the shadows of their mansions. They point to their prosperity as a sign of heaven's approval. And it is war they plan, not for security but for gain, and when they wage it, *you* will be the casualties. People of Shum, beware. Your winking at evil in any degree can only serve to open wider the door of destruction. For you've allowed evil to creep in among you unchallenged, and when the lust for power, pride, and greed at last converge, this people will be annihilated suddenly, in a moment.

I marveled that a man so given to gentility could proclaim a warning with such boldness. As I listened to him, I strained to perceive any malice in him, but his demeanor was like a parent cautioning an errant child from pending danger. I sensed that he had a true concern for us, and this drove him to deliver his message in the clearest language.

He asked, Do not those in authority shoulder a responsibility of moral example? Can a society prosper while upholding leaders who see themselves as beyond law? Can a people survive without moral principles?

Enoch said much that was new to me. He said that if a society travels the road to ruin long enough, it will eventually collide with its destiny—ultimate destruction.

—As long as a society produces poverty and ignorance, or allows them to exist, he said, That society teeters on the verge of extinction. What ultimately causes a society to be worthy of annihilation? The willful and sustained rebellion against God.

As I considered what I'd heard, I saw two men creeping toward Enoch with knives drawn. I knew not what to do. Springing like a lion, one of the men rushed Enoch, brandishing a knife. Some people shrieked. Quickly, Micah leaped at the would-be assassin, wrestling him, sinking a big fist in the man's face, and rendering him unconscious. Then the other man charged. With little thought, I jumped to my feet, bounded over those still sitting, and knocked the second man to the ground. Rolling to his feet, he flashed his knife and lunged at me. His knife tore my clothing and pierced my shoulder. Trying to hold his weapon away from me, I grappled with him, but his strength exceeded mine, and soon he was upon me, cursing, thrusting his

knife. Then suddenly Micah ripped the attacker from me and heaved
him into the trunk of a tree. The stunned man gasped for breath and
tried to recover, but Micah was upon him. Grabbing the man by the
neck and thigh, Micah lifted the would-be assassin over his head.
Then, as he readied himself to drop to the ground and break the man
over his knee, the assailant's face went ashen. Together, Enoch and I
shouted for Micah to stop, and I rushed to hold back his arms. I could
feel his muscles tighten and twitch. Then he looked at me, and an
expression of dismay washed over his face. Enoch hurried to Micah's
side and helped me gently lower Micah's arms. The terrified assailant
dropped to the ground and, for a moment, didn't move.

Enoch reached out to help the would-be assassin to his feet, but
the frightened man jumped up and fled toward Shum. I sat next to
Micah, his eyes fixed in their gaze and his chest heaving. Enoch knelt
beside me and touched my wound.

—This needs attention, he said.

I looked at the gash in my shoulder, and immediately my hand
went to it. As Enoch wrapped the wound in linen, a remarkable thing
happened. Micah slumped, but Enoch caught him. Then Micah
began to sob like a child, saying, I swore off violence, but I was ready
to kill that man.

As Micah shook with grief, the stunned people began to hurry
away. I stood and examined my wound, feeling the dull weight of
shock settle in my brain.

—Wait a moment, said Enoch. Let me finish dressing that wound.

—I'll be fine, I said, trying to ignore my sluggishness of thought.
You should stay with Micah, and I'll go home.

Enoch began to protest, but I turned, sensing that if I didn't move
on, I might faint. As I started for home, my palm pressed into the
bloody cut. I glanced heavenward and saw that dusk was closing fast.
I looked back. Micah was still weeping, despite his being consoled by
the seer. At the brow of the hill, I sat to rest and watched the sun dip
below the horizon.

The cut isn't so deep that I should be shaking, I thought.

But I continued to shake, just the same, and felt a terrible fatigue. *It's the fright I feel more than the hurt,* I reasoned. *A little rest is all I need.*

At my shoulder, my cloak had taken on the hue of a rooster comb, and I pressed my hand into it and lay back under a tree. As night came, thick clouds crept across the sky, obscuring the stars and moon. The breeze that was wont to caress the mountainside had become still. I don't know how long I slept.

—Rabunel, a voice said, rousing me. I looked up into the face of the young prophet who held a torch and was nudging me.

—You know my name? I asked.

—Micah told me, and I know your father, he said. Let me clean and dress your wound.

Pouring water into his cupped hand, he washed away the dried blood. I winced and reached out to stop him, but he urged me to allow him to clean the injury.

—Thank you for protecting me, he said.

—I didn't do much, I said, trying awkwardly to deflect his thanks. He smiled.

—I don't remember falling asleep, I said.

Enoch nodded and said, It's been a long day for everyone. I know something of these mountains, and where you've been lying isn't safe.

He pulled the skin together and began dressing the wound. As he did, my speech quavered with a series of crisp gasps.

—I grew up in these mountains, I said, trying to sound brave. I'm sure I'll be fine. I'll rest here tonight, and at dawn I'll go home.

—You're welcome to share my camp tonight. Feels like a storm's coming.

After he had rewrapped my wound, he asked, How does that feel?

I stood and tried my shoulder by raising and lowering my arm twice.

—Fine.

I gazed at the sky, then surveyed the landscape where I had lain. Enoch's comment about its being unsafe was true.

—Is your camp far? I asked

—Not very, but there's one difficult spot. Do you think you can walk?

—Yes.

As he took my arm, he said, I would appreciate your company, and your family won't worry. I told your father I would find you.

Enoch held the torch out in front of us as we started up to his camp. As we walked in the torchlight, we spoke of simple things.

—Looks like a good harvest this year, he said.

—Yes, we had a wet spring.

—You've done some farming?

—A little, I said, But mostly I shepherded with my father. Now I trade.

—For what?

—Anything valuable: metals, pottery, fabrics. Precious gems are my passion.

—Is that profitable?

—Trading for gems eclipses all my other trade combined.

—Do your children help you? he asked.

—Not much. Jerel, my second son, has the knack but not the interest. What about you? Do you have a family?

—Not yet, he said. But my wife and I hope to have a large family.

—Have you been married long?

—Not long.

That comment brought a long moment of silence.

Then I said, I can see that you miss her.

He nodded.

—Did she remain in Cainan?

—Yes. She's staying with my parents until I complete my work here. Then I'll send for her.

I felt uncomfortable having brought up a painful subject. I was surprised by Enoch's vulnerability. It endeared him to me. He seemed more approachable somehow, less intimidating. I liked him.

—I enjoyed hearing your message, I said. I admire your command of the language.

He backed away from the praise by changing the subject.

—Your father is a good man, he said. I have spent several nights in his tent sharing memories of Cainan.

—My father still mourns being taken from it, I said. He talks about returning, but I doubt he ever will. His sheep hold him to these valleys and mountains.

—Maybe someday you'll go to Cainan with him.

—Perhaps. I grew up hearing the stories of the patriarchs there—Adam, Seth, Enos, Cainan, Mahalaleel, and your father Jared. I'd love to meet Adam.

—He sometimes visits Cainan, said Enoch. He and Mother Eve have chosen to remain in the valley that they settled in after leaving the Garden of Eden.

—You've met them?

—I've spoken with them at length. It was Adam who assigned me to this mission. He instructed and blessed me.

—What are they like? I asked.

—Even though he's very old now, there's no more magnificent specimen of manhood than Adam. And Mother Eve's beauty could never be surpassed. She is elegant and dignified, truly a queen.

—The Watchers teach that the Garden of Eden is a false tradition, I said.

—It existed, said Enoch, But if you were to visit the area now, you would be hard-pressed to recognize it as a paradise. What was once a place where fruits and flowers grew spontaneously, and where the lion and the lamb lived together in peace, is today overgrown and inhabited by beasts of prey.

—I can't imagine such a place or a beginning, I said.

—I doubt anyone can imagine the Garden, he said. But it's important to know that the cradle of the human family was a more exalted place than we live in now.

—Why?

—A wise man knows his origin and his destiny, he said. Ignorance can cause a man to see himself as an aberration of nature, a being born of chance, walking the earth on an uncertain course—not as a being of purpose and destination.

—Then man should remember Eden? I asked.

—Yes, he said. It points him back to God.

We walked on.

—I wonder what it was like being the only two on the earth and starting a family here? I said.

—Rich and poor were definitions that had not entered the world. That's one thing, said Enoch.

—What do you mean?

—You're a father, he said. Each of your children is different, but do you favor one over another? Of your property, do you give to one and withhold from another?

—Of course not.

—God gave the whole world to Adam, said Enoch, And he, in turn, gave it to his children. That condition of equality existed until Cain killed Abel to enrich himself. From that point, distinctions were drawn, the earth was divided up, men began to distinguish themselves by their belongings, and inequality wove itself into the fabric of all human relations.

—You're suggesting we go back to that time?

—We're still all of the same family, he said. Nothing man has tried since Adam has succeeded as well for the happiness and progress of man as that first government headed by father Adam.

—I have trouble conceiving of your ideal society, I said. How can such a state be achieved when it's man's nature to injure his fellow beings and pursue acts of selfishness?

—It can only succeed by man's having a cause higher than himself, said Enoch.

—My observation has been that the poor, more so than the rich, crusade for higher causes, especially when it comes to working toward better society. The attempts I've seen have been squelched by those who control wealth and power. In this world, the great men of power will never allow the *higher cause* you advocate.

—True greatness is measured by one's ability to give, he said. Without giving, there can be no progress, either for individuals or for societies.

ભ

I followed Enoch to a river cascading from a tight ravine. The fast water had cut a gulf in the rocky ground.

—Be careful, he said. The water is deeper than it looks.

—Where's your camp? I asked.

—Up, he said, pointing. The widest part is here at the bottom, but it will soon become narrow. I'll hold the torch, and you follow behind me.

Although the night was dark, I could make out the boundaries of the ravine, its steep walls rising from the constricted gulf through which the river flowed. Enoch held his torch high, and I felt my way forward by its flicker, often straddling the river or leaping from one side to the other. Soon, the banks became only thin ribbons.

—Why did you choose such a remote place for your camp? I asked.

—It's safer.

—Is there another way up?

—No. That's why I chose it.

When the banks of the river narrowed, he instructed me to wait while he went ahead.

—The way becomes so narrow that only one of us can ascend it at a time, he said. I'll go up and shine the light down and tell you where to step. But you'll have to scale it alone. Can you do that?

—I think so.

Enoch leaped to the other side of the river and vanished around a corner, and I watched his torch become a dim glow reflecting off the wall of the ravine. When the light reappeared, I saw Enoch on a high ledge, shouting for me to come forward.

—Jump to the other bank now, he yelled above the noise of the river.

I crouched with my hands on bended knees to improve the angle of my vision. The black sky produced no more light than the sheen of bat wings. A sound startled me. A pair of orange eyes, round and wide, winked at me from a high spot on the far side of the river. I presumed the eyes were an owl's. As I lunged for the opposite bank, I heard the owl flap away, and my foot slipped on the slick bank.

—*Ahhh!* I hollered.

I reached out and latched onto a lip of rock, then I pulled my foot from the water and came up straight, gripping the rock wall with my fingers. The backs of my feet felt the thin ledge of the bank drop off, and I shouted to Enoch, The bank is too narrow!

—The other side is wider for a ways, but it drops straight off, he yelled back.

—If I go forward, I'll fall in!

—Feel above you. There's an edge jutting out.

I caught it and began to ease forward, the prospect of a safe ascent seeming more and more hopeless. Even the flicker of Enoch's torch above me and his words of encouragement gave me little comfort.

An idea burst upon me. I shouted over the roar of the river, I'll leap to the wider side, then jump back over when the path becomes too dangerous. At the narrow parts of the river, I'll straddle it.

Enoch shouted back, It's not possible. Do what I tell you, and you'll be safe.

Enoch's instructions were clear, but from where I was, I imagined if I took another step, I would fall into the river's current and be swept away. Nevertheless, after taking a big breath, I took my sights off the other side, grasped the wall, and began to ease forward, Enoch talking me through every step.

When I reached the top, I was exhausted and shaken, but safe. As I sat beside Enoch, he handed me a warm cup of broth and a large hunk of bread. Then, shining the torch back down at the narrow pathway, I made out the treacherous gulf below and realized that Enoch had been right: Had I attempted to straddle the gulf even a scant distance further, I might have slipped and perished. There had been no other way.

where god is found

ෆ

I watched Asher riding away, drawing a long path of broken up snow where the horse stepped. I scooted back under a pine where the ground was dry and lay back, holding my side. My wound needed suturing. I had seen it done. I reached for the string of bear claws I had hanging from my neck. Then, with my knife, I began to carve one of them into a sharp needle with a bored hole in it.

The loud calls of quail startled me. As I peeked from beneath the wide pine boughs, I beheld a covey of perhaps a hundred black-plumed birds scurrying about the area where I had lain. I remained still. Such a delicacy I had not eaten in days. As I searched my mind for a way to make a trap, several males—heads of reddish brown and bellies of white barred with black—came close. Their throats and a line above their eyes were white. At the eyes, and extending back around the throat, was a broad band of black. A quick gust of wind blew icy crystals, and as if of one mind, the covey members huddled in a circle with their heads turned outward. Slipping the bearskin from my back with imperceptible movement, I crouched, stretching my arms out to the hide's extreme edges. Then, with the motion of a fisherman casting his net, I threw the skin out over the covey and rushed to hold down the sides. Some of the quail squawked and ran. Others, flushed from the circle, took flight, beating their wings rapidly with a loud flapping sound. I jumped on the skin, spreading myself out over the bearskin, holding down the corners, gathering them toward me, tucking in the edges, and beating the bearskin with my fists. My method was not very sporting, but my hunger spoke louder. I drubbed the bearskin until the movements beneath it completely stopped. Then, as I lifted a corner, I saw that the quail were dead, and I had succeeded in catching enough for a week's meals.

As I buried the birds beneath the pine, covering them in snow and a piece of bearskin to discourage scavengers, I stopped short and realized the voice had been right—*there was another way*. A means to feed me had been in place just as I had asked, but I had not waited for it. Once more, I chastised myself for my shallow faith. I had learned a lesson in trust, and I offered gratitude for the quail. With what light was left in the day, I would suture my wound, then go after Asher and what he had stolen from me.

cs

That night, as snow began to fall, I slipped from beneath the pine and followed Asher's tracks. When the snow came with more fury, I heard the soft crackle of fire and smelled smoke. I found him near the river, sitting on his haunches, palms out before him, warming himself by a small fire. The fire popped and sputtered with the moisture from the snow. Tethered to a tree near the river was Asher's horse. If I approached the camp, clad in bearskin, I knew I would be detected by the animal, so I crouched behind a rock and waited.

I watched him—Asher, the Watcher—he who professed servitude to God, he who had robbed me, stabbed me, and left me for dead. I shuddered at the thought of my son Benjamin's desire to become a Watcher. Then I thought of how my son Enos loved the militant Rahaj that served the Watchers. I worried for my sons. For they, like me, were struggling to find themselves, caught in a world with only degrees of evil as choices, and I feared that I was losing them.

The night had grown late when the breeze gliding down the mountain shifted. The snow still fell. Asher's fire had gone cold, and he lay asleep in his tent. The horse stood a distance away, drowsing. My purpose was to retrieve my property, peacefully if I could, with force if I must. I was prepared to kill the Watcher if he opposed me. I would take the horse for recompense. Careful not to drag my leg and make noise, I made exaggerated walking motions, swinging it out to the side and dropping it forward. I skulked to a bulky rock at the fringe of Asher's camp and knelt on one leg behind it. From there, I could see the pack where he kept his food and valuables. The satchel of gems was knotted to it with a belt. Wounded as I was and weak from lack of food, I doubted I could overpower him. Surprise was my only hope.

Clutching my knife, I measured the distance from where I was to Asher's tent in the clearing. I stared at the horse, watching for signs of movement. I strained to hear the sounds of Asher's breathing. It was labored and rhythmic, a faint whistle with each release of air.

I stood. The muscles in my back were drawn tight and tense like a cat ready to spring. All at once, as I readied to move, the wind eddied. It was at my back, and before I could hide, the horse became startled and stamped nervously. The sound roused Asher from his tent, and he parted the flap and stuck out his head. I quickly crouched behind the rock and held my breath. Asher emerged from the tent and walked the circumference of his camp. Soon the horse calmed, laying its ears back, relaxing its head. Muttering, Asher knelt by the fire and stirred the coals. Then, loading tinder and logs on the flames, he wrapped himself in a blanket and retreated to the tent.

The snow was falling harder now, but the crackling fire gave off enough light to see Asher's camp. So I arose. Circling the camp to the downwind side and watching for signs of movement in Asher's tent, I stole toward him, every motion measured. I heard him stir once, and I became as stone. When I heard his toiled breathing return, I stepped forward, parted the tent, and stood over him. In the short time I had known this Watcher, I had learned to hate him. I hated his pretense as a God-fearing man, a hypocrisy made more loathsome to me by his fine robes and all the Watchers who wore such robes. I detested his willingness to cheat a person in need. I resented his seeing me as an animal and not as a man. And I hated his supposing me ignorant and easy to exploit.

Suddenly Asher opened his eyes wide, and an expression of fear washed over him. He grabbed for his sword, but I stepped on it. Then he made a fist and hit my broken leg, and as I fell back, he rolled, darted out of the tent, and dove toward the fire. Raising myself on my crutch, I hobbled after him. He grabbed the cold end of a stick from the fire and waved the burning end in my face.

—Stay back, or I'll burn you! he cried, picking up a second burning stick.

He swung and poked the sticks at me as if they were swords. I held my knife in front of me and slashed out at him. When the fire on the first stick had almost died out, he threw it at me. As I ducked, the fiery stick landed at the feet of the horse, which panicked, reared, broke away from the rope that held it, and began to thrash about in the river.

—Hear that? I yelled. Your horse is drowning.

Asher waved his remaining stick at me. Then I saw the horse break from the river and gallop off into the night.

—You're a dead man! cried Asher as he charged me.

I caught his arm, sending the burning stick into a bush, and wrestled him to his back, straddling him, bringing my blade to his throat.

—I should kill you where you lie, I said, taking him by the hair and pressing the point of my knife into the skin.

Asher tried to speak, but the movement drove the tip deeper, and drop of blood traced a crimson line down his neck.

—We had a bargain, and I will help you keep your word, I said.

He stared at me wide-eyed, and I quickly picked up a rock the size of my palm and hit him on the crown of his head. Asher groaned and reached for the spot. Then he tried to get away, so I hit him twice more until he fell unconscious, but continued to moan. Quickly,

I began to rummage through his supplies and found food and flints that I stuffed in a blanket. He began to groan and move. I grabbed the satchel of gems and searched it until I found the emerald and ruby that Asher had admired.

—I am no thief! I said, placing them in his hand and folding his fingers around the two gems.

As I cinched the satchel to my waist, I said, This is the price we bargained for, and you will receive it! Then I dragged him into his tent so he wouldn't freeze and hurried away from his camp.

I headed back to the pine where I had buried the quail, my hate for Asher still smoldering like his fire. In the stillness as I trudged, I was pricked in my heart for the course of my life. I now saw in my own life much of what I hated in Asher. I wondered to myself, *How did I stray so far away from the simple truths I had learned in my youth?* I couldn't recall the moment of departure. I hadn't discerned a change. It had happened so quietly, so gradually. But the direction was clear—I was being escorted to hell, and I hadn't known it.

My thoughts turned to my family and how my course of life had affected them. I thought of Jerel, how my pride had cost him his life. I thought of Eve's giving herself to Chaz, a young man who had no capacity to love anyone but himself. I thought of Benjamin, who loved the Watchers and couldn't discern the deceit. I thought of Enos, his being seduced by the doctrines of the Rahaj, all the while thinking he'd discovered the secret of happiness. I thought of Moriah, she who loved me and had waited long years for me to change. I thought of the honest, simple life of my father, Ebanel, and of the sacrifices he'd made to live a moral life.

—O God, help me! I cried. I am lost.

I prayed for forgiveness and for protection, for I knew Asher would waken and search for me. When I reached the pine, I bound the quail in a clutch and hung them from my belt. My leg bore the hurt of Asher's blow, and my side smarted with every step. The sky began to release huge flakes, and the powder soon piled up around my knees. I began to climb up a gentle incline, although I had no idea where it would lead me. For now, I just wanted to distance myself as far as possible from Asher. At length, I came to a steep cliff, and I began to despair, for I felt that I was trapped against it and would be easily found. For the remainder of the night, I continued up the incline. At the first light of morning, I came to a massive stony wall pocked with caves. I selected a deep opening and entered the mouth of a dark den.

If I slept, it was only for a short time. From the hole of my cave, I looked out and saw that a bright sun was overhead, about midway through morning. The snow had stopped. I could see that I had climbed up the ridge of a cup-shaped valley molded into the side of the mountain. To my right was the cliff. To my left, and at the far end of the valley, was Asher's tent. He had found his horse, for he was riding it as he combed the area, dismounting on occasion to examine things. After he had made several large circles at the borders of the valley, he rode to the cliff and spent a long time looking over it. Then, by midday, when the sun was high, he broke camp and rode off to the north.

He knows I'm lame and wounded, I thought, *I guess he thinks I'm dead.*

I ate Asher's food—dried meat, vegetables, fruit. *How long had I gone without these tastes?* I savored them, nibbling slowly and meditatively, allowing the flavor to remain in my mouth until the last essence had disappeared. Because the quail would have to feed me for several days, I spread them on the cold floor of the cave, gutted and plucked them, then buried them, covering their bodies with snow to retard their spoiling and conceal their scent. I tucked away the flints, knowing I couldn't use them until I was certain Asher had left the area. The bearskin would continue to be my main shelter.

A slim opening, barely visible to the outside world, marked the entrance to the cave. I discovered I hadn't been the cave's first occupant. Eerie drawings of hunters killing horned animals sullied the walls. The floor was covered with bones of animals. I took a sharp-edged rock and carved my own mark on a wall: one mark for one day.

I would make a mark for every day I remained in the cave. Here I would hide and heal, wait out the winter, and, in the spring, when I could walk the long distance, I would go home.

The satchel of gems seemed to weigh more than I had remembered. With the gems in one hand and all that they had cost me in the other, I made a scales and weighed what was in each hand in my mind. My empty hand weighed far more. I eyed the sash at my waist where I had tied the gems. Since the moment I had acquired the gems, they had clung to me like slave shackles, and now I wanted to be rid of them. I wanted to be *free!* I wanted to go *home,* and I felt they were holding me back. That evening, when I felt certain Asher had left, I made a decision. I struggled to the river where the water was calm and deep, then took the satchel of gems, and, without a twinge of remorse, heaved them into the river.

With that done, what was left for me was to heal and go home.

ᘓ

Winter came hard to the mountains. On many mornings, I dug an opening through snowdrifts thrown up by unrelenting winds. That any form of life could survive here astounded me. Yet, when the storms subsided, I observed a variety of edible game—quail, grouse, snowshoe hares, cottontail rabbits, and deer. Because they needed water, I set snares near the river. But I couldn't catch them. I hadn't trapped since I was a boy. I thought I was a better fisherman than a trapper and tried catching brown trout from the river but met with equal failure.

Those first days in the cave were ones that nearly cost me my life. When I had eaten all the quail and the remainder of Asher's food, I suffered four days for want of food and was reduced to gnawing away the tough hide of the bearskin to quell my hunger.

Then I asked God for help, and something remarkable happened. What was remarkable was not that I prayed—I *had* prayed for help in the past, and had received it—the miracle was in my making a specific request. For when I had done so, and I went about setting my snares, a glint of an impression entered my mind that I should discard the bearskin. My reaction to the thought was how I would suffer with cold for such foolhardiness. But I decided to experiment on the impression and leave the bearskin in the cave.

After hurrying to set the snares, I returned to the warmth of my fire and waited. *Perhaps*, I thought, *the bearskin yet carries enough of the scent to frighten off game.* Within moments, I heard a high-pitched screaming, and I rushed out to see a cottontail buck thrashing about, its back leg caught in the noose of my snare.

After enjoying the last of the roasted meat, I warmed my hands over the fire, and, without really planning to, I closed my eyes and said, O God, my Father in heaven, I thank you—

And before I could say another word, I was engulfed with a profound sense of gratitude—not for the food, not for my shelter, not even for my life, but for his being there—always. I wanted to say, *I love you.* But I tripped on the words and tried to say them again until I said them out loud. Then I felt a wonderful warmth that radiated from within my chest. I surprised myself by offering thanks for my trials. For without them, I said, I would never have found you.

I sat for a long time in my cold, dark cave, wrapped in a bearskin, nursing a broken leg and a wounded side, basking in the absolute peace I felt. I never wanted to distance myself from that feeling again. Then, without wavering and with absolute resolve, I said, My life is yours.

And I knew it would be so.

Thereafter, I made a point to ask God for what I needed. Then, as I set about going through the motions, I listened for instructions. In that manner, I learned to live day to day by the grace of God, trusting him to feed and guide me. Over the days and weeks of my seclusion, I surprised myself that, no matter the hardship or suffering I had to endure, I knew I would choose to keep the experience, for I had discovered that when life was the hardest, God was most easily found.

That winter, I set my sights on returning to Shum in the spring, but I knew Shum was not where my future would be. I had ample time in the wilderness that winter to *honestly* evaluate Shum—every detail of it. The stark truth was evident—Shum was a society headed for disaster. As surely as Enoch had said, Shum would be destroyed, and that solemn prophecy weighed heavily on my mind.

where is truth?

☙

I had just come from speaking with my father and sending my daughter, Eve, to tell Moriah I would be along later. That night I would be visiting Simeon, my grandfather.

When I entered his tent, Simeon embraced me. He offered me his big, bony hand and wrapped his lank body about me. He and my father shared many common characteristics: both were tall, sinewy, dark-skinned, with thinning white hair. Although Simeon's and Ebanel's eyes were dark, Simeon's had a piercing quality that had always made me feel uncomfortable. His eyes were black, like a moonless night is black, and lay recessed, almost hiding, beneath equally black, bushy eyebrows.

I have come to bid you good-bye, I said. My journey to Haner is imminent.

—Do you expect a good profit? he asked.

—Yes.

He asked me to walk with him to the Council.

—I haven't the time, I said. If I'm to keep my schedule, I must prepare for an early departure.

—Indulge me for a few minutes. What I have to show you will affect your trip.

Mahijah's tent was where the Council convened. As we walked, we spoke of my children, most notably his pride in Benjamin, whom he had endorsed as a student of the Watchers. He said his appointment was imminent.

—As is Enos's to the Rahaj, I said.

Simeon smiled and nodded, saying, Gad spoke with me just today of Enos's remarkable progress.

Our conversation then turned to Eve. Simeon expressed how pleased he was with Eve's being courted by Chaz. He reminded me that their marriage would make me a part of the king's family. I was not comforted by his observations.

—When the war with Sharon commences…, Simeon began.

—*If* the war begins, I corrected him.

Simeon shot me a look. *When* the war begins, he repeated, All Shum must stand with the king.

—Right or wrong? I asked.

—Do you have an opinion? he asked.

—If I'm committing my life or those of my children, I would like to know why.

—Now you're sounding like Ebanel.

—Father says the war has been contrived to put more power into the hands of Mahijah.

—And you believe him?

—I don't know.

Simeon's face grew serious. He placed a hand on my shoulder, saying, Since the death of Ramurah, no event has threatened this people more than the raid by the land of Sharon.

—No event except for Enoch's coming, I corrected him.

Simeon raised an eyebrow and repeated, Except for Enoch, he said.

We walked on.

—Other *prophets* have beset our city from time to time, said Simeon. They delivered their *disturbing* news and frightened the people, but, in time, they were exposed as frauds. Enoch is just another in a long line. An alarmist. A charlatan. I advise you to ignore the sensationalism. I expect that the *seer* will disappear back into his cave or go away and haunt another people.

—I'm not sure you can brush him aside as just another sooth-sayer, I said. You know that ever greater numbers clamor to the hillside to hear him. Many say his teachings are profound. Even Mahijah seems worried, and he has called upon the Council to do away with Enoch.

—Mahijah is a fool, said Simeon. His rash actions will bring down the city.

—But you agree with him about Enoch, I said.

—How would you know that?

I had overheard Simeon and Mahijah plotting against Enoch, and it was from that moment that I began to sense that this man was not just another impostor as Simeon claimed. To his question, I sought for a believable answer.

—You call Mahijah a fool, I said, But you stop short of disagree-ing with him.

—Take care how you interpret me, Simeon rebuked me.

I held my tongue, and soon my grandfather relaxed.

—Since when have you become so interested in Enoch? he asked.

—He's become a topic of debate, I said. When I meet with the Council, I hear stirrings about ways to take his life. Enoch's royal birthright cannot be denied, so every word he says takes on signifi-cance.

—You've heard him?

—One hears reports, I said, trying not to lie. I have no doubt that all the rulers of Shum have taken notice of what he says.

Simeon looked at me more seriously, and said, You worry about the coming war with Sharon, but I tell you that this one man, Enoch, decrying the corruptions of this city and its leaders, poses a greater threat to Shum than all our enemies combined.

—How?

Simeon wouldn't answer except to say, Better he were dead.

I let the subject drop, not wanting to get into an impassioned debate about whether Enoch was a prophet or not. For now, I decided, I was safer by remaining aloof.

Simeon had more to say.

—You seldom raise your voice in Council, said Simeon.

—It was an appointment I did not seek, I said.

—Perhaps not, but I recommended that you sit on the Council for a reason—the king needs your voice. I urge you to take a higher profile.

—For what?

—The coming war with Sharon.

—But you called him a fool. Surely this war is ill-conceived.

—A fool he is, and that's why you must speak out in support. Let the people know you support Mahijah and the coming war.

—Why me? I asked. I don't want a war, and I've never aspired to leadership. I'm content to work my trade and partner with Mahijah on occasion. Beyond that, I'm uncertain how close I want to be to the king.

—You're more a force than you know, said Simeon. The king respects you. You have his ear. Your wits and talents have added greatly to his wealth. The people know you and will listen if you'll speak out. None of the Council members can boast your public support.

—I would like to speak out against the war, I said.

—Mahijah is determined to battle Sharon. Nothing will stop that. Better to unite the people behind him than to be divided and risk defeat.

As we arrived at Mahijah's tent, I told my grandfather I would consider his words. But I also reminded him that my impending journey would preclude my doing much of what he asked of me.

When we entered Mahijah's tent, the king arose to greet me. He spread a leopard skin for me to sit on, then embraced me, and called me "brother."

—You know of the raiders of Sharon? he asked.

I said I did.

—A bad omen, he said. Then he said it again.

I asked him why.

—The Watchers have seen the stars align, foretelling the evil that has befallen Shum.

—Would you have me postpone my trip to Omner? I asked.

—No, but take care. Sharon is en route. Go to Omner as planned, but take two stallions from my stables to the merchant of Omner. Tell him that Shum has no grievance with his land. To trade is our only desire. Make the alliance, and give the horses as a gesture of assurance.

I agreed.

When I stood, some members of the Council had arrived and were milling about, speaking in hushed tones. Then, as I begged my leave, a servant approached Mahijah and announced that a citizen, with important news of Omner, had come pleading an audience.

—Who is it? asked Mahijah.

—His name is Baruch.

When Baruch entered the room, I was startled. Simeon motioned me to sit, and as I did, the remainder of the Council followed. Baruch bowed to the king, then to Simeon, then to me and the Council. Mahijah gestured for him to sit, and Baruch sat in the center of the tent, cross-legged, facing Mahijah.

—May I address the king? he asked.

Mahijah made a sweeping motion with his hand.

—Your humble servant is a trader by profession, Baruch began, And I work hard to support my family. In my trade, I've frequented the land of Omner. On occasion, I've traded in the land of Sharon. And I've encountered nothing that would lead me to believe that those peaceful people would mount an attack on Shum.

—Your prejudice is obvious, said Simeon. Your living is dependent upon trade in that region.

—That I trade there is true, said Baruch, But I would not endanger Shum for the sake of trading a few gems.

—More than a few, Simeon countered. We've heard of the incredible wealth of that land. Yours is an enviable situation—one you would be wise to protect.

—But that is not my intention, argued Baruch. I have come to plead for the people of Sharon, who are peace-loving and not the least aggressive. Perhaps the raiders are renegades from another land made to look like people of Sharon. Allow me to open a communication with Sharon in Shum's behalf, and I will report my findings to the Council. I beg you to reconsider your position of retaliation, and many lives can be saved.

When Baruch bowed and departed, a deep murmuring rolled through the Council. Then Simeon stood and motioned me outside.

—What are they discussing? I asked.

—Baruch, I'm sure.

—Why did you ask me to leave?

—You, yourself, said your journey was imminent.

—What is your opinion of Baruch's statement? I asked.

—Have you ever known Baruch to be truthful? he asked.

I thought, *Where is truth? Can truth be found in anything I've experienced this evening?*

Instead I said, In all my dealings with Baruch, no matter how competitive, I've never known him to be dishonest.

—Baruch is about to become an embarrassment to Shum, my grandfather said. If he meddles in its security, he will have to be dealt with.

I was left to wonder how.

commending my journey home to god

ↂ

On the cave's wall, I had scratched marks for twenty-nine days. The sun had shone down brightly that morning, but as I set out to check my snares, gray clouds formed quickly overhead. Soon big flakes were falling all around me, and I decided to go back to the cave and wait out the storm. Then I heard horses and dove into bushes, holding perfectly still.

The horsemen first circled the valley, then began to crisscross it, keeping their eyes focused on the ground before them. As they neared the river, I prayed they wouldn't discover the snares I'd set. They stopped at the cliff and spent a considerable time there riding up and down its rim, peering over the side. Then, they sidled their horses alongside each other and talked for a long while.

They began to circle the valley again and stopped at Asher's former camp. After they dismounted and walked the perimeter, they climbed back on their horses and headed toward me. I dug into the snow beneath the bushes and lay still.

When they came near, I could see they were covered in skins, as were their horses. They stopped to rest and eat. When the first man uncovered his hooded coat, I could see he was Asher.

—The man who attacked me wore a splint and walked on a crutch, he said.

—He still could have walked out, said the other man.

—I told you, I stabbed him in the side with my sword. He's dead.

When the second man removed his hood, I fought back the urge to gasp. It was Gad!

Gad was a powerfully built man, large in stature, dark-complexioned, a man of years yet uncommonly strong. He made two of Asher. As its captain, Gad had made the Rahaj into a force feared throughout the land. I had paid Gad courteous deference in Shum but avoided him when I could. How Gad and Asher—men of the divergent cultures of Shum and Nod—had achieved an alliance, I did not know.

—We must be certain it was Rabunel who attacked you, said Gad to Asher.

—The man said he was the son of Ebanel the shepherd and that his grandfather was Simeon of the Watchers, said Asher.

—And you're sure the satchel was filled with gems?

—Yes. I suspect we'll find them with his body when the snows melt in the spring.

—*If* he's dead, said Gad.

—Who could survive these conditions?

Gad didn't answer. He just scowled and surveyed the valley.

—What does Mahijah say? asked Asher.

—Mahijah is of no consequence, said Gad. His days are numbered. His ego is easy to massage. If I tell him that Rabunel is dead, he'll believe it.

—Finding the gems would help our cause, said Asher.

—Yes, but if they fall into Mahijah's hands, it would be a disaster, and our plans could be put off for years.

—What of Simeon? asked Asher.

—Simeon has as much to lose or gain as either of us.

—But Rabunel is his grandson.

—Let me tell you something about Simeon, said Gad. He never lets sentiment get in the way of his ambitions. Rabunel has seen you and can recognize you. Simeon won't let anything compromise his plan. Not even his own grandson.

—I still say Rabunel is dead, said Asher.

—We need proof, said Gad, And we need those gems.

—If we can't find them, we'll get more when we take over the mines at Sharon and Omner, said Asher.

—We need the gems to finance the effort, said Gad.

—And if we can't?

—That's where Simeon comes in. He'll keep encouraging Mahijah until he makes war. Then, when Shum is vulnerable, we'll make our move.

For much of the morning, they sat on their horses and spoke of the incredible wealth of Sharon and Omner. The snow continued to fall, but they didn't seem to mind.

—Those people don't know what riches they're sitting on, said Gad.

—No, but the men there are as big as bulls, said Asher.

—And as dull-witted.

—I still don't believe they can be overthrown as easily as Mahijah claims.

—That could work for us, said Gad. Simeon is convincing Mahijah to outfit every able man, woman, and child to fight Sharon.

—He's that foolish?

—Simeon has Mahijah envisioning a huge army, with *him* at the head.

—He has that much of an ego? Surely the people won't go along with that stupidity.

—They do pretty much what Mahijah tells them to do.

—Incredible.

—Yes, said Gad, But you're right about one thing: the people of Sharon will fight hard to protect their families.

—When will Mahijah attack?

—Soon. Mahijah is impatient.

—A decided weakness in a leader, said Asher.

—Yes, said Gad. He plans to make war on those lands, but he has no ability to govern them.

—It will be total chaos.

—It can work for us, said Gad.

—How?

—Mahijah sees himself as a conquering leader, said Gad. His fantasies will leave Shum vulnerable, and that will give us the edge we need. Since the day he broke his sword, we've known his weakness—his lust for power. We've used this knowledge to our advantage in the past and, if need be, we'll use it again.

—He broke the sword? How?

Then Gad revealed a secret—Mahijah's secret, the one by which Gad said the king could be controlled. Gad's cold telling made me tremble. I didn't know what few knew it; even as a member of the Council, I hadn't known it. What frightened me the most was that the security of Shum balanced precariously on a secret and a deception—and the ruthlessness of those who knew it could tip the safety of us all in either direction. From that moment, I was convinced that I must return to Shum with all haste and remove my family, what-ever the cost.

By evening, Asher and Gad had left the area, and the cave remained my dwelling for another two months.

ও

Spring came. Buds of green pushed through the melting snow. Young bucks trying new antlers staged mock fights and scraped away the soft velvet from their spreads. Dappled fawns lay hidden in thickets as their mothers foraged nearby. Daylight came sooner and left later, and rain fell instead of snow. The snow was melting, and I could now go home.

As I prepared to leave, I had the feeling I should search the river and retrieve the satchel of gems. I had learned to act on those feelings. When I returned to the river, I put off my bearskin and clothes and waded up to my chest in the frigid water. After a short while, my foot touched something soft. Taking in air, I submerged, groping with my hand in the murky water and eventually locating what my foot had touched. When I brought it up, muddy but intact, the satchel was yet filled with the gems. As I examined it, I sensed I was no longer its owner. I would carry it, but I understood it was consecrated for another purpose.

That afternoon, when I had gathered my belongings, I tested my leg. Except for a slight limp, it had healed well enough to walk. The wound in my side had mended. A bright sun warmed my face, and I thought, *This is a good time to plant.* I looked out on the valley and watched a mouse evade the sharp talons of a hawk, then scurry for cover. The sight gave me hope. I bid good-bye to the cave. If it were ever occupied again, its resident would find a wall with one hundred and eleven marks. In long days past, I had said good-bye to Jerel, but I said it again. Then, turning myself downhill and commending my journey into the hands of God, I stepped forward. I was going home.

worlds in collision

ℭ

Although I walked with a slight limp, my leg was strong enough for running. Even so, I chose to stay on the byways, thinking that this course would be less fraught with hazards. After my experience with Asher and Gad, I had no desire to come into contact with humans. I had discarded the splint, but I kept the bearskin. Its rank scent would serve to dissuade hungry predators, for few would take on a bear. I decided to take my chances with wild beasts.

My decision was not a casual one. Lions in powerful prides roamed wilderness areas. It was a time when enmity between kingdoms—human and animal—was extreme. Predators—tigers, snakes, wolves—ranged the earth, stalking the weak and careless, including people. Wild men, having sunk to savagery, lived in barbarous packs. I wondered how man could regress from the most intelligent of God's creations to the most base. Considering the dangers outside the city, one thing was certain: removing my family to the wilderness would not be without risk.

Spring invigorated my senses as I descended the mountain that had been my home. Green dominated the hillsides, ranging in every direction, providing a lush backdrop for the multicolored foliage growing atop them. Although I had been reared in the midst of nature, I had never appreciated the endless varieties of flowers and plants that grew in the earth. Until that moment, I had never been in awe of their diversity and beauty. I focused on aromas, trying to attach them to their sources. I became cognizant of myriad sounds: new life in the nest, scurrying burrow animals, territorial warnings, a katydid's distant call.

As I hiked down the mountainside, I observed kingdoms large and small existing independently—many unaware of each other. At times, when those kingdoms crossed paths, they collided with profound consequences. As I made camp one night, I observed a swarm of termites break away from its mother mound and migrate toward an ant colony. The introduction of a new community bent on establishing itself would threaten the old inhabitants. I could imagine how my changed views would be received upon my return to Shum.

Converging on the broad plain of grassy pasture land, streams that had fallen off high peaks made a wide river, its current as slow as a cow strolling. As I approached it, seeking a place to cross, I saw five women knee-deep in the water with their skirts hiked up, slapping clothes on wet stones. Some talked and laughed, others hummed snippets of unintelligible tunes. In the shade of a leafy tree sat a hairless, leather-skinned old man, his bony legs splayed before him like a wishbone, his robe open at the chest, his old dugs sagging lank as a she-hound's. Three bronze children splashed naked in the shallow water near their mothers. Since Asher and Gad, I hadn't seen a human. I gazed beyond them at the open meadow spreading before me and followed the river's course into the distant horizon where another mountain range rose from the haze. A worn pathway ran along the riverbank. I didn't know this valley, but the far stretch of mountains could have been the back side of Shum's range, those where my father pastured his sheep. The washwomen would know. As I stepped toward them, a brown child with a white bottom screamed that I was a bear and tripped and fell face first into the river. When she came up bawling, a fat woman grabbed her in one arm and splashed with her in tow toward the bank. Then the other women scattered, thrashing the water into a froth, abandoning laundry, snatching a child in one hand and a skirt in the other, and scrambling for safety. I ran after them, shouting for them to not be afraid, but their screams grew more frantic, so I pulled back.

Throughout the excitement, the old man had sat quietly, gumming a wad of something black and oily, staring off at an obscure point in the distant haze. I eased toward him, staying in his full view so as not to startle him. Then I knelt beside him.

—A hot day, I observed.

He made no movement.

—Do you come here often? I asked.

The old man gazed out upon the plain.

—I'm a traveler, I said. I hope I haven't disturbed you by my appearance.

The old man just sat, staring off, and smiled.

As I stood and wished him a good day, I made one last attempt at conversation and asked, Can you point me toward Shum?

Without glancing at me, he hacked the wad to the front of his mouth where his teeth should have been and shot a stream of black in the direction of the far mountains. I took it as an answer, thanked him, and walked away, wondering if his spitting could have been more a reflex than a response.

When I came to the river to cross it, the sunlight shot back my reflection, and the view made me gasp. I looked filthy. My hair and beard were long and matted. My clothing was blood-stained, and the bearskin was dusty and ragged at the edges. In all, I looked wild, more frightening than a child's worst night terror. After seeing myself, I knew why the child had run. I gazed up at the warm, spring sky, blue and cloudless, and came to a decision: it was time to discard the bearskin and the mangy clothing and take a bath.

The washwomen had left soap made of goat tallow and beech ash. I lifted it to my nose and smelled the sweet scent of olive oil. Then I stripped, and the old man grinned and stared off, glassy-eyed. I flopped in the cold water, rolling and singing, and lathered my body until a cloudy murk ringed me and drifted away on the easy current.

I sat in the water and scrubbed gravel, ashes, insects, and twigs from my hair and beard. Once the cold river had turned me tight-skinned and blue, I stood and eyed the abandoned clothing of the wash-women. I decided that the fat woman's husband would have to make do with one less shirt and cloak, but I left a ruby in the pit of a cray-fish shell and placed it atop her wash. Then, clean and clothed, I crossed the river and walked off wet and happy toward Shum.

ᛃ

One evening, as dusk settled wan and chill, I followed the graying twilight to a gentle knoll and heard the voice of a shepherd calling his sheep. A dog was barking. I followed the sounds until I found my father, Ebanel, kneeling near a fire with a ewe and washing away after-birth from a newborn lamb. Nearby, another travailing ewe bleated. I had arrived at the peak of lambing season. My father would be exhausted tonight, but it was his happiest time of year. I stood for a moment watching him, the old man who, without a wife, had reared me, fed me, clothed me, taught me, the one whom I had rejected in my youth, accusing him as being outspoken on his views of Shum and being unbending in his devotion to his God. Now, after all I had suffered, I saw him through more understanding eyes.

—You could use some help, I said as I stepped close.

My father started at my voice and reached for his staff as if it were a sword. Dog and Teah growled.

—Who are you?

—Don't you recognize me?

The shepherd narrowed his eyes and shook his head. His knuckles went white on the staff.

—I'm your son, Rabunel.

My father just stared at me. When Dog and Teah came near, I knelt and let them sniff my palm. The hair at Teah's neck relaxed, and she licked my fingers. I scratched Dog behind the ears.

—Have I been away so long that you don't know your own son? I asked my father.

My father placed the lamb with its mother and moved toward me, pushing back the hair off my forehead, touching my face and beard, brushing.

—It *is* you, he said. I thought you were dead.

And as he said so, his eyes filled with tears and spilled down his brown, wrinkled face. Then he took me in his arms, and we both wept. My father backed away and gazed at me with a critical eye.

—Are you well? he asked.

I nodded. His brow furrowed, and his eyes shot beyond me, searching the hillside.

—Jerel is dead, I whispered.

My father lowered his head and pinched the bridge of his nose but couldn't hold back the tears. I held him again.

Suddenly the lambing ewe bleated, and my father pulled away, composed himself, and knelt beside her.

—Can you hold her at the shoulders? he asked.

I put the sheep in a tight hold, and my father tugged at two tiny feet emerging from the birth canal. Then, reaching his hand past the lamb's legs, he guided its head into the crisp air. The ewe bawled. As I adjusted my hold, my father drew forth the lamb and set it wet and helpless at the ewe's feet. Immediately the mother turned and began licking the newborn clean, nuzzling it with her nose, bonding with her lamb that she would protect and nourish until it was grown.

My father and I sat back and laughed, then started to clean up before eating.

—It's been a long time since we've done that, he said. Then his face took on a look of apprehension, and he said, You mean to go on to Shum, don't you?

—Is there a reason I shouldn't? I asked.

—Gad announced your death to the city, he said. Moriah has been in mourning, and Mahijah has been pressuring her to pay your debt to him. As you know, he has always admired her, and now for the debt, he intends to make her one of his wives.

—Then I must hurry to Shum, I said. Every moment I delay puts my family in greater danger!

—You must exercise wisdom, my father warned. Moriah has come to my camp to seek my help. We tried to persuade Benjamin, Eve, and Enos to escape Shum with their mother and go to Enoch in the mountains. But they were swayed by Simeon, and they wouldn't believe their mother was in danger.

—How could my family abandon me so soon? I lamented.

—During your absence, attitudes have sharply deteriorated in Shum, said my father. Then he riveted his eyes on me and said, Your children have mourned your death. There has been no disloyalty. But they were deceived by Simeon's lie. Be wise. Simeon has encouraged Mahijah to pursue your wife, and he has also counseled her to submit.

—My own grandfather?

—Why are you surprised? Surely you know by now that Simeon does whatever he thinks is expedient. His loyalty to family depends on what his family can give to him. You've been away. You're expendable. Mahijah's passion for Moriah is a way for Simeon to manipulate the king.

—And what of Moriah? I asked.

—She fears for your children. If she doesn't yield to Mahijah's demands, she believes he'll harm them. She's coming to the end of her forty-day mourning. Then Mahijah will press her to pay your debt. When she cannot, he'll insist that she submit to him as the price.

—I can easily pay the debt and save my family, I said.

—You don't understand, said my father. Mahijah has his heart set on Moriah. If you reveal yourself, he won't be inclined to spare your life. He'll just take your property and your wife, then find a way to kill you.

—What should I do?

—You won't be recognized, given your appearance. Go into Shum, and pretend to be a beggar. Observe the conditions. Find a way to reach your wife and children in secret. Gain their support. Convince them of their peril. Then bring your family out, and I'll help you.

The thought flitted through my mind that an appeal to Simeon might save my family. But I sensed what my father had told me was true: Simeon would first choose to serve his ambitions rather than help me or my family.

—Simeon has a secret purpose, I said, But I don't know how it will impact my family.

—To be sure, a conspiracy exists, said my father, But I don't know the extent of the plan. I know that Simeon is redefining the powers in Shum. Mahijah may wear the title of king, but lately he's no more than an agent of Simeon.

My father had always been remarkably aware of Shum's goings-on, continually gleaning information from travelers and a few trusted friends. When he stood and lifted me to my feet, he said, Before you depart for Shum, you should follow me. I need to show you something that will help you in Shum.

I gazed up at the darkening sky of evening. Gray clouds had formed a hazy window through which a slice of moon was framed. Heavier clouds were billowing and moving east from the western horizon. A few stars studded the opaque heavens, and a quick gust of wind tousled Dog's fur. Teah yawned and went to her belly, her head resting between her outstretched forelegs.

—Is the place far? I asked. Wouldn't waiting until morning be better?

—Night is best. Where we're going isn't safe in the light.

I agreed to follow him, though I still doubted the wisdom of it.

We walked two abreast. All sorts of grasses and flowers on Shum's mountains had recently awakened and blossomed. Sweet smells of pollen buoyed on a cool breeze invigorated me. A warm spell had duped fruit trees into budding early, and my father worried that the ensuing cold snap had surely ruined the crop. I smelled the newness more than I saw it. The veiled moon provided a dim beacon along an otherwise dark path. At times, glints of light glanced off a smooth stone or a shiny leaf. I carefully moved forward, touching my father's belt, listening for the tap-tapping of his shepherd staff. At the crest of a steep ridge, I bade him stop to rest.

—How much longer? I asked, holding my knees and panting.

—A bit, he answered.

He beckoned me on, and we started again, hiking parallel to the flat plain below.

—The path leads to a canyon, he said.

As we ascended a steep, loose-graveled hill, the calves of my legs burned, and I gasped for air. I leaned into the incline as though I were a man trying to make headway against a stiff wind. At the rim of it, we dropped down an easy slope and stopped at a level landing.

—We've arrived, said my father, pointing a finger at a dark expanse. I straightened and lifted my head. Then the moon broke free of the clouds and cast a dusty blue glow on what appeared to be a dense thicket of trees lying on a dark plain—a circular clump of forest surrounded by an open field.

—It's called the Grove, said my father.

A rampart of rocks hid us. From that vantage point, we could see without being seen. We had waited for a long while before my father guided my eyes to a distant point beyond the Grove. I saw the flickering of torches coming in a long procession.

—What does it mean? I asked.

—When power is abused, the innocent suffer, he answered.

I wondered what he meant and would have asked, but he hushed me as the procession drew close and entered the Grove.

—What happens in there? I whispered.

—It is for the carnal desires of the Watchers and the Rahaj. They press women to submit to them.

—I had heard rumors, I said.

—The Grove was used infrequently before you left. Now it's widely used among the Watchers and the Rahaj.

—But Enos is part of the Rahaj! You don't think…?

—I'm getting old, said Ebanel. I've seen too many things. I'm sick. When I left Shum years ago, I thought the perversions could get no worse. But now those abominations are accepted without question, and wicked minds have thought up all sorts of vile mischief. They're addicted to evil and will never be satisfied, no matter how far they take their experimentations. You see the Grove?

—Yes.

—Debauchery with a divine twist is its purpose.

—What do you mean?

—During your absence, the Watchers have started professing that they're superior to man. They now claim to be the equivalent of angels on earth, so everything they do has the presumed sanction of God. They practice deviance and tell those who participate that their actions are divine sacrifices and what results is sanctifying.

—Have the people ceased to think? I said. Where is reason?

—The spiritually depraved are easy prey to outrageous doctrines, said my father. The Watchers have honed the art of telling a lie, and once it's believed, the people are enslaved. Now, husbands *lend* their wives to the Rahaj and Watchers as a token of consecration, believing that offspring so sired are holy. Under the guise of being *purified*, virgins are culled from an eligible crop and compelled to submit to the Watchers and Rahaj. The submission is supposedly necessary before they're *worthy* to be given to husbands.

—I can't believe that the people would blindly set aside virtue and do it in the name of God, I said.

—You've traveled many places, said my father. Yet you may not have observed that most of the evil and violence in this world is done in the name of some god.

—So, what is the Watchers' motive?

—To gratify their appetites, for one. But more than that—they want to stay in power. There's no better way to gain and keep power than giving followers sanction to do evil.

—They want to be above the law?

—Of course. Tampering with the forbidden is their way of life. Enoch was threatened with his life for speaking out against such wickedness.

—Do you know his whereabouts? I asked.

—A small group of followers fled with him into the mountains where they remain secluded. They've established a community. I'll take you there when the time is right.

—With all my family, I insisted.

—Yes, with all your family.

When the file of torches disappeared into the Grove, an eerie, sallow light haloed the trees, as though it was a hot wave rising. I felt sick. We were close enough to hear the voices of protest, the throbbing drums, the chanting. I wished I hadn't come.

—I've seen enough, I said.

—Wait a little longer, my father said.

With reluctance I sat back. Mauve light began to gather on the eastern plains. The bright luminaries of night winked and vanished, leaving the morning star alone in the sky. My father had laid his head on folded arms and appeared peaceful as he rested. I couldn't sleep. At the first glimmer of dawn, I sat up. The smell of night still lingered. Soon, motes of hovering pollen became visible in the morning air. Then, through the mist, a vague figure stepped from the near side of the Grove and paused. I gasped.

—Enos!

My father roused.

—What is it?

—Is Enos part of this?

—I don't know. I've seen him entering and leaving the Grove.

—For how long?

—A month.

We sat in silence and watched. Soon Enos was joined by a companion. They talked a moment, then the man turned so I could see his face. Gad! Soon the main body of the Rahaj emerged, and Enos and Gad joined them. I watched until my son's red robe of the Rahaj finally blended into the distant haze.

I turned to my father and said, You could have told me. Was there a reason to torture me with this sight?

—Would you have believed me?

I didn't know. If my father's purpose was to shock me, he had succeeded. With my own eyes I had seen what a parent never wants to see in his child. I didn't want to believe my son capable of such actions, but the truth was gaping at me, and nothing could obscure the sight.

—For the sake of your family, my father said, You must act quickly. I showed you this sight so that you would not underestimate the hold Shum has on your family nor minimize the difficulty you'll encounter in trying to remove them. You must not allow yourself to be dissuaded from your purpose. Rationalizing the corruption of Shum, in any degree, will defeat you.

—Can you get word to Enoch? I asked.

—I can.

—Tell him I've returned. Tell him I'll escape Shum within a week. Then I'll come to him and, if I can, I'll bring my family. If Mahijah tries to stop me, I swear he'll feel the point of my knife. I won't let him have Moriah. I will no longer allow Simeon to influence my children or tolerate Shum to own my family in any way.

—There are others who want to leave, my father said.

—Who?

—Miriam, your brother Jared's daughter.

—Jared is in Shum?

I had not seen my older brother nor his family for ten years. He had moved to the north country, a land covered with rivers and lakes, rich in beaver, fox, and otter. Miriam was a child of eight years when I had seen her last.

—Simeon sent for your brother, my father said. He intends to introduce Jared to the profession of the Watchers.

I remembered my brother as being fascinated by the outdoors and trapping, hardly the priestly type.

—Should I bring Jared out with me? I asked.

—You won't find him in Shum. He departed in pursuit of Miriam. She fled into the wilderness after Jared made of her an offering to the Watchers. Her young womb now carries the child of a Watcher, but Miriam would not yield further nor agree to release the child to the

Watchers when it was born. So she ran. Baruch's family has taken her in and is hiding her.

—Why should Baruch help my family?

—You've always seen him as a competitor, but you've never truly understood the man. He places people above possessions.

—I can't believe I'm hearing this from you, I said. You've seldom mentioned Baruch, and Leah has always annoyed you with her gossiping.

—True, but she has a good heart. When Miriam first came to me, I hid her in my tent as long as I could, but my camp was too obvious. As she always does, Leah found out what was going on and came to me, insisting on helping. I asked her not to get involved. Despite my insistence, she and Baruch came the following day to fetch Miriam. They said they'd keep her in their tent until we could come up with a plan to get her away to safety.

—Baruch and Leah! I said. It's amazing.

—You haven't known them as well as you thought you did.

—No, I said.

But I wanted to say I was ashamed for judging Baruch and Leah so harshly.

—I can only imagine what sacrifice they have made to keep Miriam safe, said my father.

—Does my family know about Miriam?

—Not yet. For everyone's safety, Miriam asked me to keep her location secret.

—Was she frightened because my sons are so closely tied to the Rahaj and the Watchers?

—I think that worried her, especially after her experience with the Watchers.

—Why didn't you take her to Enoch? I asked.

—His people were attacked by the Rahaj, and Enoch led them away. Now they're safe in the mountains, and he has returned.

—Can I betray my own brother by taking away his daughter? I asked.

—Remember that Jared came to Shum at Simeon's bidding. The covenant that binds the Watchers and the Rahaj takes priority over family. Be wise. Get your family out. Go to the tent of Baruch, and bring out Miriam.

—What about Baruch and Leah?

—They're expecting me to send them a plan for Miriam's escape. You'll be the bearer of the message.

I felt the gravity of the situation more keenly than I ever had. Where will I meet you? I asked.

—On the west side of Shum, just outside the city, stands an arbor.

—I know the place, I said.

—I'll meet you there within a week. Then I'll lead you into the mountains and conceal you until I can take you to Enoch.

I agreed, realizing that what he had suggested was fraught with danger.

My father then faced me, took me by the shoulders, and said, When you see your family, you'll want to run and embrace them. I counsel you to be patient. Take time to observe each of their situations and the climate of Shum. Be certain of your tactic, then implement it with the greatest care.

I nodded, then loosened the knot that held the satchel of gems to my waist. As I handed it to my father, he gave me a quizzical look, then opened it.

—Mahijah would kill you if he knew you had this! he said.

—That's why I leave it with you for safekeeping.

We stood and gazed at each other, with the realization that this might be the last time we would see each other. I loved the old man, but I had only learned to appreciate him since my return. Now I was leaving him again.

—What have you decided to do? my father asked, at length.

—To be a beggar in Shum, I said.

the test of an observer

og

I came upon Shum as the sun had finished traversing the broad sky and dropped off the western horizon, causing an eruption of oranges and reds in wispy, low-lying clouds. I had the impression that the heavens were alive and aflame. As I neared the fringes of the city where the poor staked their tents, I draped my father's old sheep blanket about me and hooded my head in case I happened on a familiar face. As dusk gathered, chickens went to roost, bats wakened, cows with heavy udders headed to be milked, bawling for relief. Activity had slowed by the time I entered the center of the city. Children were being called home. Dogs barked here and there. The Rahaj patrolled the streets.

At the well, I came upon a small gathering of women fetching water in fine ceramic crocks, glistening with the glaze of chipped obsidian. I recognized some of them and hid my face. They recoiled at my presence and moved to the far side of the street. One mentioned my odor. Another said there was no excuse for a person to be indigent, adding that laziness was a disgusting sickness and that she was grateful her husband was industrious. A brave one crossed the street and confronted me, saying I had come to the wrong city if I expected to beg. Shum had laws against such things. Then she ordered me to leave.

—In my homeland, I'm a man of means, honor, and high standing, I said to her. A misfortune while on my journey brought me to this.

The woman's mocking laughter encouraged her companions to join her, and soon some men of the city assembled. I found myself in a circle, being crowded upon and pushed until one man shoved me to the ground. Another kicked me, saying I would leave Shum if I had any sense. As they left, I lay in the dirt, catching my breath, and I felt a pair of strong hands take me under my arms and lift me to a sitting position.

—You've come to a difficult city, said the young man.

He sat beside me and asked if I were all right. When I said I thought so, he looked about, as though what he was going to do was dangerous, then slipped a small potato in my hand.

—Thank you, I said. I brought the potato to my lips and bit off a corner. After what my father had fed me, it tasted bland and starchy.

—If you value your life, you'll travel on, he said.

—May I know your name?

—Joshua, he said.

—Of what family?

—Baruch. I'm the eldest son of Baruch, the merchant.

I gazed upon him, astonished. In only months, the boy I had last seen in autumn had become a man. His face had produced hair, and his body was lean and muscular. Once known for his squeaky voice, he now spoke with resonant diction, both fluid and deep. I imagined young women would find him fair, not handsome, pleasant-looking. His light complexion and mahogany-colored eyes gave him the visage of kindliness. Thick auburn hair hung down to his shoulders, and I found myself musing that its thickness wouldn't last—his father's hadn't. Except for the hair, I could have been looking at his father at a younger age, for Joshua was maturing with the distinct features of his father.

I had known Joshua to be a quiet, young man, uninterested in following his father's commerce, more inclined to studies that required deep thinking. It was said of him that, whatever the task,

Joshua would work at it diligently. And that was a point of pride for his gossip-prone mother, for she noised it about to Joshua's evident embarrassment. Still, Leah was fair in her assessment of her son's virtues, for she was often heard to moan that she would have preferred him to demonstrate more "awareness of public issues."

—You're Baruch's son? I asked. When I said it, I thought I'd made a mistake. I had to continually remind myself that carelessness could give me away.

—Yes. Do you know my father? I saw him search my face for recognition. I lowered my eyes and sought a gruffness in my voice.

—I know his name, I said. My response seemed to satisfy Joshua.

—Are you all right? he asked, touching the place I'd been kicked.

—Yes, I said, holding it.

He helped me to a barracks of wisteria vines near the well.

—Will you get into trouble for helping me? I asked.

—I can't stay long, that's for sure, he said. Shum has recently become intolerant of beggars, and you'll receive little help.

—What will happen?

—If the Rahaj doesn't kill you, you will be escorted to the border within a month. You can remain here for a few days to recover, then you should move on.

—Sounds like good advice, I said.

He pressed walnuts into my hand and drew me a dipper from the well.

—Thank you again, I said. You've been more than kind. Now, you really must leave.

He nodded and said, I'll come in the morning, if I can, and see you safe on your journey. I wrapped my hands around the dipper and sipped as Joshua stood to leave. He said, In better times, I would have liked to have known you.

As I moved into the deep cover of the wisteria, I deemed it more than satisfactory as a shelter. Thick with leafy foliage, it was an ancient plant, winding about a failing trellis. Its long, gnarly branches were as thick as a man's forearm, and from them hung clusters of violet flowers and elongated pods. Overgrown at the edges, it bulged at the middle, forming an arched covering through which one could see the sky as a backdrop to the broad, green leaves. From the refuse on the ground, I suspected I wasn't the first indigent to use the wisteria for shelter. For a bush, it was comfortable, better than many of the shelters I had been in recently. Water was easily obtainable, since the wisteria grew within earshot of the well—the water source for Shum. Most of the people came to the well at one time or another, often lingering to talk.

When I'd settled and was watching the evening light grow gray, I heard a familiar voice near the well, and my eyes became wet. The voice was Eve's. I pulled branches around me, lowered my head, and lay still. She had come to the well, shouldering two buckets on either end of a sturdy pole. Her delicate features masked her hardiness. I heard her hum as she dipped the buckets into the well. Then, deep in the wisteria, a voice startled me. Its first words were, Is it one maiden or two?

—Who's there? I whispered.

—One or two? the voice repeated in a more demanding tone.

—One, I answered, peering into the shadows. Are you of the Rahaj?

I heard the voice return a muffled laugh that I took to mean no. My companion said, I am Danbenihah, a condemned man like yourself.

I would have countered by saying I wasn't a condemned man, but my attention returned to my daughter at the well. She had tarried long enough to dip a ladle into the well and drink the cool water. Then, after wetting a cloth and wringing it out, she dabbed her cheeks and the back of her neck. With the backs of her fingers, she touched her face where she'd washed and fanned the dampness dry with her palm. Then, seemingly satisfied, she stood, repositioned the buckets on the pole, and started for home.

Joshua found her then. I had witnessed young men around Eve before: gallant gestures, each fellow, whether burly or slight, offering to muscle whatever she carried. As was typical, she would decline the invitation with a smile but would seldom dissuade the attention. Since before my departure, Eve's beauty had been a topic of discussion. She had captured the attention of Shum's male population and provoked the envy of other females.

—A warm evening for such a burden, said Joshua. Eve turned and smiled. She and Joshua had been friends since childhood. At five, she had kissed him on the cheek. Joshua had never recovered.

—Now, what would people say if they saw us talking? Eve said, flirtatiously. From where I hid, I could see Joshua's face turn red.

—I know what my mother would say, he said. They both laughed. Then Joshua asked, May I carry the water for you?

—Dare we risk it? said Eve.

Eve had always admired and respected Joshua. She said his eyes reflected the kindness of his character.

When Joshua moved to carry the water, Danbenihah nudged me and asked, What's happening?

I shushed him.

—The voice is of the young maiden who feeds me, he said.

I was surprised at his comment but whispered back for him to please lower his voice. He grumbled an unintelligible response.

A husky voice from beyond my vision called out, Eve!

She and Joshua turned, and I leaned forward. In a moment, the figure of Chaz stepped into view and moved toward Eve. He wore fine, white linen, open at the chest. His head was covered with a turban of the same fabric, and his feet were shod with leather sandals, crafted for swift running. His legs were bare to the knees, revealing defined muscles, and over his shoulder hung the blue sash of royalty. He offered Joshua slight acknowledgment as he moved past him to the maiden with the sloshing buckets.

—I arrived just in time, he said, lifting the pole from Eve's shoulders.

—Yes, said Joshua. He looked up at the prince of Shum and repeated, Just in time. Then Joshua stepped aside and addressed Eve.

I can see everything's in control, he said. Will you excuse me?

Then, without waiting for a reply, he turned and walked away.

—Joshua! Eve called after him.

But Chaz put a finger to her lips and said, I need to talk with you.

—That was arrogant! Eve chided him, pushing away his hand.

—Why?

—Joshua is my friend. He was trying to help me.

—Trying to win you, I think.

—That's a comment of jealousy not worthy of you.

—Is it? Chaz had the look of discomfort. He set the pole and buckets on the ground and drew Eve near him. I am next in authority to my father, said Chaz.

—I know.

—Someday this valley will be mine to rule. Don't you understand what I'm trying to say?

Eve took a posture of patience and offered a tiny shake of her head, No.

Chaz reached out and took her face in his hands and gazed into her eyes a long time without speaking.

—Share it with me, he said. You must know by now how I feel about you. Stand with me as my wife, and help me rule this kingdom.

Eve took a short breath and pulled away, putting her hands to her cheeks where his had been. Chaz began to apologize, but she reached out blindly and took his hand in a firm grip. Then she threw her arms around his neck, buried her head in his shoulder, and began to cry.

—Does this mean *yes?* said Chaz.

Eve didn't answer. She just held him and shook and cried.

—She should run! Danbenihah whispered. He's an evil man.

Once more I hushed my companion. I knew my daughter had only allowed herself to dream of this moment, never believing that marriage to Chaz was possible. As a young girl, she had alternated between adoring and hating him. Secret love came first. Then, as she grew into adolescence, she disdained him as an arrogant braggart. She reversed herself when Chaz discovered *her*—a once-gangly girl who had become a beautiful woman. Flirting began, then a campaign to win her affections. But she hadn't decided if his intentions were real. I had hoped that during my long absence their relationship had ended. But as I watched my daughter in the arms of Chaz, so in love, so openly adoring, so accepting of his proposal, I knew I had lost her. I was an observer, imprisoned in a bush, unable to do anything.

—Why have I found favor in your sight? Eve asked Chaz.

—You are everything to me, said Chaz.

I gazed upon my future son-in-law from the wisteria. As much as a man can be, Chaz was elegant, even gallant. I could not blame my daughter for her feelings. I saw her hesitate and search him with her eyes.

—Some of the ways of our society are vile to me, she said. One hears rumors—even about the prince…

She became quiet then and paused. I leaned forward and watched for him to flinch. Among the qualities Eve had desired in a husband, chastity topped her list. She considered that chastity was a reliable indicator of other desirable virtues and traits: honesty, integrity, courage, kindness.

Chaz held himself straight. He said he understood what she was implying. Then he took her hands, held them in his, and asked, Would you accept my answer if I gave it?

She nodded.

—I admit I've been tempted, he said in an even tone, But I have refrained.

Eve's long gaze searched him—the motion of his eyes, the stance of his body—and I saw Chaz grow restless at her silence.

—Will you torture me when I come to beg your hand in marriage? he asked.

From behind me, I heard Danbenihah's whispered plea: Don't believe him. He's a liar!

I felt the same urgency. Eve searched Chaz's face a moment longer, and I prayed she would see the deceit.

—If I marry you, she said, I will be giving myself to you

completely. I have known no man, and, for all my life, I promise I will have no other man but you. That is my solemn vow. Can you make the same promise?

The look in Chaz's face made me feel uneasy. I couldn't decide if he told the truth or if he had become so skilled in lying that I couldn't read it in his face. Still holding her hands, he went to his knees at Eve's feet and said, By all I hold sacred, I swear my love now and forever. Please believe me when I say I'm clean. When I take you to wife, you may rest assured that I have known no other woman and will have no other except you. I do not lie to you now; I will never lie to you. What can I do to convince you?

I wanted to cry out, Be careful! But Eve believed him. I watched her body relax at his words. Then she embraced him again, and he kissed her.

I remembered her once saying to me, I know Chaz is the prince. I know he wields power and demands respect. But I love him for who he is. Despite my counsel and Moriah's protests, Eve said she was convinced that Chaz had a good heart. Wasn't he gentle and honest? she asked, as though she was trying to convince herself. Couldn't he command the people and bring prosperity and peace to the land?

Her answer to Chaz's proposal filled me with dismay.

—I will be your wife! Eve exclaimed.

I heard Danbenihah bury himself in the wisteria and utter a low groan. Chaz gave a great shout of delight, and I felt my heart sink.

—We must tell my father, he said, as he took her hand and started to pull her forward. Then he stopped and asked, Whom shall I ask for your hand?

I knew the reason for their pause. They looked at each other with the awkward realization that custom demanded the father be asked for his daughter's hand.

Then I heard Moriah's gentle call as she searched for our daughter.

—Eve. Eve. Do you need help with the water?

Eve's eyes brightened as she pulled Chaz forward. Although the sunlight remaining was but a purple glow, the dim light that outlined Moriah made my heart quicken and tears flow. Time had dulled my memory. She was even more beautiful than I recalled. She wore her hair loose, allowing it to cascade down her back like a veil against her satiny robe. I remembered the nights of winter I had lain freezing, sometimes near death, and had summoned the vision of my dear wife, praying I might see her once more. Now she stood near and, for the sake of her safety and that of my children, I could not run to her, take her in my arms, and feel the embrace I had longed for those many long, cold nights.

—Hello, children, she said. Chaz bowed, and Eve kissed her cheek.

—Oh, Mother, may we speak with you a moment? Eve asked, her voice rising in excitement.

—Here? asked Moriah.

—Please, said Chaz, motioning to a spot by the well.

Moriah looked at him, then at her daughter, then at the spot, and an expression of understanding came over her.

—Oh, no, I can't have this conversation with you, she said, Not without your father.

—With respect, said Chaz, Your husband is dead.

—I refuse to believe that, said Moriah.

Sighing, Moriah sat at the well. Eve took her mother's face in the palms of her hands and gazed into her mother's eyes, imploring her indulgence. Then Eve pushed Chaz forward.

He looked away at some obscure point, as if to measure his words. Then, with a shaky voice, said, I ask, I mean I *humbly* ask for your daughter's hand in marriage.

Moriah stared at him, her brow furrowed. Then she looked at Eve, who tipped her head down as if to invite a response. Chaz's discomfort grew apparent. He said he would be good to her and love her all his life. He began to list his qualifications as a husband: He had wealth; Eve would never go without; he would never deceive her or hurt her; and so forth.

—Yes, Moriah interrupted him, I can see you feel deeply for my daughter.

—More than I can express, *Mother*.

At *Mother*, I bristled. To her credit, Moriah held her eyes level on the young man and didn't react. She had a gift for diplomacy. She could put differing parties at ease while masking her own emotions. On the other hand, *my* face could be read as a scroll when dealing with such important matters. Had I sat in Moriah's place, I doubted I could have hidden my disdain for Chaz, notwithstanding the obvious feelings he had for my daughter. Having been man and protector in my little girl's life was not a role I was ready to relinquish. As a father will, I found myself thinking, *He's not good enough for my daughter.* On the other hand, the empathetic part of me saw my daughter's eyes, the look of love in them for her choice of husband, the look of imploring when she looked at her mother as he begged for permission to wed.

—How do you feel? Moriah asked Eve.

—I have agreed, if you will give your blessing, Eve answered.

All during our marriage, Moriah and I had only wanted our children's happiness. Regardless of what worries she may have had, I knew she had no choice but to take Chaz's heart-felt plea seriously. I could only imagine the emptiness she must have felt in making such a weighty decision alone.

—Your pledge of honor, then, Moriah replied at length. Promise me by all you hold sacred that you will love my daughter with all your heart and allow nothing—neither person, nor power, nor circumstance—to stand between her and you. Pledge it now, and, as I live, she will be your wife, and I will be your mother.

I felt the tears return to my eyes. Everything about the situation was wrong: the man, the time, the place.

Chaz knelt at Moriah's feet, and, taking her hands in his, said, I pledge all this and more. May my life be forfeit if I turn in any degree from this promise I make to you.

Although I had heard his words, I doubted them, but proving the moral unworthiness of the man was no more within my power than predicting he would keep his word. Nevertheless, I couldn't rid myself of the foreboding feelings that Chaz wouldn't keep a lifelong vow, that he wouldn't put Eve's happiness before his own, and that he wouldn't sacrifice his own comfort for hers. Moreover, if he had lied to Eve about the past or to Moriah about the future, I knew that no enduring or meaningful relationship could be built on such a foundation. As I had heard my father say, Every downfall and every evil starts with a lie. I wondered, *If he betrayed Eve's trust, would he betray the people's?*

Moriah moved so that her thumbs touched the tops of his wrists, as if to feel in his pulse any hint of falsehood. I could never have imagined anything so difficult as giving away our daughter, she who was most precious to us—our sweet Eve.

—Then go and take your bride, Moriah said, her voice faltering.

Eve let out a shout, and Chaz embraced Moriah. When Eve joined them, they appeared as a tangle of arms.

—We must go talk to my father, Chaz said. Then a big voice froze him in mid-sentence.

—Moriah? the voice bellowed from a distance. The three stepped back from their jubilant embrace and stood motionless.

—Oh, no! Moriah exclaimed.

What? Eve asked. Moriah hushed her.

—Moriah! the voice came again.

—Who is it, Mother? Eve whispered.

—Leah!

A look of panic crossed my daughter's face.

—What shall we do? Eve said, holding tight to Chaz's arm.

—Hide behind the wisteria, Moriah said.

I felt my pulse quicken as Eve and Chaz ran toward me. I quickly lay beneath the wisteria, scooting as far back as I could, and feigned sleep. My backside bumped up against something soft that shifted at my presence, then went still. I suspected it was Danbenihah, but I dared not move.

—Stay quiet, called Moriah in a whisper. I'll talk to her. All we need is for the whole city to know about you two before you have announced your engagement.

Eve and Chaz dove beneath the wisteria vines, and Eve's knee brushed my head, startling her.

—I'm sorry, she said, I didn't know someone was here.

I shifted, mumbled, and turned my head, as if I hadn't wakened but had only been disturbed.

—Some sorry old sot, said Chaz.

—Leah! exclaimed Moriah, as the large woman approached. What an honor, and you look so well.

I cracked an eye to watch.

—You're too kind, Leah replied. But I've had a bad ache in my back lately. She pivoted and pointed to a place at her lower spine, then said, Here.

—Poor Leah, said Moriah, in a coddling tone. You must rest yourself. Let me help you back to your tent.

Moriah took Leah's elbow and tried to steer her away.

—Oh, thank you, no, said Leah, resisting the aid. It's a burden I must bear. If only I had more help from my husband and children. A man is such a bother sometimes, don't you think? How ever do you manage, dear?

—Manage?

—With your husband always gone on trading expeditions, leaving you alone to tend the family.

Moriah looked away.

—Oh, there I go again, speaking my mind. They say he's dead, don't they?

Moriah straightened and said, I'm sure he's just delayed and will be coming home soon.

—But you're in mourning.

—By law, not by choice.

Leah put her hands on her hips and pressed further. And what of Mahijah? He wants you, you know.

—How would you know that?

—Oh, my dear! Everyone knows!

—You mustn't think that I have any interest in the king, Moriah protested. I'm a married woman!

—You don't have to be strong for me, dear, Leah interrupted. I have eyes, don't I? Such a pretty woman as you. Why, as an unmarried woman, you're the catch of Shum. What could your husband have been thinking, leaving you alone this long time?

Moriah took in a big breath and let Leah's comment float away on the evening breeze. Then she said, I wonder if you'll excuse me? I need to finish preparing the evening meal.

—But how can you think of food when your daughter has been seen with the prince?! cried Leah.

Moriah pretended ignorance. You must have heard wrong! she said.

—With my own eyes, I tell you.

—You don't say, groaned Moriah.

—I do say, and, if I may speak my mind, nothing good can come of this.

—I'll carefully consider what you've said, and when my husband returns, we'll discuss it. Thank you for bringing it to my attention, said Moriah, smiling politely to end the conversation.

—What kind of a friend would I be? replied Leah. Then, as she turned to walk away, she added, Our husbands may be competitors, but our friendship is deeper. Now don't forget to tell me everything. It will just be between you and me. You know I'm a person of the strictest discretion.

As Leah left, she kicked up a trail of dust that followed her like a yapping pup.

—Is it safe, Mother? Eve whispered from the wisteria.

—Yes, you'd better hurry away.

As I pretended to sleep, I heard Chaz and Eve joke about their close encounter. After saying they were lucky, Moriah shooed them away, admonishing them to be quiet.

Eve muffled her laughter, kissed her mother, then turned and frowned at Chaz, crossing her arms in mock disgust.

—Some husband you'll make, she said.

He responded to her comment with a questioning look. Eve pointed at the buckets still lying on the ground and said, Forget something?

—If this is what marriage is going to be like…, Chaz laughed with chagrin, as he hefted the pole and buckets to his shoulders.

Eve put her hand over his mouth and said, Not another word, sir! You're addressing the future queen!

They both seemed to enjoy the joke, laughing and sloshing away in the direction of our tent, but Moriah let her face grow serious as she sat again at the well and began drawing circles in the dirt. I came to an elbow to watch her. I could hear the soft grumbling of my companion behind me in the wisteria. The blanket of night had long ago eclipsed the last traces of a tired sun. I looked up through the leafy vines of the wisteria and noticed dusty clouds drifting across the moon, making the sky appear to move. The sounds of the city traveled on the same night breeze that carried the smells of supper's meats and vegetables cooking in fired clay ovens. Light from tallow-fat candles shone through seams in the tents. Moriah wept at the well, dried her eyes, then wept again. My heart went out to her, sitting lonely, crying in silence. Her family didn't know. Shum didn't know. I knew, and I couldn't go to her. Not yet.

When I next gazed up through the thick branches of the wisteria, I noticed that the moon had coursed a quarter of its way on its night's journey, and Moriah yet sat crying. Then a voice caused her to raise her head.

—I've been searching for you, said the voice. It belonged to Mahijah. During my absence, I had learned to hate the man. He waved on two guards of the Rahaj who had accompanied him and walked toward my wife.

Moriah dropped to her knees and bowed her head. Mahijah lifted her to her feet and said, Such an honor is not necessary for two who share feelings as do we.

—You assume too much, she said.

—Your feelings for me will grow over time.

Moriah took a step back, then asked, Have you heard the news of Chaz and Eve?

—Yes, just now. I must call a celebration to announce the betrothal.

Moriah nodded and wiped her eyes. Then Mahijah moved to where the light of the moon reflected off her face.

—You've been crying.

—For the happiness of the children and because I miss my husband, she said.

—He's dead! said Mahijah, bringing her to him in an embrace.

She moved away, saying, Please honor my period of mourning.

—Fourteen days more, then I'll come to you.

—Such an inopportune time to be talking of this, she said. Shouldn't we be celebrating the happiness of our children?

—Very well, Mahijah said with frustration, For the sake of the children, I'll wait. But, for the sake of your husband's debt, you won't make me wait beyond your time of mourning.

—What you ask of me, I cannot give, she said. I could never love another man as I have loved Rabunel.

—Does it matter?

viewing life from the bottom up

೦೪

—What did the young man give you? asked Danbenihah.

I supposed he referred to Joshua's gift of food to me.

—A potato and walnuts, I said, holding the walnuts out in a cupped hand.

He stared forward, not moving his head. I shifted so I could see his face in the moonlight. Two shadowy pits lay where his eyes should have been, and the discharge from them bore a scent more rank than his ripe sweat. He seemed a man of some age. Long strands of white hair hung below his shoulders. The stubble that bedecked his face was equally white, and his cracked lips outlined a sparsely toothed mouth. He was filthy and sallow-skinned, a spare rack of bones covered by a sagging leathery hide. Barely kept from nakedness by a set of rags that didn't fit his lank frame, Danbenihah was the poorest of beggars I'd seen. By the way he halted and groped, I could see he was blind.

—Are you going to share them? he asked.

—I ate the potato, I said, But you're welcome to the walnuts.

I split a shell and placed the meat into his outstretched palm. As though he would suck the flavor from every morsel, he ran it around his mouth, savoring it awhile before he chewed and swallowed it, then extended his hand for more. We repeated the process until he ate without urgency.

—Have you had your fill? he asked.

—I've had what I wanted, I said, though I had given each of the nuts to him.

He seemed satisfied with my answer and said, Oh, how I've grown to appreciate the taste of any form of nourishment.

—You look as though you've been a long time without food, I said.

He didn't answer. Instead, he asked if I would describe the maiden who had dropped the walnuts.

—Eyes the color of the sky at noon, I said. Hair as yellow and fine as milkweed silk. A smile that could melt winter's worst frost.

Danbenihah settled back, mined walnut fragments from back teeth with his tongue, and said, You're a poet, friend. I smiled, but he couldn't see it. He said he had left his family in the land of Abel to settle a dispute between his country and the land of Sharon.

—You know the land of Sharon? I asked.

—Yes. A difficult people, but they're easily pacified. In my country, I was a judge and often spoke in behalf of my people.

He asked if I was surprised. I was. He was also a teacher in his land and had many students. I asked how he had come to his present state—impoverished, starving, with only wisteria vines to shelter him from the elements.

—Last year, I led a contingent of fifteen men—merchants, leaders, men of learning—to the land of Sharon. A series of events had threatened our peace. Our mission was to repair the rift and renew relationships and trade. Those who called themselves the Rahaj of Shum swarmed us en route and killed all the men except for me. The dead were stripped of their clothing, redressed, painted as warriors, then paraded through the streets of Shum as raiders from Sharon. I alone was left alive to stand trial for Sharon's pretended atrocities. I told them I was from the land of Abel, a peaceful place, an ally to Shum, but a large man struck me and said I was lying. At my trial, false testimony was given. For my acts of aggression against this land, I was condemned to die by degrees on the streets of Shum. An old priest, acting in the authority of a judge, pronounced the sentence. He ordered that my feet be broken and that my eyes be put out. The strong man who leads the Rahaj had the pleasure of maiming and blinding me.

As Danbenihah told his story, I felt an emptiness in my stomach, but not from hunger. Gad had executed the judgment, as surely as Simeon had issued the sentence.

—At the penalty of death, said Danbenihah, An edict was pronounced that no one should assist me in any way. But anyone can mock and scourge me, up to the point of death.

—A blessing, I commented sarcastically.

—Yes, he agreed, with equal sarcasm, But I have spoiled their amusement.

He puffed out like a strutting cock.

—How's that? I asked.

—I have not died yet.

I shared a small laugh with Danbenihah, but the tragedy of his plight made me gaze upon him and ache with pity.

—You've lain here five months? I asked.

—Yes, a long time.

—How do you yet live?

Danbenihah paused and tipped his head, as if contemplating the wisdom of answering.

—I'll tell you because you fed me, he said, Because I perceive in you a goodness. You won't betray me, I trust?

—No, I said. I'll keep your confidence.

Danbenihah lowered his voice and beckoned me to lean in toward him. He said, For three days, I lay in the street near this wisteria bush, pleading with anyone who walked by to help me. But no one would listen. They said I was a babbling fool. When thirst and hunger had consumed me and I had lost all hope of surviving, women came—the maiden, sometimes a mother and daughter—and they fed me. When it was cold, they gave me an old animal skin that no one would miss. As I cannot see them, I came to know their voices. When they come, they pretend to show disgust for me. Then as they slap my face, they drop morsels of food in my lap. At other times, they come at night and leave food nearby. For these long months, I have survived by their kindness.

—By risking their lives, you mean!

I forgot Danbenihah's trouble and thought about Eve: *What would happen to her if she were found out?*

Danbenihah let my comment slide and shifted the subject to politics. He said, If they knew what I know, they would kill me.

—Who would kill you? What do you know?

—The king, for one. I hear things in the bush—how Mahijah plans to attack Sharon and how he has set up a deception to rally the people.

—He has the might of the Rahaj, I said. Sharon is a small land, easy to conquer. Why the deception?

—Wars are expensive, answered Danbenihah. If lives are to be lost, the people must support the cause. What better way to call them to arms than to have them fear for their lives?

—Mahijah has always been tolerated, but never loved, I said.

—So much more the reason to drive fear into the populace. Unity and resources come easily when survival is in question. But Mahijah needed an incident to confirm the crisis.

—So his Rahaj went in search of travelers near our borders, I said.

Danbenihah guessed that he and his contingent of peace seekers had served Mahijah's purpose as well as any.

—The brilliance of Mahijah's plan, said Danbenihah, Was keeping me alive. My presence has provided the people of Shum a daily reminder of impending doom if they do not unite under Mahijah.

—But why Sharon? I asked. What treasures it may have, we already trade for. Can conquering the land make that much difference?

—You don't understand, said Danbenihah, Sharon isn't the objective. Yes, Mahijah wants unrestricted access to the wealth of Sharon, but its centrality to Omner, Hanannihah, Abel, Haner, and the trade routes, makes it invaluable. Conquering Sharon leaves an open door to controlling the region.

—The people in those lands won't lie down while Shum occupies their lands and robs them of their resources, I said.

—For both sides, there will be a terrible cost in lives, said Danbenihah. But the poor will be made to suffer the most.

—How?

—The poor have always been used to fill the front lines of battle. The rich can buy a safer spot.

—And what will happen to Shum? I asked.

—Shum will obtain her objective, he said. She will feign allegiance to neighboring communities and convince them to join her and take vengeance upon Sharon. Then, when Sharon is isolated, it will be easily conquered, and Mahijah will create another reason to expand his campaign. I expect he'll accuse the other communities of aiding Sharon. Thus, they also become Shum's enemies.

Danbenihah's predictions seemed plausible. I knew the characters of Mahijah, Simeon, and Gad and knew the men that made up the Council. I knew that their greed and ambition had no bounds.

—There's still a greater conspiracy, said Danbenihah.

I searched his sightless eyes and pondered his perceptions.

—I served as a judge in the land of Abel, he reminded me. Some considered me wise, a man who understood the fabric of government and the human condition. I doubt you would understand, he said, For as a poor man, you have never known privilege as have I.

I could have corrected him but chose to keep my background concealed for the moment. Remaining as a beggar was safer for us all and would be so until I was certain of my course.

—Why do you flaunt your former position? I asked. Do you think, here in the bush, you have some special position over me? You sound like the elite of Shum you claim to disdain.

—That's just my point, he said. I have spent my life looking on my fellows from the top down. Now that's reversed. This new perspective is one I'd never expected. In my life in Abel, I knew the poor, congratulated myself for the mercy I extended to them, and took pride in championing their cause. But I never really knew them. But now I live life as they do, and I'm beginning to see things more clearly— from the bottom up.

—And what do you *see*, old man? I asked.

—I *see* this place clearly, even though I'm blind. I hear the whisperings of wives in pain who are treated worse than the beasts of burden in their husbands' stables. I sense the hurt of children whose lives are torn because the adults in their lives cannot keep marriage vows. I feel the anguish of those who fear the corruption of Shum but fear more to leave it. I know how wealth is gathered—I hear of whispered alliances, those who will be victors, those who will be defeated. I sense the hopelessness of those who have never had and who never will—those who endure a lifetime of hunger, disappointment, and tears, never quite having sufficient to live a life of even minimal dignity. Yes, I *see*, my friend, and viewing life from the bottom up is a perspective I would never want to lose. I see more clearly than I have ever seen.

—What do you know of another conspiracy? I asked.

—I've only heard whisperings.

—When will it happen?

—Soon.

For six days, I sat with Danbenihah beneath the wisteria. Not since the hollow had I felt the pangs of hunger as I did with him. When Leah or Rachel or Eve dropped nuts or fruit, I savored the morsels as if they were a feast and cried at their generosity. Sometimes we moved to the edge in full view of the street and begged. At other times, when the sun was hot or the nights were cold, we slipped beneath the thick, sheltering branches and talked. At such times, I listened to him impart his wisdom, and I watched and waited for a way to approach my family. At times, he would suddenly roll on the earth, writhing in pain, holding the sockets where his eyes had been. I would rush to the well, retrieve water, and bathe the cavities. Then, sponging his face, I would wait for the anguish to subside. On some nights, I worried that he would perish because his body temperature would rise to frightening levels. I cooled him with water, and when he chilled, I held him. When the fever broke, I occasionally bade him talk, in order to focus his mind away from the pain.

He said he'd traveled to many lands. He'd seen kingdoms rise and fall and knew the signs of a civilization's impending death—just as he knew he was dying. When I argued that he wouldn't die, I knew I couldn't fool Danbenihah.

—When I first received my sentence to starve on the streets of Shum, he said, My condition became a topic of discussion. Each day, people would gather to watch me die and would guess the number of days till my death. Some said I'd starve within fourteen days; others speculated a month, no more. My circumstance became a curiosity and provided plenty for the people of Shum to talk about. I heard many say, No one can live for such a long time without food; he must be eating. They marveled at how I could bear starvation for so long. Leah and her daughter Rachel were the first to feed me. I came to know their voices. Leah's brash way of speaking to me brought laughter from those watching, but she had used her mocking to slip me food. Eve followed their example, using similar tactics. To the astonishment of all Shum, I have survived to this day by their kindness.

Like Danbenihah, I became a recipient of Leah's and Rachel's charity, being fed by them as I sat under the wisteria observing Shum. Turnips and beans were a typical meal, and I ate them as gratefully as I would fine venison. Eve came less regularly, but when she did, she slipped us nuts and fruit. Twice we were dragged into the street by the Rahaj and hit and kicked. When they left, I carried Danbenihah back to the wisteria, washed his wounds, and tended him as he suffered. The odor of the man that had once repulsed me had now become sweet, and what rags he wore for clothes seemed to me the robes of royalty.

—I'll tell you a secret, said Danbenihah.

He said it one clear night when a warm breeze delivered the fragrance of blossoming jasmine. We were relaxed beneath the wisteria, sharing a turnip Leah had sneaked to us.

—Have you a secret left? I laughed.

For long days, I had listened to Danbenihah impart his history, his travels, his brushes with death, his successes and failures. I knew he had a family in the land of Abel—two daughters and a son, all married. His wife was a skilled potter. Five grandchildren had come to them, and when he had departed Abel last, his second daughter was expecting a child in autumn.

—Yes, he answered, I have a secret.

—Then tell on, old man.

—This is my secret: I hated being a judge.

—Why? It would seem to be an honorable profession.

—Except for one problem, he said.

—And that is?

—Deciding where justice ends and mercy begins. For all the years I have judged people, I have never seen opposing parties go away satisfied, feeling that their position has been fairly arbitrated. They say the reckoning was too lenient, or the judgment was too harsh, or the offender's punishment was too little, or he received too much.

I said, As a father, I've found myself as judge for the situations of my children, and usually I've allowed emotion rather than justice to decide.

—An honest answer, said Danbenihah, And therein lies the dilemma: justice demands that a price be paid for a broken law. Fairness lies somewhere between death and ignoring the incident altogether. But fair to whom? To one, judgment will seem lacking; to another, it will seem severe.

—I would lean toward mercy, I said.

—Yes, he said, But what about justice? How do you balance the two? I tell you, my friend, I've never found a way to balance these, and I've often wondered if it can be done. Now you know my secret: I hated being a judge.

Then I said, Now I'll tell you my secret.

—Let me guess, he said. You hate being a beggar.

I laughed, then cleared my throat and became serious. I said, I've been your companion these six days, but you haven't asked me my name.

—I just supposed you had a good reason for not telling me, he said.

—I am Rabunel, son of Ebanel, the shepherd.

Danbenihah nodded, but the expression on his face made it clear he didn't recognize my name.

—I dared not reveal myself, I said.

—Why?

—In Shum, my name is one of consequence. I have a seat in the Council of the rulers you abhor. It's my daughter who has fed you and is betrothed to Chaz, prince of Shum. It's my wife, Moriah, who comes to the well and is pursued by Mahijah.

Danbenihah's face shifted to a look of concern. He reached out a groping hand and felt for my bearded face, then shifted it down to my shoulder and arm.

—Did they send you to spy on me? he asked, his voice wavering.

—No, I said, taking his hand.

His body relaxed, and he said, These six days have made us brothers. What happened to cause your poverty and make you a beggar on the street?

—I've supposed it to be the chastisement of God.

—His blessing or punishment?

—Perhaps both.

—I cannot see you, friend Rabunel. Are you changed so much that your family cannot recognize you?

I felt warm tears come to my eyes, and I couldn't answer him. He brought his hand to my face once more and wiped tears as they spilled down my cheeks.

—You have suffered greatly, he said. I may be blind, but some things I can see.

At his kind words, I dropped my head and pushed back tears.

Then, taking a deep breath, I said, There's more. Simeon, who sentenced you, is my grandfather.

Danbenihah made a slight movement, as if to cringe, and his face went blank.

—I apologize for any pain this revelation causes. I only share this so you'll know my predicament, and I hope you'll still trust me, I said.

He nodded and found my hand to clasp.

—For the safety of my family and for my own life, I dared not reveal myself, I said. There are those who still hunt me.

—Then you hide here for a purpose, he said.

—Yes, to observe Shum and find a way out for my family.

—Have you a plan? he asked.

—Yes. I've watched the Rahaj and can anticipate their movements. I've also watched my family, and their routine is predictable. I believe I can reveal myself to them with little risk. My father is to meet us outside Shum tomorrow night. He'll aid us in our flight.

—What if your family won't go?

—I've thought about that. Seeing me alive will be a shock. However, they're used to traveling to my father's camp. I'll try to convince them to go that far with me and counsel together about our future.

—Do you really think you can escape this place?

—Yes, but the danger is real.

—Will you take me with you? asked Danbenihah.

I paused and gazed upon his empty eye-sockets and broken feet. I touched his hand and asked myself, *Would I take him?*

I answered, Yes.

the seat of justice

 C3

In the early morning before first light, I stole through the streets of Shum to find my father and give him my plan for escape. For Danbenihah, I had gathered what food I could scrounge. As I had tended to his wounds, I worried over the red streaks that had channeled up the swollen calves of his legs. The vacant eye-sockets had discharged matter recently, and he said his head drummed with more pain. Now, he rarely sat up. After I had filled a flask with water and set it beside him, I left, vowing a quick return.

As the guards of the Rahaj had gathered at the well to talk in days past, I had heard them complaining that Danbenihah yet lived and how weary they were becoming of checking on him. Sometimes they mocked and threatened me, but usually they passed me by. For all who came to the well, no one, not even my family, recognized me. In recent days, the Rahaj had increased their patrols to see if they could detect the secret of Danbenihah's survival. But Leah, Rachel, and Eve continued to find ways to feed him and me, though Eve's visits were becoming less frequent. As beggars, Danbenihah and I had become adept at hiding the food they gave us and bringing it out at safer times.

As the eastern sky began to lighten at the horizon, birds wakened, and crickets quieted. I neared the edge of Shum and heard a woman screaming. Her shrill cry stopped me, and I sought its origin. The woman's cries were words I could not discern at first, but I ran in their direction.

—*Rachel!* came the cry of a woman's voice.

I sprinted toward the center of Shum and saw heads shoot from behind flaps of tents and peer into the dim light of dawn. My appearance startled some, but most ran into the streets and ran toward the source of the screaming. As I neared, I witnessed a flurry of excitement. A band of the Rahaj wrestled in the dust with several people, one wailing hysterically. As I came close, a burly man struck me with a club and sent me sprawling. When I looked up, I saw the Rahaj drag Danbenihah from the wisteria, strip him naked, and begin to beat him. Two men had forced Rachel to her knees and were binding her hands behind her with cords. Leah was screaming that her daughter had done nothing; it was *she* who had fed the beggar. Joshua lay prostrate in the dirt, groaning, a bloody gash at the back of his head. I assumed he had rushed to his sister's aid and had paid for it. When I cried for mercy on those being battered, the man with the club shoved it into my stomach and said, She was caught feeding the condemned.

A guard of the Rahaj took me by the hair, raised me to a kneeling position, and looked me over.

—This man was with the spy! he said.

Then he spat in my face and kneed me in the chest. The spittle dripped off my cheek and caught in my beard as I reeled on the ground, gasping for breath. Then four large men pounced on me, bound my hands behind me, and dragged me next to Rachel. When I opened my mouth to speak, I received a fist to the side of my head, and once more I fell into the dirt. A great, dark shadow covered me, and a deep voice asked my name and business in Shum. When I looked up, my eye caught the sun, and I turned my head. The voice repeated the question and nudged me in the side with a foot. Again I lifted my head and tried to see through the slits of my eyes. Moving to block the glare, the figure became a silhouette, and the sun at his back framed him as though he were haloed. Then I recognized the face and the form. They were Gad's.

—Let the maiden go, cried Danbenihah. She has done nothing.

Danbenihah was struck for his comment, and I held my tongue.

Gad lifted my chin with his club, stared at me, and asked, Who are you? Why are you in the company of this condemned man?

—In my land, I am a wealthy man, I said. I can pay for the release of these people.

—Yes, of course, said Gad. You're a gentleman, and don't you look it!

His statement was received with laughter.

—It's true, I said.

Gad threatened me with his club, and I shrank.

—Beat Danbenihah, and burn the maid who fed him, ordered Gad.

—No! cried Leah, breaking free from the guards and running to her daughter. A strong man of the Rahaj caught her, swung his club, and struck her at the base of the neck. I heard a snap, and her body crumpled into the dirt, her head lying askew, her eyes glazed. Leah was dead before she hit the ground.

Rachel began to wail. Joshua crawled to his mother, buried his head in her shoulder, and wept. I gazed upon Leah, her lifeless body lying unnaturally contorted. She was the one I had criticized for being overbearing. I had abhorred her appearance and avoided her. But she was the one who had fed us beggars, Danbenihah and me, and in doing so had shown more courage and charity than all Shum combined.

A huge crowd had formed about us. Someone cried, The spy is being beaten!

I looked over at my friend and saw him being bludgeoned without mercy. Once a powerful man, now blind, lame, starved, Danbenihah was no match for the six men who pummeled him. Then I heard Baruch's anguished cry. He rushed forward, tight-fisted, flailing arms like weaponry, beating his way through the Rahaj, and wrestling Gad to the ground. When aid came, Baruch had wrapped his hands about Gad's neck in a death-grip. He was not subdued until the bulk of the band had grasped his legs and arms and had stretched him on the ground like a skin for tanning. He struggled and wailed, calling out, Leah! Leah!

Rachel sank and sobbed, Oh, Mother! What have they done?

Joshua, who still held Leah, tried to rise and run to Baruch's aid, but was restrained.

—Have mercy on them! Eve cried.

I turned and saw her running toward us. Gad had recovered enough to be raised to a sitting position. As he rubbed his neck and took in big breaths, Eve fell at his feet and began to beg him to spare us. One of the Rahaj pulled her back by the hair. Then Gad made a motion with his hand, and the beating of Danbenihah continued. Three powerful men pounded him with their fists and kicked him with their feet.

—You're killing him! I shouted.

But it had no effect. There was no mercy in them. I watched them break his body, aim their wicked blows at open wounds, kick him until he went limp. When they left him in the dirt, his face was swollen beyond recognition.

As if from nowhere, my son, Enos, came running to Eve and attacked those who held her. He lunged into one of them, knocking him to the ground. Then he ripped Eve from the grasp of the other. As he held her in his arms, the man on the ground shouted, You are of the Rahaj!

But Enos stood between Eve and them and yelled, I am her brother first!

—It is enough! a voice cried above the uproar of the brawling and shouting.

The voice belonged to Chaz, the prince of Shum. He pulled a member of the Rahaj away from Danbenihah, saying, Stop beating him. He's barely conscious.

Then he rushed to Eve, took her from Enos, and held her in his arms. Leah lay at their feet, and I watched his eyes as he surveyed the dead woman and the bound prisoners. When he gazed on me, I felt the tiniest hope that perhaps I had misjudged the boy and he would stop all the insanity.

—What is happening here? he shouted.

Gad stepped forward and bowed low to the prince. He pointed to Baruch and said, This man's wife and daughter were caught feeding the spy from Sharon. By your father's decree, it is treason.

Chaz gazed on Leah's body once more. Then he turned to Rachel. Is it so? he asked her.

Before Rachel could answer, Baruch cried, The law is an abomination!

Then Eve faced Chaz and said, Show the people that the prince of Shum is both just and merciful. Let the chastisement of these people and the death of this woman be enough. Certainly the broken law is now satisfied.

But as she said it, my hope that Chaz had changed dissolved, for I saw a look cross over his face that perhaps only I could interpret. I now realized why Chaz could not show mercy—he was part of the conspiracy. Chaz knew his father's plan to invade Sharon, and he knew how Danbenihah figured as such a major part of that plan.

As for Baruch, from the moment he had gone to the tent of Mahijah to vouch for the peoples of Omner and Sharon, his life was forfeit. He was seen as a threat to Mahijah's objective. Simeon had said it well, *If Baruch meddles in Shum's security, he will have to be dealt with.* Now, the incident Mahijah and Simeon had needed to discredit or destroy Baruch was before them: he had struck the captain of the Rahaj, and his wife and daughter had broken the law of the king.

The prince of Shum did not respond to my daughter's plea. Instead, he looked past her to Gad and gave a slight nod of the head. At that, Gad clapped his hands, and we prisoners were dragged to the center of Shum, with the entire city following us.

—Let them burn, was the cry of the multitude.

Eve tugged at Chaz and cried, These are my friends! Stop this travesty! Upon your love for me, I beg you to exercise mercy!

Chaz stopped, looked into her face, and, without looking away, said, Let it be enough!

Those of us who were fated to die sighed, and I sensed a hush fall upon the people. We arrived at the Seat of Justice as Mahijah and Simeon emerged from the king's tent. Mahijah motioned for Chaz to continue with the judgment, and all the people waited to hear what he would say.

Gad spoke first. He stepped between Chaz and Mahijah and cried, Is the prince of Shum greater than the law of the king?

Eve gripped Chaz's arm. He stood erect but visibly shaken, unable or unwilling to speak. Gad took his silence as an answer, for he turned to the Rahaj and commanded, Let the guilty burn!

With fists raised high, the band of the Rahaj shouted, Let them burn! Let them burn!

At once, the people joined in the chant. A pole was brought forward, and Rachel and Danbenihah were dragged toward it. Rachel screamed and tried to wrench herself free. Danbenihah, barely conscious, offered no resistance.

As the two were bound back to back to the pole, Eve grabbed Chaz by the arm and turned him to her, crying, Do something!

Chaz seemed anxious and confused.

Taking no chance that the prince of Shum would waver, Gad shouted, May Mahijah and his son rule long over the land of Shum!

The people applauded Gad's shout and in one voice repeated it. Chaz appeared paralyzed. Eve shook him, but without effect. The Rahaj had piled a high mound of dry sticks around the pole holding Rachel and Danbenihah.

—What have these people done to deserve this? cried a loud voice from atop Ramurah's scaffold. The people hushed and turned to see Joshua balancing high above the Seat of Justice. He shouted, Nothing that was done is worthy of death! You have the body of my mother. Let that be enough. Restore this daughter to her father. Put the beggars at the borders of the city. But do not kill them!

Once more, Eve begged Chaz, Help them! Rachel is my friend!

Again Joshua cried, Release them now! They are *not* worthy of death, and this city is *not* worthy of this deed!

—Will you die with them? Gad shouted at Joshua.

I wrenched myself from my captors and ran toward the people, crying, People of Shum, you must not commit this act!

The two men who had held me soon caught me, pushed me to my knees, and roped my hands behind me.

Joshua pointed at Chaz and yelled, You are the prince of this people. The Rahaj serves you. Use your influence to stop this injustice!

—Get that mad man off the wall! cried Gad. Who dares speak against the prince and his father?

Three of the Rahaj wrestled Joshua from the wall and held him facedown in the dirt.

—Pile on more wood, and light the fire! ordered Gad.

Danbenihah raised his head and, in a voice that was hardly a whisper, begged his executioners for Rachel's sake, pleading, Let me die, not this maiden! She did nothing but show me kindness.

As the plea was ignored, I saw Rachel's face grow white and her legs buckle.

—Father, help me! she cried out.

Baruch tried to run to her but was held back by four large men. When the Rahaj lit the edges of the pile with torches, all Baruch could do was watch and wail.

The tiny flicker soon took hold, and the smell of fire seared the morning air. The people's cries to burn the condemned yielded to the loud whistles and snaps of dry wood succumbing to heat. Abruptly, an explosion of flames drove the multitude back. Some fell. Others shielded their faces. Children bawled but were ignored. The once meager blaze had suddenly become a raging inferno with flames leaping skyward above the tent-tops of Shum.

—Save me, prince of Shum! cried Rachel. What I carry is holy— it is your child!

Eve gasped at Rachel's revelation and, looking dumbfounded, stepped away from Chaz.

—Stop the executions! Eve insisted, her voice stern.

—She lies! She lies! Chaz shouted.

Then, in the midst of the crowd, I heard my wife cry for clemency. Benjamin and his family had come with Moriah, running. I saw the look of horror on my son's face as he held his mother back and hid the faces of his wife and son. Rachel screamed.

—Stop the executions! Eve cried again.

—I…, Chaz began, I am not above the law. There is nothing I can do.

Chaz tried to take Eve's hand, but she wrenched away and ran to Moriah, weeping. A wave of heat surged over the executioners, and they quickly retreated. For an awful moment, the crowd fell deathly silent. As the flames leaped at the tender skin of Rachel and Danbenihah, they shrieked. Danbenihah pled for a quick death, as the fire started to char and burn away his flesh. A man raised his bow to give Danbenihah mercy, but was chastised by Gad, saying, Not until justice has had its way.

When the flames reached Rachel's hair, she shook her head violently and screamed. Baruch slumped down on the pole and pled, O dear God, let her die quickly!

I took up the same prayer as even the most callous of the Rahaj shuddered at the sight and withdrew. A stiff wind whipped the flames, and hot drafts carried the stench of burnt flesh out over the gaping crowd. My heart pounded within my chest. The charred bodies made flailing movements, then, as one last whimper came from Rachel, she too hung slack from the binding pole. Finally, both of them fell into the crimson coals below. Except for the sound of the blaze, all stood quietly transfixed. We had not seen people burn in Shum before. Some turned their heads and covered their noses. Others ran behind tents and retched. Children softly cried. As I scanned the faces of the onlookers, I saw expressions of uncertainty, horror, excitement. Some became frenzied by the sight, the way a wolf pack is aroused by blood. Eve collapsed into her mother's arms and both wept. Enos had fallen into the ranks of the Rahaj, but turned his face away. Benjamin continued to hold Sarah and cover the eyes of Nathaniel. He stood stoically watching the scene, and I wondered, could he be a Watcher now? A judge to the people? One who could pass this type of punishment upon another?

—Stoke the fire, ordered Gad. There is yet another execution today.

He pointed at Baruch. The men that stood over Baruch lifted him off the ground and dragged him toward a binding pole. A murmuring droned throughout the crowd. Gad's shout rekindled the hysteria of Danbenihah's and Rachel's burning. Some of the people took up the shout, calling for Baruch's death.

I rolled and struggled to my knees, loudly crying, No! No!

My shouts interrupted the execution, and quickly I rose to my feet.

—I have urgent news of Sharon, I yelled, And it is meant only for the ears of the king.

The guard near me looked to Mahijah for direction, and Simeon whispered something to the king.

—Bring the prisoner forward, ordered Mahijah.

The guard took my arm, dragged me to the Seat of Justice, and forced me to my knees at the feet of Mahijah. Then the guard stood back.

—Mahijah, king of Shum, I said in a low voice, It is to your advantage to let me speak.

—You assume to have rights here, he said.

—I know your secret and will reveal it.

Mahijah laughed.

Simeon glared at me and said, Who are you to threaten the king?

—A friend.

—A friend? said Mahijah. A *friend's* head is as easy as an enemy's to detach.

—Then you would be killing your daughter-in-law's father, I said.

Mahijah eyed me and motioned Chaz to bring Eve to the Seat of Justice. Chaz obeyed by taking Eve by the arm and escorting her forward. When she tried to protest, she could not free herself from his grasp.

—Young love! said Mahijah to the crowd.

They laughed with the king as Chaz pulled Eve forward. Then Mahijah spoke quietly to me, saying, The king's only secret is the betrothal of his son to this young woman.

My daughter's face was streaked with tears, but she summoned strength, straightened, and took on a look of dignity. As I gazed upon her, I felt a love for her beyond my ability to express.

—She cannot be betrothed without her father's blessing, I said.

—Her father is dead, said Mahijah.

—Then the dead walk among you!

Eve turned to stare at me. She pulled away from Chaz, came cautiously toward me, then took my face in her hands, and studied me for a long, quiet moment, touching my cheeks, pushing the hair back from my face, tracing the shape of my chin.

—Say something, she said inquiringly.

I thought for a moment and said, Once, when you were a child, you climbed a tree to free a butterfly from a spider's web. When you stretched out over a limb, you slipped and fell and received a gash on your elbow.

Eve glanced at the small, white scar on her elbow, then threw her arms around me and began to cry.

—The butterfly survived, I whispered.

—It's Father! she shouted to her mother and brothers.

—Rabunel! cried Moriah.

The guard held her, but Enos pulled her from him, and they and Benjamin's family raced up the steps of the Seat of Justice. When a guard stepped between them and me, Simeon whispered to Mahijah, Let the family come up, and we will hear him out.

As Mahijah made a motion with his hand, the guard stepped aside, and my family embraced me. We cried in each other's arms.

A deep murmur rolled through the assembly, and I looked to Simeon, still hoping he would help me. His face had gone ashen, and he grabbed for Mahijah's shoulder to steady himself.

—By what magic are you alive? asked Mahijah, visibly astonished.

—By a power greater than yours, I said. Now, I tell you again to let Baruch go!

Then Gad stepped to the Seat of Justice and said in a loud voice, This man was the companion of Danbenihah, the spy from Sharon.

—Grandfather, I appealed, It is I, Rabunel. Tell them I am no traitor.

Simeon just stared at me, offering no response.

Moriah took my arm and said to Simeon, This is your grandson! Help him!

—Stand away from that man, Mahijah ordered her.

—I will not. He's my husband.

Mahijah's face became the color of the embers that still smoldered. Simeon stood yet in silence, glaring at me, and I felt my stomach become tight.

—Will you not give your own grandson aid? I begged Simeon.

He said nothing.

I directed myself to Mahijah and asked, Will you give me audience?

The king looked to Simeon, who returned a small nod, and Mahijah motioned me forward. The guard at my side nudged me forward with his club.

—Loose my hands, I said to Mahijah.

—No.

—What are you afraid of? You have your entire army before you. Loose my hands.

Mahijah nodded, and the guard cut my bands. I rubbed my swollen hands. My wrists bore the deep impressions of the ropes.

—Where is the fortune you promised me? he asked.

I didn't answer.

—You're a thief, and now you sneak back into Shum to betray us.

—I am no traitor, I said. I have never had a passion for government or the military. You know this. A tragedy occurred on my return journey from Haner. I was delayed for months.

—You have returned as a spy, said Mahijah.

—As an observer! I shouted.

—Lower your voice, said Mahijah.

—As an observer, I repeated in a low voice.

—You have come back as an enemy, said Mahijah.

—I have come for my family.

The king laughed and raised his voice so that the assembly of Shum could hear, saying, Rabunel shares the company of a known criminal and seeks ways to betray us, and now he thinks he can take his family and leave.

Gad stepped forward and said, I say this man is in correspondence with the enemy.

—There is no enemy! I cried.

Simeon took Mahijah aside to consult with him, and I turned to Moriah and whispered in her ear, You must trust me. No matter what happens to me, you and the children must flee to the arbor outside Shum tonight. Ebanel waits for you. He will hide you. If I can, I'll come and help you. But don't tarry. Promise me you'll go.

The people had begun to stir at my saying that there was no enemy, and a guard stepped forward and slapped me for insolence. My family tried to reach me, but they were held back.

—Move them away from here, Mahijah ordered, motioning guards to remove my family from the Seat of Justice.

—Father? cried Eve.

—It's all right, I said. Go with your mother.

When they had moved back with the crowd, I whispered to Mahijah, Beware! You don't want the people to hear what I have to tell you. But if you'll allow me, I'll make you an offer that you'll find profitable.

Mahijah looked to Simeon, and I was motioned forward.

—Tell the guard to leave, I said.

Mahijah waved the guard away, and Simeon drew near.

—Say what you will, said the king, But be quick about it.

—Let my family go free, and release Baruch, I said, And I will pay you for their lives.

Mahijah pursed his lips into a thin smile and said, You're in no position to bargain. If you have anything of value, which by your appearance I doubt, it's mine for the debt you owe me. You cannot use that which is not yours to negotiate with. But the fact remains that Baruch struck Gad, and by so doing, broke the law. It is within Gad's rights to have Baruch burned. I will not deny Gad his revenge. As for claiming your family, they're dead to you now. Moriah is mine. I claim her for the debt you owe me.

—She is not property, I said. She is her own person and a married woman.

—I remind you of the law: debtors have no rights, said Mahijah. Yours is a fool's errand. Eve belongs to Chaz now. As for your sons, you're welcome to them, if you can persuade them to follow you. But will Benjamin abandon being Simeon's apprentice? Will he forfeit assured prosperity and position to risk his family's lives wherever you might lead him? Will Enos leave the Rahaj and betray Gad, who has afforded him the affections of a father? Go back into the mountains, Rabunel, and count yourself lucky you still have your head.

—You misunderstand my intention, I said. I am not *requesting*, I am *demanding* that you do as I say.

Mahijah took a step toward me with fists clenched and said, Draw another breath, and tell me why I should not order you killed where you stand.

—Because I know your secret—how you gained your power, I said. If the people knew, do you think they would continue to support you?

Mahijah looked past me into the faces of his subjects and whispered, They believe what I tell them to believe.

—They may believe what I tell them, I said.

—You lie, said Mahijah. You know nothing, and your threats will die with you.

—Do you think I would make this threat without proof? I said. What if I have told others?

—Extortion is a dangerous game, said Simeon, stepping near.

—Now speaks my grandfather! I said. How say you, Grandfather? Will you defend your own blood or stand with this excuse for a king?

—If you insinuate that I should abandon my office for the sake of familial affections, said Simeon, You have sorely misjudged me.

—Since when have you subscribed to duty and morality? I asked.

—There is too much proof that you have consorted with the enemy, he said.

—Do you persist with this lie? I said. There is no enemy! Everything that has happened—the bodies made to appear as warriors from Sharon, the mock trial and execution of Danbenihah— all of it was intended to whip the people into a frenzy and raise an army to invade Sharon and Omner.

—You travel a perilous road, said my grandfather. I urge you to forsake your threats and yield to reason. If you stand before the people now and endorse the king, you may still reclaim your former position, and I will arbitrate the charges of treason against you, help you settle the debt with Mahijah, and restore your family to you.

Mahijah began to protest to the offer, but Simeon raised a hand to silence him. I was astonished that my grandfather had that much sway with the king. I carefully observed Simeon for a long moment, especially his eyes and the position of his body. Then I straightened.

—You lie, I said. Your course is set. I can sense it, and it does not include aiding me or my family.

Then I turned to Mahijah and said, You hold me and my wife in bondage for a debt you think I cannot pay. But no one—not even Moriah—knows the extent of my wealth or resources. I will give you all my wealth—twice what I owe you—for the freedom of my family and Baruch's release. Then we'll leave this place forever. I'll keep my silence, and you can keep your secret.

—You're more dangerous outside of Shum, said Simeon. You know the city and its defenses. If you go to our enemies in Sharon there will be a bloodbath. You're too great a threat.

—What say you, king? I asked, turning my attention away from Simeon. Will you agree to my terms?

—Who would believe your claim anyway? he said. I will deny everything you say. No one will believe you.

—Are you willing to wager your crown? I asked.

—Are you willing to wager the lives of your children? he answered.

—My children?

—You force my hand, he said. I will order them executed before your eyes this very day, and the people will sustain me. They have seen your family embrace you, a known traitor, the companion of Danbenihah, the spy. Your family is as worthy of death as you are.

We stared at each other a long time, posturing.

Then Simeon said, I urge reason. Rabunel, my grandson, you have little choice. Talk to your sons. If they will go away with you, take them. But Moriah must stay in Shum to ensure your silence. Eve is betrothed to Chaz and must stay also. She is royalty now. To take her would incite war. We'll order Gad to not punish Baruch, but Baruch will be chastised by one of the Rahaj. Baruch's life will be spared and placed into your hands to do with as you will. You'll be allowed to leave Shum, but you must never return. If you attempt to come back or if you betray us to our enemies, we have your wife and daughter.

—And I'll keep your property as you suggested, said Mahijah. As for Moriah, she is not negotiable. She is mine for your treason.

—I will not allow this! I protested.

—You have no choice in the matter, said Mahijah, clapping his hands.

Two guards came and pulled me away, and Simeon summoned Gad and gave him instructions. The captain of the Rahaj cursed his displeasure and reluctantly issued the order to draw lots for one of the Rahaj to whip Baruch.

All at once, the Rahaj shouted, Enos! Enos! I looked up and saw my son being pushed to an opening in the midst of the throng. Enos was handed a whip, and he stood alone, opposite a lashing pole. Baruch was dragged to the pole and bound to it.

—Enos! No! cried Moriah.

—Do not do this thing, cried Eve.

Chaz stepped to her side and held her back. Again, she could not break away from him.

A great hush of anticipation fell upon the people. A rush of anxiety knifed through me like a hot blade, and I saw Enos's face become as pale as a dead man's. He stood, quavering. He held the whip so that it lay slack in the dirt, taking a serpentine form, his knuckles having turned white from tightly grasping the handle. The muscles in his forearm twitched. By his expression, I knew he was struggling. I prayed for God to reach out to him and give him courage to walk away from the awful act.

A restlessness shuddered through the assemblage. Then Gad stood forth and ordered Enos, Be done with it. Similar pleas rumbled from the crowd, and Enos slowly raised the whip. As the people quieted, Baruch's body arched and trembled. Suddenly Enos let go with the whip. It snapped in the air and struck the ground at Baruch's feet. A harmless puff of dust rose where the leather length had cut a long channel. Dropping the handle of the whip, Enos rent his robes of the Rahaj, then walked away to stand with his family.

Moriah wept.

With a look of anger and determination, Gad ran to pick up the whip, positioned himself, and cocked his arm.

—No! I cried. Then, turning to Mahijah, I said, You promised that Gad would not punish this man.

Mahijah shot me a look of indignity and raised his hand to stop Gad. He said, Very well. Follow me.

Puzzled looks and voices spread throughout the multitude as Mahijah and I stepped from the Seat of Justice. Baruch was roped to the lashing pole, beaten but conscious. Mahijah ordered a guard to lift Baruch's head so that he could see his face. The guard forced a rod under Baruch's chin and thrust his head back so that he looked into Mahijah's eyes.

—Do you recognize your old competitor? Mahijah asked Baruch.

He made no effort to reply.

I said, What are you doing?

Mahijah did not respond to me but continued speaking to Baruch.

—Your *friend*, Rabunel, has returned from his journey to Omner where he bought your supplier away from you. He intends to destroy you and your family. It was he who gathered evidence against your wife and daughter and exposed them. Now, he has paid for the privilege of lashing you for your crimes. But before he does, I wanted you to know your executioner.

As he walked away, I followed him, saying, You lie. Is there no decency in you? Why do you do this?

—I want you to feel every lash as much as he does.

—I will not do it!

Mahijah stopped, handed me the whip, and said, Ten lashes. It's either you or Gad. It's your choice.

I took the whip. Then, returning to Baruch, I said, You must not believe him.

Baruch looked up into my eyes and said, Is it true? Did you go to Omner?

—Yes, but you must not believe what the king has said.

Baruch bowed his head and said, What else can I believe? You're the one holding the whip.

—I'm sorry, old friend, I whispered. I would gladly trade places with you. But if I'm to save your life, this is all I can do. Forgive me and live.

—You may beat me, answered Baruch, But I will not forgive you.

I said no more, stepped to my position, removed my outer wrap, and readied the whip. My family cried for me to stop, but the people cheered me. I stood for a long moment, as had Enos, assessing the options. I tried to decide what effort I should expend: to lash him too hard would cost him his life; too soft and Gad would cry injustice. I gazed at the frightening instrument in my hand. I wondered at what would possess people to fashion something so painful and lethal—and to craft it so handsomely, intricately, and artfully. Balanced and proportioned so exquisitely, the handle fit in my hand as though the artisan had measured it for me. Lengths of leather had been wound in tight braids, long and serpentine.

As I arched my arm to deliver the first blow, I sensed a feeling of anticipation leap through the crowd. The flesh of Baruch's back twitched just before the lash struck, and when it hit, the snap carved a long gash. Baruch's head jerked back, and he cried out in pain, gasping for breath through clenched teeth. The multitude cheered. As I fought back tears, I wondered how I could deliver nine more lashes.

—Forgive me, Lord, I prayed. Save this man from what I must do.

When I let the whip fly again, small bits of bloody flesh cut away from Baruch's back and flew toward onlookers. By the sixth blow, Baruch no longer cried out. His head lay back; his eyes were glazed and senseless; his mouth hung open as though he were dead. At ten lashes, he was cut down and fell to the earth.

Joshua rushed to him and cried, Water! Will no one give him water?

Eve broke free from Chaz and ran to retrieve a vessel of water. Enos ran with her. Moriah broke away from the Rahaj, as did Benjamin and Sarah. They rushed to help Joshua care for his father. Benjamin lifted Baruch into his lap, while the women washed away the blood and cleaned the wounds. The people became loud, milling about, intrigued, confused, excited.

In the confusion, I knelt beside Moriah and whispered, Will he live?

—Yes, he's strong.

—Can he walk? I asked.

—No, he'll need to be carried, she said.

—His life is as much in danger as is ours, I said. We must get him out of here.

Gad deftly grabbed the whip from my hands and said, Be gone from this city!

As he motioned for a guard to escort me from the city, I quickly turned to my family and said, I must leave now.

Joshua stared at me with a look of confusion and hurt.

—I hope someday you can understand, I said. For now, you must move your father far from this city.

Joshua nodded, and I discerned in his face a glimmer of clarity.

I turned to Benjamin and whispered, We haven't much time. Get your family to the arbor tonight.

—I don't understand, he said. What are you suggesting?

—Shum is dangerous for us. We must leave, if only temporarily.

—This is insane!

—Benjamin, I said, We have no time to argue or debate. Will you risk the lives of your wife and son? Meet at the arbor tonight! This is all I ask of you. Once you hear me out, you may choose to do what you will. But for now, son, it's too dangerous for any of us to stay.

—We'll be there tonight, he replied with reluctance.

I turned to Enos and said, I'll need your help to bring out your mother and sister. They will be guarded.

—I'll meet you at the arbor, said Enos.

—Chaz won't let me go, said Eve.

—The guards are coming! said Enos.

—Tonight, Eve whispered.

Then Chaz stood before the people and said, Go back to your tents.

As I arose to depart when the guards came, Chaz extended a hand to Eve, but she turned and walked away from him. He followed her, took her arm, and spun her around. She wrenched away, crying, then rushed to Joshua, who was trying to lift Baruch into his arms.

—Help me carry him! she cried to Enos.

Chaz held Enos back in order to help Eve. As Chaz stooped to help Joshua lift Baruch, Joshua said, I would rather you didn't.

Chaz stepped back, and Enos knelt down by Joshua, saying, I have a cart. Stay with your father while I fetch it.

Joshua nodded.

—You shouldn't have seen this, said Chaz to Eve. He held her at her elbow.

Crying, Eve looked past him to her mother and pled to stay with her. Moriah made a motion as if to go to Eve, but Chaz raised his hand to stop her and said to Eve, Come with me, and we'll talk. I cannot bear to see you this way.

—Can't you? Eve said in a strong voice, looking at him through tears.

Chaz flinched.

—Do you fear I have exposed you? If what Rachel said was true, you lied to me. You lied! And you allowed the mother of you child—*the mother of your child*—to burn! Is this what you would build a marriage on? Lies? Cowardice?

Eve searched his eyes deeply. I knew her. She was searching for the truth, the truth that was so important to her. But I knew she wouldn't find it. As Chaz gazed back at her, steadying himself, gathering about him the look of confidence, his eyes shifted away from hers for the tiniest moment, and she had her answer. Her face, flushed and wet, suddenly became very clear.

She did not cry, but spoke with an even voice, saying, Your oath of chastity to me meant nothing. Rachel was my friend. I loved her like a sister. Will the Rahaj put me to death too?

—What a thing to say, Chaz said. I wouldn't allow it!

—What if I were to tell you I also fed Danbenihah?

Chaz hesitated, as if examining her to see if she told the truth.

—You must not say such things! he said.

Eve rebuffed his words with a challenge. What say you, prince of Shum? I, Eve, daughter of Rabunel and Moriah, have sinned a great sin. I have fed a poor beggar!

Chaz grew quiet, straightened, then clapped his hands. Guards of the Rahaj came, and at Chaz's order, they escorted Eve and Moriah to their tent. Then, as Chaz turned to walk away, the guards nudged me toward the border of Shum. Enos and Benjamin were left to help Joshua, and Sarah held Nathaniel, who was crying.

I glanced at the lashing pole and beyond to the Seat of Justice. Mahijah and Simeon yet stood on it, with backs turned, speaking in whispers. Then they left. With the excitement over, the people of Shum had gone home, and the city began to hum as if nothing had happened. I mourned for Danbenihah, for Leah, for Rachel, for Joshua, and for Baruch. As I stared off at my wife and daughter being escorted away, I remembered watching Eve's heart go out to a poor man. I recalled her giving him food to save him from starvation. With a little more imagination, I could see her burning for her "indiscretion."

escape from shum

ભ

A chilling blanket of fog snaked down the mountains of Shum as afternoon became evening. Chickens roosted early, and the setting of the sun in the western horizon produced a faint glow. Outside the city, I lurked in the shadows until darkness came thick with the fog. Then I began to search for Miriam. I had no idea where to begin. First, I checked around Baruch's tent for clues. Then, I felt my way to her father's tent to see if she had hidden there in his absence. I checked around the well and even checked the wisteria. Having no success, I decided I would need more help, so I went to the arbor to find my father. He and Enos were there, sitting by the flickering light of a small fire. Enos had told him of the executions, my confrontation with Mahijah and Simeon, and my whipping Baruch.

—Rabunel! exclaimed my father as I entered the arbor.

—I'm safe, I said, embracing him.

—A guard is posted at Mother's and Eve's tent, said Enos.

—We'll go back together, I said.

—The Rahaj is as thick as the fog, said Enos.

—Why?

—Mahijah has put them on alert to guard against our entering the city.

—Where's the rest of the family? I asked.

—They haven't arrived, said my father. Eat something before you go back.

—I haven't the time.

—Take a few moments to eat. You'll need your strength.

We settled at the fire and ate my father's beans and mutton. Except for my worrying about the safety of my family, I might have had a wonderful experience. My instruction for them to meet at the arbor was now imperiled by the fog.

—Father, you and Enos must try to find Benjamin, I said. I'll go for Moriah and Eve.

—By yourself, you can't get past the guard, said Enos.

—In the wilderness, I became a fair stalker, I said. I won't take undue risks. If I can't find a way, I'll come and fetch you.

ᛢ

I never wanted to see Shum again. Dim in the fog, the city looked as foreboding as a crypt. Slipping in and out of shadows, I crept the lone pathways. The fog was a blessing. Even when it ebbed, one could not see but a few strides beyond. I used it for cover and relied on memory and stealth to make my way to my tent where Moriah and Eve would be waiting.

It was late that night, and Shum was asleep except for the Rahaj that prowled the streets. When I arrived at my tent, I crouched behind a stack of firewood beyond the notice of the guard, who was stationed at the front. The man was large, clad in red, and held a huge club. While he stood, he shifted his weight from leg to leg. He had the look of determination, and I knew by his training that he would stay awake at his post and guard it all night. I also knew that such an assignment would not go to the incapable or unseasoned.

I heard Eve and Chaz talking inside the tent. She was crying and saying, I love you, yes, but I don't know if I can trust you anymore.

—What do you want from me? asked Chaz.

—Time.

—You're not backing out on the marriage, are you?

—I'm so confused and tired. I need time to think. Why did you come here tonight?

—To reassure you of my love, he said. Today, you were too upset to talk rationally. Tonight, I hoped we could talk things over.

—I don't think you can defend what happened today.

—The issues of government are complicated, said Chaz. We do hard things that the populace may not readily understand. As my wife, you must learn to occasionally hold your tongue and look the other way.

—Not when it concerns my family and friends. Not when it comes to fairness.

—What is fair? asked Chaz. The people cannot decide what is fair. Fair is what we leaders tell them.

—Fair was not what I saw when Danbenihah was burned, said Eve. Fair was not what I saw when Baruch was whipped or Leah clubbed. Fair was not Rachel's being executed. Fair was not your swearing to me that you were morally clean and had known no other woman. Isn't it true that Rachel carried your child?

—No. She was lying.

—She lied as she was dying?

—Of course, to save her life.

A long pause followed, then I heard Moriah say, Children, let sleep take the emotion out of the day. Tomorrow will bring clarity.

I heard murmuring that I could not decipher, and soon the vague figure of Chaz exited the tent.

—I think I will never understand the female mind, he said as he left.

Outside, he stopped to speak with the guard, then walked away holding a torch. The guard remained at the entrance.

The thick haze that hovered along the ground of Shum was now my friend. Hiding in it, I watched glimmers of Moriah's fire escape the seams of the tent. As I slipped to the rear, I took my knife and quietly clipped the stitches that held together the layers of fabric that covered the tent. I heard the snap of a twig and froze. The guard paced, and I sensed Moriah and Eve grow completely quiet. When the guard had settled, I whispered to them, I'm here.

—Are you taking us now? whispered Moriah.

—Yes.

I continued snipping the seams until the first and second layers were loose and I could open the flap. Another distant noise brought a shout from the guard.

—Jubal, is that you? he called out for a comrade.

—Be still! shouted Moriah from inside, How can we sleep with all the noise?

I crept to the side of the tent and saw the guard pace, return warily back to the tent's entrance, and stand uneasily, alert like a gazelle at the whiff of danger. When he quieted, I slipped to the back of the tent, drew back the flap, and motioned Moriah and Eve to step out.

We hurried through the dark, foggy streets of Shum. I held Moriah's hand as she held Eve's. Sometimes we ran from one hiding place to another. Other times we crept along quietly, sliding behind tents, blending in with the shadows. At the edge of the city, I led my wife and daughter through the fog to the arbor, where we found my father, Enos, Benjamin, Sarah, and Nathaniel waiting.

—Where is Miriam? asked my father.

—I saw no trace of her, I said. The tent of Baruch was plundered.

—Miriam is in Shum? asked Benjamin, surprised.

Until that moment, neither my father nor I had informed my family about Miriam.

—Yes, Miriam has been in Shum, said my father. She's been hiding in the tent of Baruch, and she is with child.

—Then we must find her, said Sarah.

—I've tried, I said, But I don't know where she could be.

I put my hand on Benjamin's shoulder and asked, Can you lead the family to your grandfather's camp?

Benjamin nodded and asked, What's your plan?

—I will take Enos and your grandfather and return to find Miriam.

—But one cannot see beyond a few paces in the fog, he said. How will you find her?

—In the wilderness, I found meat and drink when I thought I would perish. I don't know how we'll find her, but I know there is great power in asking God for help.

—Father? asked Eve, Where is Jerel?

I looked to my father as if to ask, *You haven't told them?*

He shook his head, and when Eve saw this, she burst into tears.

Moriah looked heavenward and cried, O God, what else can you demand of this family?

I took her in my arms, and each of my family wept.

Drying my eyes, I said, We will mourn Jerel, but not now. We still have family somewhere in the dark, likely scared, cold, wondering who will rescue her. At grandfather's camp, we will gather and give Jerel, Leah, Rachel, and Danbenihah the honor and remembrance they deserve. For now, we must concentrate on the task at hand.

As I gazed upon my family, emotions welled up within me. On the one hand, I had longed for this moment during my long absence—being together, being at peace with each other, being able to see and touch them all again. On the other hand, all the feelings I had tried to bury surrounding Jerel's death returned with the full intensity of that first day. I had thought I had dealt with the hurting and put it behind me. I had no idea how tender and how near the surface my emotions were. I gestured my family to gather in a circle and to take hands. Praying had not been a common practice in my family. When I knelt on the earth and brought my family into a circle of worship, I was met by looks of puzzlement, my father's excepted. He smiled.

I tried to summon language worthy of the honor I felt for the God of heaven. I commended the lives of our deceased family and friends into his hands. I pled for our deliverance, that we could find Miriam, that each of us could find answers to our individual concerns. When we arose, I delivered my wife and daughter into Benjamin's care, then my father, Enos, and I headed back to the city.

෨

As the fog crept along the ground, its eerie shapes betokened terrors of the night. As we neared Shum, we took care to communicate in gestures and whispers. To find Miriam was our goal, and we had devised a plan to increase our line of vision, hoping to remain safe. As Enos and I moved forward, searching the fringe of the city, my father remained in the high grass with his bow readied to protect us, keeping us in sight, watching for danger at our flank.

We guessed that the deep part of night was moving toward morning, but without the light from the moon and stars, we had no way of knowing. We decided to search the outer limits of Shum first, reasoning that Miriam might have escaped there during Baruch's lashing. But our chances of finding her were remote. Miriam had managed to remain hidden in Shum for a very long time, and the number of places to hide was overwhelming.

The fog would billow, then part long enough to see a ways in front, then close in, thick and damp. Sounds seemed as distorted as sights, muted, haunting, removed. Our sense of direction became skewed at times. I couldn't see, and as my senses failed me, I sought for guidance and a quickening of my spiritual senses. I drew upon my experience in the wilderness. I had discovered that a quiet communication exists that surpasses understanding. I had learned to detect and trust it. I knew it as peaceable, coming as a stroke of intelligence, something I struggled to translate through my physical senses. Prayer was the key to invoking it, and that process had been my source of survival in the wilderness.

I sought it now, petitioning God, then searching my mind, casting off distractions, listening, *feeling* for direction. Not long after, the tiniest brightness burst upon my thoughts. I envisioned an abandoned, bowl-shaped hut made of dried mud and covered with flax-colored hemp. I could see it in my mind's eye—a perception I equated with physical sight. From the impression, I knew Miriam hid in the hut, and I could *see* the route to find her.

Signaling Enos, I beckoned him to follow me. We slipped into the mist, threading our way cautiously between the tents of Shum.

—The Rahaj is everywhere, whispered Enos.

—Go slowly so your grandfather can keep us in sight, I said.

My son knew the training of the Rahaj and led me in evasive movements. As we skulked through the city, we faded into shadows and padded as softly as panthers stalking prey. From time to time, we would turn to locate my father. When the fog waned and we could see each other, he would wave, and Enos and I would move on.

At the outskirts of the city, I knew we were close, and soon the earthen hut that I'd seen in my mind earlier stood before me. Enos and I came near. I felt certain it was the place of Miriam's hiding. We paused and listened. The Rahaj was close. We had heard their talking. Up till now, we had evaded them.

I whispered to Enos, I'll go inside and talk with Miriam.

—I'll stand guard outside, he said.

—Keep your grandfather in view, I said.

As I moved to the entrance of the hut, Enos reminded me that my appearance was anything but reassuring. I nodded. I seldom thought about it. The harsh garb I had worn as a beggar had become as natural to me as my soft robes of former days. I prayed Miriam would believe what I had to tell her and come away with us.

I wondered how I could silently remove Miriam. A call to her, no matter how discreet, might frighten her or alert the Rahaj. I decided to burst into the hut, cover her mouth, explain my purpose, then release her. But just as I touched the loose flap of the hut and made a movement to step inside, I felt a dagger at my throat.

—On your knees!

The voice was that of a young woman. I felt the point of her weapon dig at the flesh under my chin, and I obeyed and went to my knees.

—Will you allow me to speak? I asked.

—Who are you? Why have you come?

—Miriam, I said, hoping to calm her, Lower your voice. It is I, Rabunel, your uncle.

As I said it, I cast my eyes upon her, and I felt tears come to my eyes. The little girl I had loved and not seen for years had grown into a woman. She was small of stature with a creamy complexion, blue oval eyes, and soft raven hair braided to her waist. By the roundness of her belly, she had carried a child for many months. When she moved, she occasionally moaned with discomfort, but her condition had not made her less feisty.

At the mention of my name, Miriam drove the tip of the dagger into my flesh until I thought the pressure would break the skin. She nudged me toward a small fire and studied my face.

—Douse the fire, I said. We might be seen.

—You're a liar and a wild man, she said. You smell like the carcass of an animal long dead.

—I agree with your last statement, but put out the fire.

She hesitated.

—Think back on the days at your grandfather's camp, riding a dapple pony, frolicking with your cousin, Eve, in just-sheared wool.

Miriam moved so that she looked at me straight on. From my hair to my chin, she examined every part of my face.

—I don't recognize you, she said.

—You have changed too, I said. You were a child when I saw you last.

—I won't go to my father, she said. If that's your purpose in coming, you won't succeed.

—Ebanel, your grandfather, sent me, I said. I've come to help you escape.

I carefully moved the point of her knife away from my throat. The fierce look in her face became soft, and she relaxed her body. Again, she studied my face and clothing with a look of doubt.

—I'll explain later, I said. For now, you must trust me.

I threw dirt on the fire, took her hand, and helped her to her feet.

—I'm not very fast, she said.

—Just as long as you're quiet, I replied.

We stepped from the hut into the dense haze.

At seeing Enos, Miriam moved to hug him, but he put a finger to her lips and motioned us to follow him. I sensed worry in his demeanor, but dared not speak. Enos gestured toward a murky spot that I took to be a stand of trees. By my son's look, I could tell he had detected the Rahaj lurking there.

As we crept toward the edge of Shum, we employed any cover we could find. We watched my father as he moved before us, stopping, crouching, then motioning us on. We learned to step softly as a feather floating to the ground. We heard sounds—the voices of the Rahaj, we thought—sometimes the cry of a child, the popping of embers burning. We stuck to the shadows. A dog barked close by, and we went to our knees until the animal stopped. When we felt safe, we moved on, crouching forward as though we were walking into a stiff wind. Miriam held her belly as though it were a bundle of clothes to wash.

When we reached the extreme edge of the city, she whispered, Where are we going?

—To your grandfather's camp, I said.

—But they'll search for me there.

—We'll take you on to Enoch, I said.

—Enoch?

I perceived by her tone that she had heard rumors of him—the wild prophet who sought to lure disciples into the mountains and pepper their minds with fantastic teachings.

—Is Enoch our destination, Father? asked Enos.

I detected an uneasiness in his tone.

—We don't have the time to discuss it, I said. But I will say this much—the hearsay you've heard regarding Enoch is false. I know him, and I know there's safety in his camp. But the choice is yours. At your grandfather's camp, we'll discuss the future, and each of you can follow your heart.

Enos stopped abruptly.

—What? I whispered.

He raised a hand, and I became quiet.

—Can you run? he asked Miriam.

—I don't think so.

He pointed a finger at an obscure site at the border of the city. I strained, but shook my head that I couldn't see.

—Wait for the fog to part, he whispered.

I focused on the spot, and soon the mist thinned, revealing two faint shapes. As I watched, I discerned the familiar robes and clubs. Then the haze folded in around them, and they were gone from my view. I searched the fog for my father. When he arose from the high grass, he motioned for us not to move.

—Can we go around them? asked Miriam.

—Unlikely, said Enos. We would just run into other guards, maybe more than these two.

—I could distract them, I said to Enos, Then you could run with Miriam to your grandfather.

—I can't run, Miriam reminded me.

We became silent.

Then I finally said, The fog will have to suffice. We'll crawl along the ground using the grass as cover.

—It might work, said Enos.

—You'll have to run a short distance, I said to Miriam.

—I'll try.

Again, the guards of the Rahaj appeared from the ebbing fog. They paced, raising their torches, speaking in low tones.

—They're archers, whispered Enos. Wait until they've settled.

When the mist covered the men and their voices dimmed, we dropped to our knees and waited for my father's signal.

—Now! said Enos, pointing us toward a clump of bushes.

He took the lead, feeling for sticks or pebbles, anything that might make a sound. I worried over Miriam's labored breathing that turned involuntarily into groans. I followed her as she followed Enos and hoped her sounds were dampened in the murk about us.

A boulder, then a tree were our next goals. Reaching the tree required a short dash through a clearing. After achieving it, Miriam lay back, rubbed her stomach, and blew quick puffs of air. The spasms in her stomach lasted a short while before she recovered enough to move on.

—Wait for the fog to thin, said Enos.

As the mist curled back, we could see a grassy spot where my father waited. We glanced back for signs of the Rahaj, but the haze concealed them. My father motioned us forward.

—If we can't see them, they can't see us, Enos whispered, hopefully.

—But they can still hear us, I said.

—If the fog thins, we'll have a problem, he said, Especially in that small clearing ahead.

—Do we have to run? asked Miriam.

—Only through the clearing, said Enos, But we'll help you.

I had crouched until my feet began to tingle. Enos stood first and supported Miriam to her feet. Then I stood, and Enos and I lifted Miriam at the waist as she draped her arms around our shoulders. At our first steps, she grimaced and faltered, and I feared she would collapse. Bringing my free hand to her belly, I tried to give her support as we ran. When we had run halfway to my father, Miriam's foot clipped a stick that snapped under her weight, and we all tumbled onto the ground. Miriam cried out as she rolled. At once, a squall of activity started where we had detected the Rahaj, and the blurred glow of torches began to move toward us.

My father ran to us and said, Run for the arbor!

A flurry of arrows suddenly fell about us, and my father shot his bow at the torches. Again, arrows landed near.

—Get her away! said my father, filling his bow.

Enos and I lifted Miriam as though she were sitting in a chair.

A distant voice from the fog shouted, Over there!

I heard the pounding of feet. More torches joined the two, and another set of arrows lit around us. My father launched his own, and the torches sank to ground level. Then I heard the dull sound of an arrow striking flesh. My father fell back. I dropped Miriam, and she cried out in pain.

—Father? I said.

I strained to see his face in the thick darkness. Then I touched the shank of an arrow buried deep in his chest. As his heart pumped, warm blood seeped from his body. He gasped for air. I broke into a sweat as I grasped the shaft with both hands to pull it loose. But my father stopped me.

—It's too deep, he said.

—No! I can pull it out.

Enos took his grandfather's bow and began to launch arrows in the direction of the torches.

—Raise me up, said my father, wincing.

I brought him to a sitting position, and he closed his eyes.

—Father! I shouted, shaking him.

He opened his eyes and coughed.

—Escape to the hills, he said in a whisper.

—I can't leave you! Let me pull out the arrow!

My father touched my hand and said, Let me go, son. You have others to save. Now, lift me to my feet, and give me my bow to lean on.

Placing both hands under his shoulders, I raised my father and steadied him until he could stand. He groaned and cried out, and as I was about to let him back down, he squeezed his eyes shut and shook his head. The blood from his chest filled my hands. Swaying, with his weight on my arms, he took his bow from Enos and steadied himself on it.

—The stump of an old tree lies near my camp, he said. At its base is a great stone, and beneath it you'll find the satchel of gems.

I nodded.

—Now, run! he said.

—I cannot go, I said through tears.

—You must. I don't have the strength to argue. Get your family away from here. I love you, my son.

Then he backed into the thick brush, notched an arrow in his bow, and said forcefully, Go now!

—We must go, said Enos.

He turned my face and made me focus my eyes on his. I nodded, and together we lifted Miriam and began to run. When I slowed to look back, Enos said, We must keep going, or Grandfather will have died in vain.

I knew he was right.

My muscles burned carrying Miriam's weight. Far behind us, we heard shouts, the sounds of scuffling, and finally a single cry. We stopped to listen, and I was struck with an overwhelming sense of loss. I considered my father's final act of love. He was dead. I knew it. I also knew Mahijah would not allow him any dignity in death. My father's body would be paraded through Shum as a traitor and planted where birds and animals could pick at it. Then, when it had rotted, the remains would be thrown upon the refuse heap outside the city where they would be burned.

My vow that night was not one of revenge but of resolve. By my decision to leave Shum, I had stepped to the front lines of battle. That decision had come at a terrible price, and separating myself from Shum had proven violent. At that moment, however, I didn't know that the most exacting test of my conviction was yet to come.

taking a stand for right

ℭ

Dawn burned away the fog and left a crystalline sheen on the landscape. My family, Miriam included, had traveled the night and lay exhausted in my father's tent. We mourned his death. When Dog came sniffing, I cuddled him. Then, burying my head in his long fur, I wept. Even my family's company and their consoling didn't comfort me. I had not known the loss of a parent. My mother had died before I was weaned. My father had fed me goat's milk for a year.

When Nathaniel began to cry, Sarah pressed him to her, and I thought of the nurturing a child needs and how exacting life is in the wilderness. I looked at my oldest son, Benjamin, and could read the concern on his face for his young family. I glanced over at Miriam, large with child, aching with every movement. I then observed Eve and Moriah. A hard life of being exposed to the elements was foreign to them. Only Enos was experienced in outdoor living.

At mid-morning, I invited my family to follow me to my father's high mountain camp. The Rahaj would certainly seek us at the lower camp. My insistence met with rancor and reluctance.

—How long must we stay in the mountains? asked Eve.

Moriah looked at me the way a wife will and beckoned me to answer.

—We may not be able to return to Shum, I said.

—Surely our stay is temporary! said Benjamin. We are here only to counsel about our future. When things have settled down, we'll return. Or do you expect me to make a home in the wilderness for my family?

—I can't return, said Enos. I've rejected the Rahaj. Forgiveness isn't a part of their creed.

—My place is with my husband, said Moriah to her family. If I return, Mahijah will kill your father and take me captive. I know what that would mean.

—The people wouldn't tolerate such treatment of you, said Eve.

—Some would speak out, Moriah answered, But Mahijah has a way of justifying his actions, even in complete public view. After some resistance, the people would believe what he tells them. No, I cannot return.

—I have no life in Shum, said Miriam. Neither has my unborn child. If my father finds me, he'll give the child to the Watchers to rear, and I'll be sacrificed to their gods.

—Simeon will help us, said Benjamin.

—You saw what happened yesterday, I said. Do you really think Simeon would choose family over his position?

—I could talk to Chaz, said Eve. Maybe he would…

—…keep us safe? Enos interrupted. He didn't listen to you before. Why would he listen to you now?

—You're not thinking of going back to him, are you? Moriah asked Eve.

—No, but so much has happened, and I'm so confused.

—A woman deserves complete loyalty from her man, said Moriah.

—I know, said Eve, But I still hurt.

Sarah lifted Nathaniel onto her shoulder and patted him. Her eyes welled up with tears as she said, I can't travel in the wilderness with a child. I wouldn't even know what to do. I only know how to live in the city.

—We'll help you, I said, But we've already been here too long.

Mahijah is probably searching for us now. I beg you all to come with me up to the high camp. Then we can discuss each of our situations.

Before we began our hike, I walked to the river and found the old tree stump my father had described. At its base, beneath a great stone, I retrieved the satchel of gems. As I held them and thought of their history, I wondered if they were to be my never-ending curse, tied to me as a weight that I must drag everywhere throughout my life, a constant reminder of my follies.

CB

At my father's high camp, in full view of the flock, we found rest, food, and shelter. Newborn lambs frolicked on the grassy slopes, as mothers, thick in wool, grazed and watched. An old billy with long whiskers and a rank odor butted heads with younger competitors and discouraged their bothering the females. Eagles spread wide their wings and rode the sky in search of hares and marmots. The comfort we felt on the high, peaceful mountains tempered the sorrow we felt for my father's death. We could have remained there had we not known that only time stood between us and the Rahaj.

Each day of that week, we discussed our future. We spoke kind words to each other, though I sensed little change of opinion. I used much of the time to become reacquainted with my wife and children. One morning, I took my wife's hand, and we strolled along the mountain peaks to nowhere in particular.

—The memory of you kept me alive, I told her.

She laid her head on my shoulder, and I put my hand around her waist.

—I missed you too, she said. I couldn't imagine life without you.

—From this moment forward, our lives may be hard, I said. I don't know how I'll support you.

—I don't care, as long as the family stays together. I could never go back to Shum.

—Because of Mahijah?

Moriah became quiet and weepy. We walked on, and I held her.

—He is the most vile man I've ever known, she said, finally.

—He put a lot of pressure on you?

—If you hadn't come when you did, he would have forced me to be one of his wives. And for the sake of the children, I would have had no choice.

—I couldn't bear to see you in the arms of another man, I said.

—And you're the only man I could ever love.

Holding her then, I felt closer to her than I had ever thought possible.

—I'm concerned about keeping the family together, I said.

—But you can't force them. They'll resent you. Each of the children has a tangle of emotions to work through.

—I'll try to be patient, I said.

—Time and more discussion is what they need, said Moriah.

—More talk is easy; it's *time* we don't have.

CB

That night as I gathered my family together, Benjamin said he and Sarah had decided to return to Shum.

—To be a Watcher? I asked.

—I'm not ready to give it up, he answered.

I stood and paced, then said, Your brother Jerel is dead, and so is your grandfather. We have seen the deaths of friends. You must trust me when I say that you won't be safe.

—Speculation, said Benjamin. Your perspective is prejudiced.

—I have come from a wilderness experience worse than you can imagine. I can't bear to lose you. Risking your family for your ambitions can result in terrible consequences. I, myself, have carried a heavy burden.

—What burden?

I had said nothing to them of the gems. When I produced them, my family was shocked.

—You've had these all along? said Benjamin. They could be used to buy our freedom.

—To ensure our deaths, I said. Mahijah would murder anyone to obtain these stones.

—It's worth a chance, said Benjamin.

—I would gladly give them to you if I thought they would help. But they won't.

—I think they will.

I looked at the rest of my family and said, What of you? Is this what you want?

Each, except for Eve, shook their heads. Eve just stared at the gems and finally said, I want to believe the stones will help, but I don't think there is any price we can pay to repair what has happened.

I turned to Benjamin and said, You're a man with a family. I respect your decision and will give you the gems. But before you depart for Shum, I must ask you to help the rest of us cross the valley and find Enoch's people. Will you do that?

—Yes.

—What shall we do with the sheep? asked Enos.

—We'll leave them here. Dog and Teah will tend them. We'll return for them later.

ᘔ

A valley, rich in grasses and wooded at the borders, extended between my father's high camp and the mountains where Enoch had settled his people. As we entered it, Miriam pointed into the distance and said she saw people. I shaded my eyes, then lowered my hand and smiled.

—It's Enoch teaching, I said.

The seer stood on an outcropping of rock, speaking to a small group of people.

—I hope that isn't why you brought us here—for us to be led away by Enoch, said Benjamin. I won't stay here if that's your design.

—You can make your own choice, I said.

—Not from what I've heard, said Benjamin. Enoch mesmerizes people, and they follow him blindly.

—Who told you such a thing? I asked.

Benjamin didn't answer.

—Enoch is a man of God, said Moriah.

—How do you know? asked Benjamin. Have you heard him?

—Yes, said Moriah. Several times. When he first came to Shum, I went out with Eve and your grandfather to hear him. What Enoch says is really quite profound.

—You're not serious! said Benjamin.

—I most definitely am!

I took Benjamin's arm and said, At least come with us to where he teaches the people. Then you can take the gems and leave if you want.

When we had crossed the valley and approached Enoch, the seer turned from his teaching and called out, Rabunel! Bring your family up here!

Benjamin gave me a sharp look, but I smiled, trying to reassure him. Then, before we could exchange greetings and sit to rest, Micah stood and shouted, I see spies from the Rahaj!

We all spun to look out into the distance. Three men clad in red were running out of the valley and into the trees, and the sight made Enoch's people stir nervously.

Benjamin said to me, By leading us to Enoch, you have guaranteed our deaths. We'll be massacred.

Micah rushed toward us, swooped up Miriam in his arms, and said, Follow me. It's Enoch that Mahijah is after. We've seen his spies lurking about. We think he has amassed a large army.

—Mahijah hasn't moved on you? I asked.

—Not yet. His objective seems to be Sharon. But he'll come after us first. We must hurry!

—Hurry where? asked Benjamin. To be killed with Enoch?

—To be saved if you don't delay, said Micah.

—Father, said Benjamin, This may be our one chance to set things right by demonstrating our allegiance to Mahijah. Let's give him the gems and go back to our homes in Shum.

I looked at my family, their faces showing expressions of doubt and fear. I said, Benjamin, I'm your father. If you can't trust me, then take the gems and go to Mahijah. But your mother and I are staying with Enoch.

—To be killed?

Without answering, I loosed the satchel and offered it to Benjamin. As he took it from me and looked inside, he said, You would give all these to me?

—Compared to you, Sarah, and Nathaniel, they mean nothing to me, I said. Do with them as you will, but make your decision now.

Benjamin looked at me, then at his wife and son, then at the rest of the family.

—These would buy us our freedom, he said to them.

No one moved.

—We're free *now*! said Enos. Gems or not, are you sure Mahijah will give you freedom?

Benjamin paused, looked at his brother, then slowly shook his head.

—Enough talking! Micah said.

—Mahijah is coming with a great army! Moriah cried, pointing out into the valley.

We looked, and just as Moriah had said, a huge force was entering the valley and advancing upon us.

—Run to the foothills! Micah shouted.

Enoch was standing on a plateau, watching the movements of the army. He said, Mahijah's army comes a poor way.

I looked out and saw a steep-walled gully where the army had slowed.

—Maybe they'll turn back, I said.

—Not likely. They want my blood, said Enoch. Your father would know where we could hide.

—My father is dead, I told him. They killed him.

—When?

—Last night.

Enoch looked down and away, and his eyes became moist. My children looked on with expressions of wonder, for they hadn't known that their grandfather and Enoch were friends.

—Mahijah will kill us if he finds us, I said.

—We should run and hide, said Enos.

—There's no place close, said Enoch. It appears that the time for us to take a stand has come.

—Take a stand? Benjamin asked, incredulously.

—Yes, said Enoch, And to trust God.

Benjamin turned to me and said, Father, this is insane!

೮ঽ

While I surveyed the clear skies over the valley, a warm breeze carried with it the scent of mint and clover. The sun made a bright circle in the west, shooting rust-colored beams of light through the dim horizon. The calmness of the day contrasted sharply with the sight of Mahijah's army surrounding us. Caught as we were between Mahijah's military might and the harsh wilderness, I contemplated my family's future, and I wondered if I had led them to their deaths.

—Hail Enoch! cried Mahijah when he came into view.

Enoch acknowledged the king with a nod.

Mahijah climbed the mountain at the head of the people. At his sides were Gad and Simeon. The Rahaj and the rest of the army marched behind. From where Mahijah stood on the mountainside, a small outcropping of rock rose the height of two men. Enoch stood on it, and Micah and my family gathered around him. Likewise, Mahijah's people circled the outcropping, forming the shape of a crescent moon. Several thousand men made up the contingency. The bowl-shaped valley that we stood in resonated the sounds as though the assembly had converged between smooth canyon walls. Mahijah turned to his army and, with outstretched arms, beckoned them to come closer. He bared his sword and raised it over his head.

—The sword of my father, Ramurah, be upon your neck, Enoch! We know you are the agent of our enemies. We know you have aligned yourself with Sharon. You have come to torment and confuse this people with your lies. I denounce you as a fraud. Tell us plainly why you are here and who you are.

—I come from the land of Cainan, cried Enoch, A righteous land to this day.

—A lie! shouted Simeon. I was born in that land and escaped only with my life.

Enoch raised his hand and said, I am the son of Jared, he who taught me in all the ways of God. As I journeyed from the land of Cainan by the sea east, I beheld a vision. I saw the heavens, and the Lord spake with me and gave me a commandment to speak forth these words. The Lord who spake with me is the God of heaven, my God and your God, and we, all of us, are brothers and sisters.

—The Watchers know God, cried Mahijah, And he is not the one you claim to know.

—The fathers from Adam to Jared have all declared the same God, said Enoch. There is no dispute is this. But your Watchers have perverted the knowledge of God and have taught this people to worship gods who cannot respond and who have no affection. Why do you deny the true God of heaven? Your every perversion of truth is an act of rebellion against him. If you were ignorant, God would grant you a reprieve from destruction, but you know the truth. Because of your pride, you corrupt it, and destruction is at the door.

Mahijah made a move toward Enoch, but he raised his hand, and the king stopped.

Enoch continued, saying, The Watchers counterfeit the power of God, then use his name falsely to justify their actions. They have taught you to swear secret oaths to uphold each other in your lies and vile deeds. They have taught you to use the sciences to emancipate yourselves from dependence on God. You insult nature. The earth itself lays an accusation against you and pleads with God to rid her of the sins that you have polluted her with, and all the heavens weep as they share the pain of a violated world. The Watchers pretend to be as the angels but choose the violence of the Adversary. You fill the earth with blood and horror and destroy everything that God has made true and beautiful. For carnal pleasure, you men of Shum force your wives and children into vile acts. In this society, the son lies with the mother and the father with the daughter. Husbands and wives commit adultery and make a mockery of sacred vows taken before God. You leaders of Shum say, *We can lie and make it sound like the truth, and we can tell the truth when we want.* You accuse me of coming among you to be a king over this people, but I serve the King of heaven, whom you reject. That God, the God of my fathers, your God and my God, will destroy Shum. I come with a voice of warning to tell you to repent and save yourselves.

When Enoch had finished speaking, he stood silent and steadfast, not shrinking from attack or persecution.

—Let this man who speaks against us die! cried Simeon.

—By the sword of my father, I will spill Enoch's blood! shouted Mahijah.

—Make ready! Gad commanded the Rahaj. Show no mercy to any of them!

When the Rahaj moved, readying themselves to turn the accusations to violence, Micah stepped in front of Enoch, a club in one hand and a knife in the other.

—Stand back, friend, said Enoch, touching him on the shoulder.

—If my lot be to die today, said Micah, Then let it be with you. But I won't leave you.

Mahijah's voice rose above the sounds of the assembling Rahaj. His words were directed at me.

—What say you, Rabunel? Shall I also slay you? Or shall I thank you for capturing Enoch, the criminal?

—You have a gift for presumption, I said. As for your threat to kill me, where I stand is where I stay.

—Do you speak for your wife and children?

—They can speak for themselves. Ask them.

Chaz called to Eve, Come down while I can still save you.

Eve looked at me, then Chaz, then shook her head and looked away.

Simeon said to Benjamin, The order of Watchers is yours. Do not be deceived by your father, who has been deluded by this false prophet. No good can come of this. If you stay, your wife and child will be beaten and burned before your eyes.

Sarah took a step behind Benjamin, holding Nathaniel in her arms. Benjamin gazed at Simeon a long while, then said, You've been like a father to me. Why do you threaten my family?

—It's not a threat, but a fact, said Simeon. You have no future with fugitives. Come down now, and save your family.

Benjamin looked at the satchel of gems tied at his waist, then at me, and said, Father, what shall I do?

My mind raced. From the time I had returned from the wilderness, I had made a commitment to follow Enoch. I believed what he taught was the only sanity left in the world. I had never considered my decision greater than an individual resolve to wrest my family from Shum. To take a public stand was quite another thing. But, as I gazed at my family, who needed my courage, and as I looked on the young prophet, who stood bravely against the adversity, I realized my days of private conviction were over and that the time to openly declare what I believed was at hand.

I stepped to the side of Enoch and, in a voice that all Mahijah's forces could hear, I addressed myself to Mahijah, saying, I stand with Enoch!

Although I feigned courage, I feared the king. I truly believed that once I had made the declaration, it would be my last.

—Treason! cried Mahijah, raising his sword.

—Not so! I said. In nothing have I broken the law. I stand with Enoch, not as an enemy of Shum, but as a spiritual guide to my soul. He has spoken against corruption. Who can deny that corruption in

Shum does not exist? He has warned against the imminent destruction of Shum. Would not wisdom dictate that we listen? Not one of you has proof that Enoch plots with your enemies. On the other hand, you seek his life and our lives without cause, and so we leave. You call us fugitives from justice, but we leave to find justice.

—Slay them all! cried Mahijah.

I stepped in front of Enoch and Micah and spoke to everyone present saying, People of Shum, you know me. I am Rabunel, son of Ebanel, the shepherd. My grandfather is Simeon of the Watchers, he who stands in your midst. These many years I have lived among you and served on your Council. My family is known in Shum. You thought me dead, but by the grace of the God Enoch declares, I stand before you alive. By that same God, I swear to you that all Enoch has preached to you these many months is true. I know the Watchers, I know the Council, I know the king. No one knows them better than I do, and I tell you that all of them, including Simeon, my own grandfather, will bring destruction upon you if you continue to follow them. Power is their aim, not your welfare. And though I know not how, I am certain that Shum will be destroyed if you do not acknowledge the God of heaven and turn back to him, as Enoch has said.

My words silenced the army. Mahijah and the Rahaj stood still, and I gathered more courage.

—Behold the sword of Mahijah, I cried. As God lives, he broke it not in battle but by slaying his own father, Ramurah. The king you uphold is a liar and a murderer.

—You have no proof! cried Simeon.

—Then proof you shall have, I shouted. People of Shum, go now to the Seat of Justice where lies the body of Ramurah. Remove the wrapping from his head, and you'll see that he did not die from a fall but from the blow of a sword. Look inside his skull. You'll find the fragment of metal that matches the tip missing from Mahijah's sword.

A great murmuring shot through the army, and a look of fear swept over Mahijah's face. I looked straight into the face of Gad, who had revealed Mahijah's secret to Asher months earlier within earshot of my hiding place. For a man of stoic countenance, Gad began to waver and stare at me in disbelief.

—You lie! shouted Mahijah.

But the stir among the people drowned his words, and a great confusion followed. The Rahaj fell back, and the Council members looked around at the unsettled army with expressions of apprehension and distress.

—It is desecration to examine the body of Ramurah! cried Simeon.

But already some had left, hurrying for Shum, saying, We will see if what Rabunel says is true.

Gad followed in pursuit of the people, and the leaders of the Rahaj and members of the Council stood in a knot with looks of bewilderment.

—You're a dead man! Mahijah shouted at me.

Simeon looked dumbfounded, then grabbed Mahijah by the arm and pulled him toward Shum. In moments, the entire mountainside cleared, and I stood with Enoch and the small group of people, watching the huge army of Shum hurry away in confusion.

In the commotion, a few of the army began to defect from the main body, come up to Enoch, and join with the little group of listeners. In the midst, a young man stood, tall and strong. He looked at me and I at him, and I sensed in him a character like that of my son Jerel—brave yet gentle, of an honest heart, filled with integrity. His hazel eyes didn't look away. I motioned for him to come to me.

—What's your name? I asked.

—Reuben.

—What are your intentions?

—To follow Enoch.

—Even in death?

—We all die.

—So we do. Who are your parents?

—I'm his father, said a man stepping forward. My name is Ishmael.

—Then I'll ask you, Ishmael. Will you give permission for your son to go on a daring mission?

—You may ask him yourself, said Ishmael.

—I would have been Rahaj by autumn, said Reuben.

—Yes, I said. I can see that you're very brave. Will you accept a mission?

—I will.

—Follow the people back to Shum, I said. When they examine the skull of Ramurah, observe their reactions, and bring us word.

As Reuben agreed and departed, Eve came to me and said, What's the purpose of risking that young man's life?

—I have the feeling he is clever, I said. Behind those eyes, I see intelligence.

—You can *see* intelligence?

—I think so. I've been watching him. He moves deliberately, as though he has a purpose. He'll find a way to blend into the crowd.

—Why do you care how the people react to a piece of bronze in a dead king's head?

Enoch stepped to us and replied, Because the destruction of Shum will be assured if they uphold Mahijah once they have proof of his treachery. A house built on sand…

—…will surely fall, said Eve, completing the proverb.

—Yes, and despite all you do, you cannot stop the fall. All you can do is step aside.

Moriah came to Eve and said, pointing off in the distance, Look over there.

Eve followed her mother's finger to where Chaz stood in the valley, alone with two of his guards. He gazed at her. Neither moved for a long moment. Eve made a small gesture with her hand, and when he didn't respond, she slowly dropped it to her side. A tear spilled down her cheek, and Chaz turned and walked away.

—Eve?

She turned. Enoch then spoke to her as he reached out and wiped her tear with his finger.

—A single tear may fall unheeded, he said, But if the pain that caused it continues, the tears will become many. Just like a lie—and Shum has an ocean of them.

—Then I swim in deep water, she said.

The people whom Enoch had taught and those who had remained—some two hundred of them—came to Enoch then and appeared as though they wanted to speak with him.

—What is your desire? he asked.

—We would stay with you, they said.

—For what purpose?

—To be taught the truth.

—You'll be considered traitors, he said, So you must make a decision. I'm willing to teach you, but this is no time for the curious. Every word I speak from this moment on will condemn you if you return. Better to go back now than to be undecided.

The people conversed among themselves, then Ishmael stepped forward and said, We are the poor of the city. We believe all the words you've told us. But if we follow you, what will become of us?

When Enoch didn't answer the question, I grew nervous. I was certain he had a plan, but what it was I didn't know.

Another man said, We will follow you, but let us return to our tents and bring supplies. Then we'll come to you tomorrow.

Enoch said, You must not return to Shum. The danger is too great.

Murmurings rose from the group, and a few walked away.

—What of the rest of you? asked Enoch, speaking to the people who had remained.

—We desire to stay, said Ishmael.

—Then come up into the high mountain, said Enoch. We cannot stay here. We need to find a safe place to camp tonight.

Micah led out and bid all the people to follow.

—Are we going to the City of Enoch? asked Enos.

Over the months of Enoch's ministry, people, such as Micah, had splintered off from Shum to establish a place of gathering, a city high in the mountains. They called it the City of Enoch because Enoch lived among them and taught them.

—Not tonight, I said. It is still far.

As we started up the mountain, I looked into the faces of my family and saw acceptance. Given the chance to leave, they had resisted, and *that* gave me reason to *hope*.

—We're still here, said Benjamin.

—By your own choice? I asked. Or do you feel coerced?

—By our own choice, he said, But that doesn't mean the decision is easy.

—What changed your mind?

—I thought of Baruch watching his wife and daughter burn, and I began to wonder if that could happen to me. I still don't know what I believe, or how deeply I believe it, but I know I feel safer here than I ever felt in Shum.

—Even with Mahijah threatening to murder all of us?

—I know it sounds absurd, but, yes, that is how I feel.

I took Moriah's hand and helped her up a gentle incline. Benjamin took Nathaniel from Sarah, and Enos helped Miriam.

—You have all felt something new today, I said, huffing. These motions of joy, this hunger for truth, cannot find expression with the human tongue. This unspeakable gift comes from the Spirit that God extends to all those who sincerely seek him. You feel the Spirit but cannot see it. The Spirit works upon your senses, like the unseen wind caresses your skin and ruffles your hair. The Spirit is just as real.

—Where will we sleep tonight? asked Miriam.

—I have spent many nights under the stars, I said.

—Easier for a man than a woman, said Moriah, indicating Miriam's condition.

Now that we had cast our lots with Enoch, we were all enemies of Shum. We would be hunted. I looked at Sarah, whose face showed worry.

—What will become of us now? she asked.

Moriah forced a brave smile and answered, We'll survive.

We walked on. Miriam held her stomach and moaned. Nathaniel

laid his head on his father's shoulder and drifted off to sleep. Night had brought the chill of a cool mountain breeze.

—Father? asked Eve. Where is heaven?

She pointed at a bright star, and I looked up and found it.

—Maybe it's heaven, I said.

—It seems far, she said.

—Yes.

—Too far?

—I don't know.

—Perhaps we live at the edge of heaven, she said.

I lifted my eyes toward the silver points of light and considered the smallness of man. The scope of eternity was so immense that it seemed to eclipse all earthly troubles. I wondered at God's ability to govern it all and still be aware of the tiniest cry for help. Like Eve, I too wondered where heaven was, and I longed to be there.

As we made camp that night, the people were ill-prepared. We managed fires. Some had brought food that was shared. But few had blankets or adequate clothing.

Enoch approached me and said, The people will perish without supplies, but they can't go back to Shum. We must hurry and get them to the City in the mountains.

—Is it far?

—Several days for this many people.

—Do the people in the City have enough reserves to help us? I asked.

—Yes, said Enoch, But this group exceeds the number who live there. And there are more people who are waiting for me in another valley.

—More?

—Yes. They come from the land of Omner. Maybe a hundred. I left them to find the small group you saw me teaching. Our plan was to join up and travel together to the City.

—What shall we do? I asked.

—I need to return to the other group, he said. Their need for me is greater than this people's. In the morning, I'll take Micah with me, and we'll move the group from Omner up to the City. We'll prepare the people for your arrival.

—You're going to leave us?

—Only for a few days. Then Micah and I will meet you along the way and move you up to the City. Rabunel, will you lead this people?

—Me? I'm weak! You need a leader like Micah.

—He's needed elsewhere, said Enoch. You must not underestimate the power of your example to this people. Will you lead them?

I found courage to say yes, but from where I did not know.

a small beginning

ಀ

—It isn't much, said Enoch as he removed his pouch of food and handed it to me.

Micah gave me his food, saying, I hope it helps feed the people.

I received the food, knowing I faced an imposing challenge.

—I've seen a caravan moving southward that will most certainly carry food, said Micah.

I nodded, but was doubtful. I knew the type that traveled the caravan routes, hard men capable of braving the wilderness, ruthless in trade.

—They may sell you provisions, he said.

Then Enoch raised his voice to the people, saying, People of God, hear me. We have a destination before us, but the journey is fraught with hardship and danger. To be certain, Mahijah will return, and next time he will not be easily dissuaded. Our existence undermines his power. But God will protect us if we are one and unite by a covenant of mutual protection. I present to you Rabunel and call him to be the leader during your journey. Micah and I must leave you for a few days to rescue another group of people like yourselves. Once we move them to the City and prepare a place for you, we'll return and lead you there. Let Rabunel guide you, and soon you'll join with the others in the City and dwell in peace.

—How do we proceed? asked Ishmael.

—Our entire effort must be to survive, said Enoch. We must quickly move to a place of safety—but in an orderly fashion. Bring together all the resources you've brought with you—food, extra clothing, tents, tools, weapons. Then let us make a covenant to be one people, binding ourselves to each other, sharing equally in the resources of the camp, every person as interested in his neighbor's circumstance as in his own. This is the covenant that your brothers and sisters in the City have made.

With hands raised in a sign of affirmation, the people entered the covenant. With that foundation laid, Enoch proposed that we divide the assembly according to families, five families—including widows and orphans—making a company.

—Let us appoint captains for each company to help the fathers, said Enoch, And let the captains be upheld by covenant.

The captains were to assess individual needs and to divide provisions accordingly. Ishmael became the supervisor over all the resources of the camp. As captains needed to draw upon those resources, Ishmael gave approval, to assure that no group received more than their needs. Ishmael was to report to me.

—No captain shall receive compensation for his service, said Enoch. Service alone can be the purpose of leadership.

On the following morning, Enoch and Micah departed, and the seer received the people one by one as they came to him and embraced him. From the tears he shed, it was evident he loved them. As for myself, I felt the terrible weight of responsibility settle on my shoulders. As Enoch and Micah disappeared, I doubted I had the capacity to lead the people and maintain the trust that Enoch had placed in me.

Moriah, seeing my worry, encouraged me, saying, Enoch has set the pattern. Just make it work, and we'll do fine. Let your family help you.

Her words helped me focus my mind, and instantly I saw a way to take charge and bring order to the people. As Moriah had suggested, I gathered together my family to help me.

—The people will perish if we do not act, I told them. Although we've been in this remote place only a brief time, I must ask each of you to shoulder a weighty load. Can you do it?

Each agreed.

To Benjamin I asked, We need meat and clothing. Can you herd your grandfather's flock by yourself?

—With Dog and Teah, yes, he said.

—Lead them east to where the valley rises up to a lone peak. There on the foothills we'll meet you.

Benjamin knew the place, for as a child he had spent many days shepherding with my father.

Benjamin turned to Sarah and said, You know I love you. Without your blessing, I could not go.

—You have it and more, said Sarah. None of us have any hope of survival without the sheep. Go and do what you must, and I'll be waiting for you.

Benjamin kissed her and hugged Nathaniel. Then he said, Father, they're yours to protect.

Then Benjamin set out. His countenance bore the image of humility and determination. That he was outwardly affectionate with me brought me to tears, for it was an expression we had not shared in years. I put my arm about Sarah when he left and saw tears in her eyes.

—Don't be afraid, I said.

—It isn't fear, she said, I'm missing him already.

As Benjamin disappeared into the pines, Sarah patted Nathaniel to sleep and said, If Miriam can watch my child, I can help you with the people.

—It's the emotional care of the people that concerns me, I said. Go with Moriah and Eve. Move among the people, and minister to their needs.

—While I rest here, I can watch him, said Miriam.

I looked at Eve, whose eyes were red. Moriah motioned Sarah to follow her and then said to Eve, We will start now. Come help us when you're able.

—I can come now, said Eve.

—Better that you talk with your father first.

When the women left, I pulled my daughter close.

—Your heart is broken, I said.

—Why does love hurt so? she said as she wept.

—Great love carries with it great possibility, I said. But the risk is worth it.

—I'll never let myself be hurt again. Nevermore will I give myself completely to love.

—Yes, you will. *Completely* is the only way you know how to love.

—I'll never love anyone as I did Chaz.

—Probably not. You'll love someone *more*.

—You seem to have an answer for everything, she said, pulling away.

—No, I said. But I've lived enough years to know that seasons change, spring follows winter, and life begins again. What feels so painful now will pass. The only way I know to ease the pain is to lose yourself in serving others. You must help others bear *their* sorrows. I can try to comfort you, but true peace comes from another source, and you'll never know *that* peace until you give your pain to God. That doesn't mean you won't mourn, but you'll receive peace, and that will give you the courage to move forward.

I kissed her and invited her to find a quiet place to gather her thoughts and talk to God.

—I don't know how, she said.

—Yes, you do. Talk to him just as you're talking with me.

ଓ

My family and I ministered among the people throughout the day, instructing the captains, assessing particular needs, inventorying supplies. In the late part of the afternoon, I handed Enos the satchel of gems, saying, Go to the caravan, and buy all the food and provisions you can. Be frugal and cautious. These are the kind of men who, if they knew, would kill you for a fraction of what you carry. Hide the satchel, and take only a few gems with you. Use the rest if you must.

—Will you walk with me a ways? Enos asked.

—Yes.

As we walked, Enos turned his head from me and was silent. As a father, I had learned to wait quietly in such moments. Soon we reached a crossroads and stopped. Then Enos turned to me. His face was wet, and he reached out to me.

—Sometimes I feel as though my soul is being seared by a hot dagger, he said. It's a torment I can't escape. I've tried to keep myself busy, but I can't forget what I've done.

I placed my hand on his and asked, What have you done?

—Those of the Rahaj take oaths, he said. Breaking the oath of loyalty has the penalty of death. The oaths are riveted down by rituals administered by the Watchers in a place called the Grove. A sacrifice is demanded of initiates…

I waited as Enos bowed his head down for awhile, unable to continue.

—The sacrifice is virginity, he said, Something I realize now is precious and sacred and cannot be replaced. I swore an oath of allegiance to the Rahaj. I received a secret name and special robes. The Watchers anointed me with blood. Then I made my sacrifice. I lay with a young woman, a virgin, one who had been brought to the Grove by her father, a Watcher. She was as terrified as I was. Neither of us knew of such things. But the sacrifice demanded that I forfeit what was most sacred to me and take what was most precious to her. She wept and begged her father to save her from this thing. She pled with me to refrain, but I fulfilled my oath and made my sacrifice. I became Rahaj that night, and I sent away a young maiden sobbing. To this day, I do not know her name.

I held my boy as he wept.

—Since that day, I have had no peace, he said. My companions of the Rahaj claim that such actions are liberating, but I am only enslaved.

Enos couldn't look at me. But as I looked at him, my first emotion was anger. I had taught him better than this. Then I felt disappointment. Perhaps I had failed him, and I searched my mind for where I had gone wrong. I was filled with self-doubt. His failure was my failure. Then, as I considered his remorse, I realized my reactions were selfish. What my son needed was a father who loved him despite his sins. My heart broke for him. As his father, I would have gladly taken his pain and shifted it to myself. But I could not.

My father used to say, *Pain is a great mentor. We'll avoid what causes it and embrace what keeps it at bay.*

I wondered what I could say to Enos. I wanted to ease his pain, but wisdom demanded that pain be allowed to teach its lesson.

—Have you tried to make amends? I asked.

—It's impossible. Her father married her off to a trader. She's gone from Shum now.

—Often we can repair the damage we've done, but some offenses are impossible to rectify, I said.

—I don't understand.

—If you steal, you can replace the stolen property, I said. But if you murder, how do you replace life? If you sacrifice your virtue or take it from another, how do you replace it? By yourself, you have limited ability to repair the damage you have done. Setting things right requires that you draw on a Power greater than your own. The peace you seek can only come by reconciling yourself with God.

—I don't know him.

—But he knows you.

As I bid my son farewell, I returned to camp and found that Eve hadn't returned, and I supposed she was still seeking her own peace. I ached for her and Enos, and I knelt on the earth and pled for my children. I pled for strength to lead the people, to find food and shelter for them, to lead them to a place of safety. When I arose and returned, Miriam had made a fire and was tending Nathaniel. Moriah and Sarah still ministered among the people, seeing to their comfort.

—Will you be all right if I leave you for a moment? I asked Miriam.

She nodded, and I walked down among the people who were preparing for the night. I raised my voice so all could hear.

—By what name shall we be called? I asked.

—Enoch's Camp, said Ishmael.

—So it shall be, I said, We are Enoch's Camp until we arrive at our destination. Then we shall become part of the City of Enoch and live in peace.

That night we managed a meager meal and slept on the ground. Though scantily fed and outfitted, the people seemed happy, bound to each other in mutual love, with leaders who had pledged to care for them. A feeling of calm and security had spread throughout the camp. Moriah and I slept last. We surveyed our little flock and spoke softly about recent events that had brought us to this. For all that had happened, we hadn't had much time to talk, to express our love for one another, to feel gratitude for our being reunited. That night, we fell asleep in each other's arms, a dream that had sustained me many harsh nights in the wilderness. As I drifted asleep holding my wife, I thought to myself, *If I died tonight, I would die a happy man.*

Dawn came, changing the misty mountaintops from gray to blue. Peaks in the distance majestically appeared as the rising sun burned away the mist. Babies' cries were the first sounds in camp. A gentle rustling among the people followed. Mothers rose, suckled infants, stirred embers, straightened campsites, coaxed older children awake. Fathers counseled with their captains, received rations, then formed teams to scout for food. Some set out to hunt. Others dug roots or picked berries.

At mid-morning, I asked Ishmael to call the captains to counsel. Their reports were of little food remaining, and I hoped Enos would return soon with provisions. I charged the captains to inventory the skills of the people. We discovered that we had among us tent makers, artisans of wood and metals, hunters, and men who had lived in the wilderness and knew survival skills. Some knew how to prepare edible roots and plants. From the outset, adequate clothing and shelter was a problem. We formed groups of experienced people as tailors and tent makers. Craftsmen were assigned to make tools and weapons. Ishmael was commissioned to keep a journal of Enoch's Camp. I asked the captains to prepare their people as much as they could, so that we could begin our journey to the City of Enoch, for by this time we were feeling the urgency to move on before Mahijah returned.

Eve awoke and knelt by the fire. Moriah beckoned me to go and talk with her. I shook my head. Moriah scowled and motioned in Eve's direction with her head. I sighed. I truly was home.

—May I sit by you? I asked Eve.

She patted a place at her side.

—Do you want to talk? I said.

—Not now. Just sit with me awhile.

She smiled, took my arm, and laid her head on my shoulder. I felt more like a father in recent days than I had in a very long time.

—A runner is coming! a captain shouted.

—Can you see who it is? I asked.

After a pause, he yelled, It's Reuben!

—Bring him to me at once.

When Reuben ran into camp, he knelt at my feet, breathing hard.

—Do you have news? I asked.

He nodded and tried to speak but still couldn't catch his breath.

—Take your time, I said.

He raised his hand, then when he could, he said, You won't believe…

—Believe what?

—Father, said Eve, Let him recover.

—Yes, of course, I said, handing Reuben a dipper of water.

—If I hadn't gone to Shum, I wouldn't believe the report I give you now. For as I crept into Shum yesterday, some men of the city had taken the body of Ramurah, unwrapped it to reveal his bones, and discovered a piece of bronze the size of a thumbnail in the skull.

—And the skull?

—Obviously pierced by a sword.

—And what of the people? asked Eve.

—The men who had found the fragment of bronze were enraged. They ran through the streets of Shum shouting that the king had lied and had gained his power through murder. Mahijah was forcibly taken from his tent by a mob that had formed, and the Rahaj was held back at the threat of the king's life. Someone brought Mahijah's sword and, before the entire city, fitted the broken tip where it had been broken off. Then, something incredible happened. Mahijah asked to speak to the city, and, at the point of his own sword, they placed him high on the Seat of Justice. He said, *My father was a mighty king, but weak among our enemies. Many years ago, I discovered that the king of the Aramites had formed an alliance with Omner and Sharon, our old enemies. Together, they were combining against us. My father wouldn't listen to reason, and as we argued, he came at me with his sword. When I managed to wrest it from him, he slipped, and the point of it pierced his head and broke off, killing him. For these many years, I have kept the secret of his incompetence so that he might have the honor of his people in death. As for me, my only desire has been to rule this people justly. With my own hands and the sword of my father, I took the head of the Aramite king, and from that day on we've lived in peace, and Shum is feared. Have I not led you to be a mighty people? Have I not led you to be prosperous? Will you let an old shame, which I have protected you from, erase all the good I have done for this people?*

—What did the people do? I asked.

—They supported him. Simeon stood and endorsed him, as did Gad, all the Council, the Watchers, and the leaders of the Rahaj.

—They believed him? I asked.

—No, I didn't say they believed him. They *supported* him. No one believed his lie, but they heard what they wanted to hear.

—How do you know?

—When the people walked to their tents, I spoke to some of them. I listened late into the night. The people figure it's better to support Mahijah than cause an insurrection and overthrow him. He may be corrupt, but his story soothed them, and that's what they seem to have wanted.

—You're very astute, I said. You have a keen understanding. Where did you learn it?

—I had a good teacher, said Reuben. My father Ishmael, although a tiller of the ground, is a student of the law. He taught me it.

—Then you must go now and tell him everything, I said. He'll be most pleased.

When Reuben had left, I turned to Eve and said, What do you think of my spy now?

—A stroke of luck, she laughed.

ଔ

After hiking a long distance, the people of Enoch's Camp settled in a wooded area for the evening and ate a meal of roots and berries. Then watchmen ran into camp with news of the Rahaj scouting the area.

—We are too many to hide, I said. Our only option is to hasten and join up with the City of Enoch.

The captains assembled. Then I said, Make your people ready. We must leave at once. We'll travel by the light of torches. Assign people to help those sick or with child.

—Such a march could take a terrible toll, said Ishmael.

—Let each healthy man and woman be assigned one or two families so that all are cared for, I said. Let them report to the captains. We'll form a net of safety to aid each person.

—What route will we take? asked the captains.

—The way to the City of Enoch is a long trek that will render us vulnerable to the Rahaj, I said. But, as a boy, I explored a nearby canyon that could cut the distance in half. The canyon has a swift river with a waterfall at its head. The route is narrow, and the climb out is steep, but I think we can manage it. I won't say following my plan will be easy, for it may be dangerous at times, but it won't be as dangerous as confronting the Rahaj. Do I have your support?

The captains said yes, and when we had gathered the people together, I offered a prayer in behalf of the camp. I expected looks of fear in the people's faces. Instead I saw calm determination.

That night, as the camp began its ascent, we climbed a gentle slope, using torches to light our way. Behind us, we could see the torches of the Rahaj. If we could see theirs, we knew they could see ours. The grassy slope became a steep, rocky incline, and we gave assistance to those who needed it. We finally negotiated the slope and stood on the flat ground at the mouth of the canyon. I led them in.

In my memory, the canyon appeared as a ragged scar in the side of the mountainside. A river flowed out the canyon mouth, breaking up rocks as it descended. We followed the path on the riverbank as we began to hike the canyon and climb to the waterfall. Walking two or more abreast was soon not possible, so we followed in each other's footsteps as we ascended along the slender bank of the river. As I stood on a high place and surveyed the canyon's entrance, I couldn't see the torches of the Rahaj, but I doubted we had lost them. By the position of the moon, I guessed that we wouldn't see first light for some time. I hoped to have achieved the waterfall at the end of the canyon by then.

Miriam lagged behind, holding her belly and groaning.

—I have to rest until the cramps stop, she said.

—Is it your time? I asked.

—I don't know. The pains are becoming more intense.

—Constant pains?

—They come and go.

I called for Eve to take Nathaniel from Sarah, and for Sarah and Moriah to pay special attention to Miriam.

When the sun broke over the eastern peaks and dropped light into the bottom of the canyon, torches were extinguished. Adults carried sleeping toddlers. Older youngsters cried as they stumbled along the rocky path. At the end of the canyon was the waterfall, and when it was in sight, the people hurried to it, some even running, then collapsed on the wide grassy area beside it.

I summoned Ishmael, saying, Send two men back down the canyon to scout for the Rahaj.

Moriah came to my side then and gazed up at the steep canyon walls and the cliff over which the water fell.

—You once climbed this? she asked.

I nodded, then shaded my eyes and surveyed the face of the canyon in detail.

—I was younger, I said.

—To be sure.

We walked near the waterfall and let the spray wet our faces. The entire terrain had changed from what I remembered—even the water fell at a steeper angle. Moriah took my arm, and we began to walk the perimeter of the falls. Massive debris at the base of the cliff and a rupture of rock at the top meant the earth had shifted since my last visit as a boy. On both sides of the waterfall, the face of the cliff was a crag of broken stone, sheered branches, and twisted and tangled bare roots.

No one could climb this now! I thought.

A scream for help startled me, and Moriah began to run.

—Who is it? I asked.

—Miriam.

—Shall I get help?

—Send for Eve and Sarah. Call for the midwives.

Miriam lay inside a tent. Several women, Moriah included, gathered around her—inside and outside the tent. I called for Eve and Sarah. Midwives followed. Moriah stuck her head out of the tent and said, We're having a baby!

When I came near, an old woman waved me off.

—You'll just fuss, she said.

Not feeling wanted, I decided to explore around the waterfall for a way out.

Behind the falls was a gap through which a man could walk from one side of the river to the other. Hoping that the opposite bank might present a solution, I moved toward the gap, but a man from the camp stopped me.

—I've seen a man in there, he said.

—Rahaj, you think?

—I don't know. His clothes were torn, and he appeared battered.

—You saw him behind the waterfall?

—Briefly. A young man pulled him back, then returned and watched us for a long time.

A shot of realization pierced me. *Baruch!*

—Shall I summon the guard? said the man.

—No, I said, This is a journey I must make alone.

As I entered the gap, the roar of the water was deafening and looked to be a continuous sheet of white crashing down into the river. I could only imagine what peril might befall one who lost his footing. I continued to edge my way along. My clothes were drenched from the spray, and I found myself continually wiping the moisture from my face. A gust of cold air suddenly hit me from a dark hole, and I felt the sharp point of a knife at my stomach.

—Take a breath, and say who you are, said a male voice.

—Rabunel, son of Ebanel, the shepherd, I said.

The speaker drove the point deeper.

—Don't kill me, I cried. I mean you no harm.

—Why are you here?

—To help a group of refugees escape from Shum.

—Drop to your knees. Put your hands behind you.

I obeyed, saying, I know it's you, Baruch. I've come to plead for forgiveness.

—That wouldn't be in your nature. You've tracked me here to kill me.

—With all these people? Not likely. A man in camp saw you, and I knew by what he said that it was you. I have come alone and unarmed. How is it that you're able to stand?

—Are you disappointed?

—No, I said, I'm pleased that you're recovering. It's more than I could have hoped for.

—Maybe I'm stronger than you thought, said Baruch. Maybe I'm not so easy to kill.

—I didn't try to kill you. I tried to save your life.

—Shall I thank you? he asked.

—I don't expect you to believe me, I replied.

—Who are these people you've brought with you? he asked. You love power. Are you a king to them?

—No, I serve them only.

—You're a liar!

—Please, I pled, My wife and children are outside the falls. These people aren't violent, and they have no desire except to move on and find a place to live in peace.

Instead of responding to my plea, Baruch asked, Do you believe in justice?

—I do.

—Then I have a question to pose, he said. Answer it well, and you may live to see the sun once more.

—Show yourself, I said.

—In time, but now my question: Suppose a man is falsely charged of a crime and he is punished for what he didn't do. Shouldn't justice demand that the one who caused him the pain suffer similarly?

—Is that your intention? I asked.

—I would be justified.

Then I heard Joshua's voice.

—Father, don't! he said. This isn't worthy of you.

Joshua pulled the knife away, and I fell prostrate on the ground before them.

—The blood of your mother and sister are upon this man's hands! said Baruch.

—Is it true? Joshua asked me.

—They fed Danbenihah and me, I said, But I did not betray them.

—You destroyed my trade and left me destitute, said Baruch.

—I'm ashamed to say that's true, I said.

—You admit it?

—Yes, and I would do anything to make things right.

—Can you replace Leah and Rachel? My home? My life?

I bowed my head and said I could not.

—Bring me a torch, said Baruch to Joshua.

—What are you going to do? asked Joshua.

—I want to show our friend what he has done.

When Joshua returned with a torch, Baruch told me to lift my head. Then he stepped to where I could see him. Joshua helped him remove his clothes so that he stood naked before me except for a garment he had wrapped about his loins. The light of the torch reflected off his body. Baruch slowly turned, his arms outstretched. He whom I had known for so many years was unrecognizable. Bruises covered his whole body, coloring his skin a sick purple-green. Where my whip had cut through flesh and muscle, a network of red slashes marred his back and the backs of his thighs. His face was swollen, one eye closed to a slit. Red lumps rose at his cheeks. After seeing all the damage, I was amazed that he could stand and walk.

Baruch slipped back into his robe, wincing as he made slight movements, then retrieved his knife, its blade glinting in the light of the torch.

—You pled for your life so that you could continue as a husband and father, said Baruch. *I* raised such pleas, and who heard *me?* You see what's left of my body, and you know what has happened to my family. I should kill you now!

—Then do it if you must! I cried with the voice of anger.

Baruch took a step back.

—You make yourself a judge, I said, So judge me now, and take your revenge. But make sure your judgement is just, old friend, for you'll have to live with your decision long after your scars have faded.

—I have a right! he cried.

—A right, perhaps, but do you have the will?

—My wife, my daughter, everything that was dear to me—gone!

He knelt beside me, brought the blade again to my throat, and began to weep. I closed my eyes, expecting to feel the point split the flesh. I measured my words and said, Do you have any mercy left in you?

Joshua knelt beside his father then and said, Father, please, let the man speak.

—Speak then, Baruch said to me. For the sake of my son, I will hear you.

—May I rise? I asked.

Baruch nodded.

I came to a sitting position and looked even-eyed into the face of my old competitor. I looked at Joshua, whose face bespoke kindness but whose expression was concern. I glanced at the knife and forced myself to look away so as not to draw attention to it.

—Baruch, I began, I'm so sorry for what I've done to you. So very sorry. In a great way, I am guilty. For years, I sat on the Council. I witnessed the corruption and growing violence. I said little. I went about my business, growing more wealthy every day—often at your expense. I justified my actions as being those of a skilled merchant, a responsible father, following the methods and tactics men of wealth and renown had followed. I never even allowed myself to consider that what I did could be wrong. Then I lost my son, Jerel, because of my greed and pride. I nearly lost my life because of my own recklessness. When I returned to Shum, I found I was losing my family because of my neglect. In rescuing them from Shum, I lost my father. In trying to rescue you and my family, I offered Mahijah everything I owned. To keep Gad from whipping you to death, I took the whip myself and beat you to save your life. I had no choice. It was either Gad or me.

—Why did you hide in the streets and pretend to be a beggar, if not to spy on Leah and Rachel and condemn them? Baruch asked.

—I had reason to believe that Mahijah and Gad would seek my life and injure my family. I hid my identity to observe the conditions of Shum and discover a way to get my family out.

Joshua walked to the edge of the waterfall where he could see around it.

—There's a great commotion, he said.

—There's a young woman in camp giving birth, I said.

—Giving birth? Here?

—Yes, I said. She's someone you both know.

—Who? asked Baruch.

—Miriam, my niece.

—Miriam is here? When they took me, said Baruch, I thought they would also find her and kill her.

—No, I said. She's here, and she's having a baby.

—The shouts I hear are shouts of terror, said Joshua.

—Then let me stand and listen for myself, I said.

Baruch lowered his knife. I stepped to the edge of the waterfall and heard the muffled sounds of men's voices, but I couldn't make out their words.

—There's trouble in camp, I said. You must let me go.

Baruch raised his knife, and Joshua stepped between us, saying, I believe him, Father.

—So many lies, said Baruch.

—I must hurry back, I said.

—Not yet! he said.

I sensed something urgent was happening in the camp, so I quickly lay prostrate on the earth before Baruch. With head down, I said, I have admitted my wrongs, but I won't admit to what I didn't do. If you can find mercy in your heart, I beg you to forgive me for what fault was mine. But I leave judgement up to you. Do with me as you will, but do it now!

A palpable silence brooded. I waited. For all he had suffered, I didn't know if Baruch had any mercy left in him. I silently implored God to touch my friend and give him peace, and as I prayed, a vision came to my mind of his being forced to watch his beloved wife die and his precious daughter burn. I imagined his anguish at each lash that I had delivered to his back. I remembered how he had cried out until he could cry no more. I thought of his pain as he endured the indignity of being labeled a traitor, being stripped naked before a vicious populace, and suffering demonic shouts for his blood. I thought of my allowing wicked men to persuade me to destroy this honest man's livelihood, silently standing by as he defended the innocent people of Sharon and Omner, holding my tongue as Mahijah and Simeon made him expendable. I thought of his heartbroken son, who carried his battered father to safety, while former neighbors and friends looted his tent and stole his belongings, a scene I could compare only to the feeding frenzy of jackals at a kill.

Suddenly, I became aware of weeping. A big hand stroked the back of my head and lifted me at the shoulder. Baruch knelt beside me and shook. I came to my knees, and he embraced me. I felt him shudder with pain as I wrapped my arms around him, but he didn't move away. Tears welled up in my eyes, and I couldn't stop them from flowing. As I buried my head in the shoulder of my friend, I felt as if every tear I shed took back a lash from that dreadful whip. There, at the edge of the falls, we wept a river of hurt until all that was left was peace between us. Joshua also wept as he watched us. Then he said he'd heard shouts again and urged us to our feet. At Joshua's words, I took Baruch by the arm and helped guide him from the dark cavern into the light.

Cʒ

—The Rahaj has entered the canyon! were the first shouts we heard.

Scouts had discovered a small contingent of the Rahaj searching for us. The people of Enoch's Camp had crowded up against the side of the mountain and looked afraid. Moriah and Eve rushed to me and gasped when they saw Baruch.

—We must find a way out, now! cried Moriah.

—How many of the Rahaj have you seen? I asked the scouts.

—Ten.

—Are they positioning for an attack?

—No, but they can hold the entrance to the canyon until the army comes.

—Can we fight past them?

—Not with women and children.

We were interrupted by a shout from Ishmael.

—There are people at the top of the cliff! he yelled.

We all cast our eyes up together and saw my son Enos and a young woman. She looked to be about the age of Eve, but I didn't recognize her. We began shouting at him, but the waterfall drowned out our words. I stood aside from the people and pointed back toward the Rahaj. Enos motioned that he understood, and suddenly he was gone. At the top of the cliff, the young woman was now alone.

the worth of one

ॐ

I chose twenty men to guard the entrance of the canyon, hoping a show of resistance would discourage the Rahaj from advancing. Our men were poorly armed, and I doubted that they could withstand an assault, but we needed time to form a plan.

The young woman Enos had left at the rim of the canyon dropped a bag over the side. It landed at my feet but didn't burst. After loosening the knot, I examined its contents. Then I dumped cabbages, potatoes, dried beef, and mutton onto the grass. The people gasped. Some began to cry. I called the captains to me to divide the rations. As I looked up at the young woman, I waved. Something had gone right. Enos had found success, but to what degree I didn't know.

Next, the young woman tossed knives and weapons of bronze. Except for the craftsmanship of Mahijah's sword, I hadn't seen their equal. I summoned Ishmael and said, Take these weapons and food to those men guarding the entrance.

The cry of Miriam drew my attention. As Eve ran past me to fetch water, I grabbed her arm and asked what was happening.

—The baby hasn't turned, she said. If we can't help Miriam, both she and the child will die.

I began to run to the tent, when Eve said, We'll tend to her. You must find a way out of this canyon.

—I'm waiting for Enos to return, I said. Let me help you.

—Enos?

—Yes. He has brought provisions and has gone to find help.

—Then come to Miriam's tent, if you want, said Eve, But don't get in the way.

Eve made a move to fetch the water, and I called her back. I'd seen Baruch hobble to Miriam's tent and enter as though he was one of the midwives. So I asked Eve what Baruch was doing.

—He has seen the women of Sharon turn a breech child, said Eve. He's trying to help.

—He can barely move! He could kill her!

—But none of the midwives has this skill, said Eve. We have no choice but to let him try.

Eve pulled away and ran to the river for water as I sprinted to Miriam's tent. I had heard birthing ewes bawl and seen them bleed as they labored. I had watched Moriah give birth to my children. I had witnessed men in battle, their bodies rent and bloodied. But I had never seen blood and pain like Miriam's. Baruch had thrust his hands inside her womb and was shouting for the midwives to hold Miriam's shoulders and legs. Her face had the look of panic. When she screamed, Baruch shouted, Don't push yet! In her pain, Miriam managed a quick nod.

Baruch looked up at me, saying, I've turned the baby. I'm holding the head, but the child is too large to be born. Can you get a knife and cut Miriam?

—I'm not a midwife! I said.

—That may be true, but not one of these women has done what I'm asking you.

—Neither have I!

—If Miriam dies, I don't want the midwives blaming themselves.

I took a knife, wiped it clean, moved to his side, and asked, Where?

—Can you see the child's head? It needs to come out.

I nodded as I looked between his arms at the blood-colored pate covered with veins.

—Make a cut half the length of your small finger, he said.

—I can't do this, I said.

—You can. You must.

Tears came to my eyes. Hurting someone intentionally was abhorrent to me, but I knew, watching her writhing in pain, I must act for her sake. Miriam shrieked when I slit the flesh.

—I'm sorry, I whispered to Miriam.

—The cut has to be a little longer, said Baruch.

—I'll try, I said.

Miriam screamed again.

—It's enough, said Baruch.

Two women lifted Miriam's legs and bent them at the knees, while Baruch repositioned himself.

—Can you push? he asked Miriam in a gentle whisper.

She cried out, unable to control her breathing.

—I'm dying! she groaned.

—No. Stay with me! said Baruch.

He forced Miriam to focus on his eyes and said, Look at me! You have to push!

—I can't!

Moriah lifted Miriam's head and cooled her face with a wet cloth.

—She's delirious, said a midwife.

—Miriam, look at me! You have to push!

Miriam looked at Baruch and nodded. Then he placed both hands on the child's head again and said, Push now!

Miriam squeezed her eyes shut and groaned. Her entire body tensed.

Moriah said, Push!

Miriam gasped for air, and the crown of the child's head forced wide the opening and began to protrude.

—Someone take her hands, said Baruch.

I nodded at Eve, who took one hand, as I took the other.

—Miriam, said Baruch, You must find the strength to push.

Her body arched, and she began to breathe in short, forced puffs.

The veins in her neck bulged, and as she gripped my hand, her fingernails dug into my skin. She yelled out.

Moriah said, We're close! Just a little more, Miriam.

—I have a head! shouted Baruch.

He turned it and, with a finger, emptied the infant's mouth of mucus and water.

—One more push, Miriam, said Baruch, You have to birth the shoulders.

—There's so much blood! cried Eve.

—We'll deal with that later, said Baruch. Here comes the baby. I've got it! I've got *her!*

When Baruch held the child up to show Miriam, all in the tent sighed. Their looks of urgency changed to looks of relief.

—It's a girl? cried Miriam.

—Yes. Dark hair and beautiful, said Baruch.

—Is she all right? asked Miriam.

—She's perfect, said Baruch, handing the child to a midwife, who brought the baby to a cry.

—Can I see her?

—Let us cut the cord and wash her first.

As Baruch pulled away the afterbirth and began to suture the cut, I gazed upon the child and felt reverence. My father used to say, *Nowhere is God's power more manifest than in the miracle of birth.*

—Where did you come from? Miriam asked Baruch. When they took you away, I sneaked from your tent and ran to the edge of the city. Then Rabunel and Enos found me.

—Joshua brought me into the wilderness to heal, said Baruch. When we heard you coming, we hid behind the waterfall. We thought the Rahaj had followed us.

—You dug your nails into my hand and made my hand bleed, I told Miriam.

—It's only fair, she said, reminding me of my cutting her.

Then Miriam closed her eyes and said, I'm so weary.

—I'm almost finished, then you can rest, said Baruch.

—My daughter and I are alive because of you, she whispered. First, you took me into your tent, and now you've saved my life.

Baruch smiled and went back to cleaning her.

—How are you feeling, Miriam? I asked.

—Exhausted. The pain was more than I thought I could bear, she said.

—And now?

—I hurt, but I feel such relief.

Eve brought in the child, washed and bundled in a soft wrap. She handed the baby to Miriam, who opened the wrap and examined the child.

—What do you think? asked Baruch.

—She's beautiful.

Baruch washed his hands and knelt at Miriam's side, then he caressed her cheek with the backs of his fingers.

—She *is* beautiful, he said. She'll need a name.

Miriam rocked the baby and cooed. Then to Baruch she asked, Would you like to hold her?

—Oh, yes, he said.

Miriam placed the baby in the fold of Baruch's arms and smiled. All of us who stood by laughed and hovered over him, but Baruch ignored us and gazed into the child's face, his eyes glistening.

—Do you have a name? I asked Miriam.

Eve leaned forward and whispered into Miriam's ear. Then Miriam smiled and nodded, looked at the baby and then at Baruch, and finally said, *Rachel.* I'll name her Rachel.

Baruch let tears roll down his face.

—Thank you, he said, as he touched the child's mouth with a finger and stroked her cheek.

When he returned the baby to Miriam, he said, I'm sorry for how badly I must appear.

—At least you're clothed, said Miriam.

Baruch's face reddened. He said, Yes, childbirth isn't very discreet for the mother, I'm afraid.

—You look as though you've suffered much, said Miriam.

—Shum can be very hard on its citizens, he said.

—Will you stay with Enoch's Camp? she asked.

—My son and I would like to stay, he said. We now are refugees, like you.

—The trek will be difficult, I said. We must climb out of this canyon, then move into the mountains to the City of Enoch. With your injuries, do you think you can do it?

—I think so, said Baruch. But I may be slow.

—Me too, said Miriam.

We laughed, and I said to Baruch and Joshua, This is your home now, and we are your family.

—My son and I would like that, Baruch replied.

Miriam looked at Baruch and once more said, Thank you.

—You already thanked me, he said.

—I know. But it doesn't seem enough. You stayed with me the entire time.

Baruch smiled, and I whispered to Moriah and Eve that we should leave. The people would want to hear of Miriam's news.

When we left, Baruch was holding the baby, while the midwives were kneading Miriam's stomach to stop the bleeding.

—New life, whispered Moriah.

—Yes, I said, The first new life in Enoch's Camp.

&

During the day, the Rahaj gathered strength, but the body of Shum's military might had not yet arrived. Because the canyon was narrow, our men could defend it from an attack for a reasonable length of time. Even so, we maneuvered our men in full sight of the Rahaj to give the appearance that we were many.

The young woman at the top of the cliff continued to drop us food and provisions. Enos had not yet returned. Men not assigned to guard the camp had devised a way to convey people out of the canyon. Ascending a short distance up the face of the cliff, a climber would secure a rope to a rock, then move higher and secure it again. The goal was to string a line to the top and pull people up, one by one. But the men had progressed only a quarter way to the rim because the face was so treacherous. By evening, the young woman had disappeared, and we thought she had run off. Two guards returned from the mouth of the canyon with news that the Rahaj had received new troops and seemed to be preparing to attack.

—When will the ropes be ready? I asked.

—By morning, I was told.

—We must reinforce the entrance to the canyon and hold on as long as possible, I said. In the morning, we'll move out as many of the people as we can.

By early dawn, a sentry shouted that the young woman had returned with three men. I quickly donned my clothes and ran to the cliff by the waterfall. There, indeed, I saw the young woman standing at the top with the three men the sentry had mentioned—Enoch, Enos, and Micah. Enoch threw down lengths of rope, then lowered a long rope that he had secured at the top of the cliff. He descended it hand over hand. News of his return spread like wildfire through the camp, and the people seemed buoyed up. After a quick greeting, he joined me as we hurried up the canyon to observe our defenses.

—It appears that Mahijah's army has taken to both sides of the canyon, said Enoch.

—Yes, I said, And now they can see our strength and easily over-run us. We won't be able to sustain an attack.

—How many men can you spare to defend the canyon?

—Ten. Fifteen at the most. But they'll be massacred at the first assault.

—Call the men to reinforce the canyon, said Enoch. We just need a little time.

—Time is what we don't have.

—I'm convinced God will protect us, but you're right. We must hurry and get the people out.

—But how?

—We have enough rope to span the distance top to bottom, he said. We'll make a harness to raise them up. You organize the people at the bottom, and I'll go back up to help Micah and Enos pull them up. Have the captains prepare their groups. Women and children first.

We made the harness of ropes, and Micah and Enos pulled Enoch to the top.

—Keep your heads about you, I said to the captains. Some of the people may panic. The climb will take courage. You must keep order no matter what is happening at the canyon's entrance. Belongings must be bundled for transport, but leave all that you can. We'll begin by sending up two strong men to help pull. Get the women and children ready to follow.

We had worked together to prepare a system of ropes to hoist people to the top while at the same time reducing the risk of injury. One rope was tied to the person's waist and held loosely at ground level to keep the person from swinging into the rocky wall. Then, as the person sat in the harness, men at the top pulled the person up. On a separate line, men raised up the camp's belongings.

After five people had been conveyed to the top, an old woman was brought forward and fitted into the harness. She gazed at the long tether stretching to the top of the canyon, then began to falter.

—I'll never make it! I haven't the strength to climb! she cried.

Ishmael ran to steady her, saying, We'll help you. You won't have to climb. The men will pull you to the top.

The old woman took in a big breath and, with reluctance, allowed Ishmael to strap her in the harness. A cheer went up from us below when the woman reached the top and was released from the harness.

After some of the women, children, and elderly were transported, we began to hoist two men to one woman or child. In that way, those at the top could rotate and share the burden of lifting others.

—You should go next, Ishmael urged me.

—Can you manage without me? I asked.

—Yes. Go to the top, and help pull.

Ishmael held the end of the rope as I stepped into the harness. When the rope went taut, I was lifted off the ground and began moving up the face of the cliff. The mist of the waterfall soaked all who stood near the area of ascent. The one being transported received the worst drenching. Midway, I heard a great confusion in camp below, and as I looked down, I saw two guards running to Ishmael, waving their arms, pointing toward the mouth of the canyon. The noise of the water prevented me from making out what they said, but as I leaned back for a better view, I saw the entrance to the canyon filling with red-robed forces. Our small force of guards was attempting to hold them back, but Mahijah's army appeared to be gaining ground. I made exaggerated signs for Enoch and Enos to let me back down, and they quickly lowered me.

Then, as I looked up, I saw a most remarkable sight. Enoch raised his head toward heaven and moved his lips as if in prayer. Suddenly, I felt a quick breeze, and the sun disappeared overhead. I touched ground and stepped from the harness. A great bolt of lightning was followed by a jolting crack of thunder that reverberated down the canyon. Those still in the camp rushed toward me as I fitted the harness onto an old man and signaled the men above to pull.

—Don't be frightened, I said to him. This storm isn't intended to destroy us but to save us. We must hurry to get everyone up. Do you have the courage?

He looked pale, but nodded and gripped the rope. His knuckles grew white, and he squeezed his eyes tight.

A mighty gust of wind shot up the canyon and into the waterfall, dousing much of the camp. Women screamed. Men fell. Children cried and hid in their mothers' skirts. As the wind spun, it raised the dust of the canyon as though it were a serpent coiling to strike. All went quiet. An unsettling stillness brewed in the sky above us like a pot ready to boil. I looked up and watched dark clouds huddle, billowing, combining in strength and fury.

I shouted at two guards, Run to the entrance of the canyon, and bring back your companions.

—The Rahaj will attack us, they cried.

I looked up again and said, I don't think so. Not yet.

To Ishmael I said, Tell the captains to calm the people, and bring them to the ropes.

Suddenly, another crack of lightning resounded, and the wind swelled with increasing force. Dark clouds fell into the canyon, and the engorged sky began to heave hail on Mahijah's army. The tempest drove the regiment back and sent them scurrying for cover. They hid under large rocks or beneath trees. So powerful was the pounding of the hail that few of the army moved, and those who had moved quickly retreated.

The absolute astonishment I felt for what was happening was beyond my ability to express. I thought I had seen the hand of God work in small, quiet ways, but never with such force and fury. A part of me wanted to stand and observe the phenomenon, but fear and duty impelled me to rush to get the rest of the people out.

The torrent continued unabated while we conveyed each person of Enoch's Camp to the top of the canyon. Ishmael fitted the harness as I held the rope. I gazed at the blisters that had formed on my hands. Most had ruptured, and blood had stained my palms. When Moriah stepped into the harness, she wrapped pieces of cloth around my hands.

—Are you coming soon? she asked above the din of the storm.

I looked back down the canyon, then at her, and said, Yes, I'll come soon.

Ishmael stood by me and helped me hold the rope as Moriah ascended.

—Are all the people accounted for? I asked Ishmael.

—Yes.

—The provisions?

—I just sent up the last of them.

—Then you go next, I said to Ishmael. I'll go last.

When Ishmael reached the top and the rope descended, I strapped myself into the harness, then tied an end of rope about my waist and the other to a stump. No sooner had I left the ground than the storm abated, and the Rahaj began to appear from their hiding places. Partway up the cliff, sitting in the harness, I watched them rush to the edge of the waterfall, point at me, and curse. One took the rope at the stump and began to pull back with it. I felt as though I was being cut in half at the waist. Reaching for my knife, I cut the supporting rope. As I did so, I began to swing out of control, bumping into the rocky face of the canyon, spinning, all the while getting drenched from the waterfall's spray.

When I arrived at the top, wet and exhausted, I peered below and saw some of the Rahaj trying to climb the face. They scaled only a scant distance, then gave up and gathered to talk strategy. Gad came to the waterfall and surveyed the face of the cliff. Then a few men, who appeared to be leaders, gathered to him, spoke for a moment, then broke off and gestured to their forces. Soon the entire army marched out of the canyon.

—Where are they going? asked Micah.

—The only way to intercept us now is to make the long trip around the mountain and meet up with us in the valley opposite Shum, I said.

—Your son, Benjamin, will be coming into that valley with your father's sheep.

—I know.

As the people gathered into their companies and their captains assessed their needs, all grew quiet. Some had expressions of anxiety. I heard soft talking, as though the ordeal had drained everyone's energy.

—I'm worn out, said Enoch, collapsing beside me.

I gazed at him, in awe at what he had done in our behalf. Enoch truly was a man of God. I had known him as a friend and as a teacher, but never as one who could speak the word of God and bring together the powers of earth and heaven. His modesty wouldn't allow him to bring attention to himself. What power he had was God's, not his, and he used that power only to serve others.

—We should speak to the camp, he said. Do you have the strength?

—Give me a moment, I said.

—Your son is a hero, said Enoch.

I surveyed the area, looking for Enos and the rest of my family.

—Mahijah will still hunt us, said Enoch. You must lead the people out of here and up to the City.

—Where are you going? I asked.

—To finish preparations in the City for your arrival. You'll need food, clothing, shelter. Without these things, you'll face more perils than you will fleeing from Mahijah. We must each do our duties, Rabunel. You must continue to lead the people, and I must prepare a place for them. You'll be safe until you reach the rise that ascends to the City. There's a valley below it, and that's where I expect we'll meet Mahijah again.

—I know the place, I said. I recall it has a spectacular view of some valleys, including a clear view of Shum.

Enoch said, You've never been to the City, have you?

—No, but I'm looking forward to it.

—Then let me tell you about it, he said.

For a long while, Enoch told me of the people of the City of Enoch, how they had come there impoverished, fleeing for their lives. He told me what covenants they had made to live in peace, how they took care of one another, and how they settled disputes. I was interested in how he had laid out the City and how the people had received stewardships of land for their support. Enoch had established schools there. Culture and efforts to beautify the place occupied much of the people's time. When he had finished telling me, I had as clear a picture of the City as if I had visited it.

Enoch stood to gather the people, and when they had assembled, he commended them for their courage and their love for one another. He sustained me as their leader and explained the challenges and destination of our final trek. Then he bade us kneel upon the ground as he thanked God for sparing our lives. Finally, when we had arisen, he took each of us into his arms and blessed us.

Micah put a big hand on my shoulder, saying, Your son has developed your genius for trade.

When he laughed and departed with Enoch, I was left to wonder. I searched for Enos and saw him hurrying about, helping Ishmael divide up the provisions he had brought among the captains. The young woman helped him. She unloaded two mules laden with food-stuffs and equipment. I was amazed at the quantity and variety.

—Do you need some help? I called to her.

She shook her head. I walked to her and thanked her for helping us. She appeared embarrassed.

—Maybe we can talk later, I said.

Nightfall was near. The captains hurried to establish a quick camp and arrange an evening meal. Judging by how I felt, I guessed that everyone else was hungry and tired too, but all were busy and seemed relieved to be momentarily out of danger. Moriah and Sarah hustled about, tending to the women and children. Joshua helped Enos and Ishmael carry blankets and food to the captains. Baruch sat with Miriam, and Eve held the baby. I overheard their conversation.

—Would you bring me some supper? Miriam asked Baruch.

—Of course. I'll be back soon.

—Take your time. Eve and I need to talk.

—We do? asked Eve.

Baruch groaned when he stood, then limped off to fulfill Miriam's request.

—He's so caring, said Miriam. From the moment he took me into his tent, I sensed his kindness.

—Yes, but you're taking advantage of his good nature, said Eve.

—Maybe he needs us as much as we need him, said Miriam.

—Why?

—He misses his wife and daughter. I think he needs someone to care for. And little Rachel and I need someone to care for us.

—That kind of caring is hard to find, said Eve.

—And that's what I wanted to talk with you about.

—Yes?

—I didn't go into the Grove of my own accord. My father forced me.

—I've heard, said Eve, And I'm so sorry for you.

—I experienced things no one should have to endure, said Miriam. I saw things no one should see—perverse, secret things. Young women like me were forced to submit to vile men. Others were willing to give themselves for advantages among the elite.

—I cannot imagine such things, said Eve. I had heard rumors, but...

—Eve, listen to me, said Miriam. Chaz not only participated, he led the ceremonies. The Grove may be used by the Watchers and the Rahaj, but it belongs to Chaz. Do you understand me? Chaz is as evil a man as I've ever known, worse than his father.

—I can't believe it! Eve said, wiping away tears.

—I'm your cousin, said Miriam. I wouldn't hurt you, but I cannot stand by and watch you give your heart to a lying, degenerate man. Please, believe what I say. Chaz has no concept of honesty, goodness, or virtue.

—Why did he want *me?*

—You're beautiful and trusting. You might have gone on forever believing whatever he told you. And he couldn't have the kingdom without a wife. You were available.

A long silence settled between the two young women, then Miriam asked, Are you upset with me for telling you this?

—No.

—What are you feeling?

—Used.

இ

From that moment, Eve began to take on a look of resolve. She seemed stronger, more dignified. She became a tireless worker, cheerful, compassionate to those in need.

That night, she came to me, saying, For all that the people have suffered and for what they yet face, we should have a time of celebration.

—I've never been one for merriment, I said.

—Then it's time to change.

That night, at Eve's insistence, we sang, rejoiced, and offered gratitude to our God for preserving us. Ishmael produced a stringed instrument he had brought with him and began to play. It appeared to be made of cherry wood, having a flat top, a gourd-like body, and a round sound hole. Along its narrow neck ran four tight strings that were fastened at the top to pegs. As he sang, the camp joined him in a folk tune, and I found myself singing what words I could remember and humming through those I could not. Eve began to laugh at me and motioned to her mother who sat beside me. Then Moriah stood on her feet and pulled at my hands.

—Will you dance with me, husband? she asked.

—In front of all these people?

—They're our friends now.

—I've never been very good at dancing.

—You can't sing either, but you don't seem to mind doing *that* in public.

As I stood, I said, *I can too sing!*

As Moriah began to skip around to the rhythm of the song, she laughed and said, No you can't!

Ishmael picked up the tempo, and the people began to clap as I tried to keep up with Moriah. Everyone was smiles and advice, singing as badly as Moriah claimed I did.

Eve couldn't stop laughing, and soon she tugged at Joshua and said, Come on, let's show them how.

More laughter shot from the crowd, and Ishmael crowed as he plucked the strings and tapped his foot.

—If any of you can do better, come on out! I shouted.

Nearly everyone jumped up and began to dance, laughing, singing, twirling partners, beating dust into the air, as happy a sight as I'd ever seen.

CB

Late that night, Enos came to me, saying, Father, I want you to meet Esther.

The young woman held her head low. I took her hand and patted it. She wore a slave band on her wrist.

—We must cut this off, I said.

She raised her head and stared at me without expression. She had smooth, tanned skin. Her long, black hair fell to her waist with the sheen of satin, soft as raven down. Her eyes were the color of mahogany, her bones slender, her lips red. For her beauty, she could have been royalty, but her rough hands and plain clothing betrayed her. Two scars—likely from burns—marred her forearms. A pale line on her calf bespoke an old wound.

I handed her food and a blanket, and she stared at them as she rubbed the blanket between her thumb and forefinger.

—Where is your homeland, child? I asked.

Enos answered for her, saying, Esther is the daughter of nomadic people—cattle breeders from the northern countries.

—How old are you? I asked her.

—She's seventeen, replied Enos.

—Does she have a tongue? I asked Enos, smiling.

Esther looked at me and said, I belong to Enos now.

—You belong to no one, he said. You're a free woman.

What he said seemed foreign to her. She wrinkled her eyebrows, then asked if she could sit on the ground and eat her food. Enos nodded reluctantly, and I motioned him to follow me.

—She looks to have had a hard life, I said.

—She won't say much, but from what I've learned, her life has been one of suffering day after day. I can't imagine what she's endured.

I swept my hand out over the camp and said, You did well. The provisions are more than I had hoped for.

—Food and supplies were what the caravan carried for trade, said Enos. They sought rare stones. Our meeting couldn't have been more fortuitous. I hid the satchel and entered their camp to trade. I received all the provisions for five sapphires and a diamond.

—And the young woman?

—She was a slave, he said, Sold as a child for her father's extensive debts. She belonged to the master of the caravan, who abused her. The master told me he would never recover the amount of her father's debt, and he intended to exact recompense any way he could. Esther paid the price of his displeasure.

—You traded for her?

Enos looked into my eyes, his own brimming, and said, As I journeyed toward the caravan, the weight of my guilt pressed upon me, and the memories of my offenses plagued my soul. I was in such agony, I wished I might die. I knew I had offended an innocent person; I had offended myself; I had offended God. I felt so ashamed. When I could bear no more, I fell on my face and begged for forgiveness. And then I had an experience…

Enos paused, and tears spilled from his eyes. He said, When I arose, I felt a rush of peace sweep over me.

—And then you saw Esther's condition? I asked.

—I couldn't stand to see her suffer.

—So you bought her?

Enos nodded, saying, I retrieved the satchel and returned to buy Esther's freedom.

—How much of the satchel did you give for her? I asked.

—All of it.

zion

൙

I led the camp the following morning along mountain dales into an open valley, a prelude to our ascent to the City of Enoch. The high valley was often a pasture for cattle, but I knew it as a place my father had sometimes moved his sheep in the spring. That Mahijah's army would be scouting us there was certain, but I doubted we would be vulnerable until we reached the far range of mountains and began to move east. On those far slopes, one could view both the valley we now traversed and the valley of Shum. My hope was to achieve the mountains by midday.

As I searched the horizon, I wondered when we would meet up with Benjamin. A miscalculation on his part would put him face to face with Mahijah. As we walked, the dew soaked our sandals. Within a short time, the sun became hot and burned the dew away. The winter I had left so long ago had been replaced by spring—cool in the mountains, warm in the valley. Tender flora that had struggled against chilly nights now flourished. Spring spawned a sense of rebirth. We saw elk calves suckling in a far meadow. Nestlings now tested young wings on soft breezes. Honeybees labored in thick colonies to nourish their brood of larvae. Mad squirrels chattered warnings to each other and scurried to restock their pantries as though winter was almost upon them.

Although the people helped each other, I could see by the looks in their faces that they were exhausted. Some sick were carried on improvised totes. Women strapped babies to their backs, and men lugged provisions. Joshua had constructed a stretcher of poles and flax for Miriam and her child. I was interested that Eve took one of the poles and helped Joshua pull. Baruch struggled to walk alongside and often stopped to rest. Moriah and Sarah mingled with the women, aiding whom they could, and Esther accompanied them. The captains bunched their companies into tight units in order to observe and minister to their needs. Enos had run ahead to scout for trouble.

The sudden blast of his ram's horn signaled danger.

—We've been spotted, I said to Ishmael.

—How many do you think? he asked.

—I don't know.

Enos sounded the horn again, and heads turned each way. A low murmur spread through the camp. Till that moment, the people had shown remarkable courage, but now a palpable sense of fear overtook them. Even the captains had the look of terror. Two of them faltered and were unable to lead their companies. I called to Baruch and Joshua.

—Relieve those two captains, I said.

—In my condition? asked Baruch.

—You are worth five men, I said. I wish I didn't have to ask you, but I need you.

—Surely I'm too young to lead heads of families, said Joshua.

—Capability, not age, is what's needed, I said. There's no time to discuss this. We must hurry!

When Enos signaled once more, Ishmael ordered the captains to move the people out at a fast pace. In the distance, at the border of the valley near Shum, we saw a cloud of dust rise. Its length was half that of the valley, and it billowed into the air as fast and as startling as a summer storm.

—Keep your heads about you, I told the captains. Panic won't help the people. We must hurry to the mountains.

—Flee to the hills! Ishmael cried to the people.

Enos caught up to us.

—Who were they? I asked.

—Spies of the Rahaj, he said.

—Could you hear them?

—They intend to kill us all, he said.

—How many are in the army? I asked.

—Most of Shum is coming.

—We'll make our stand where the hills rise up to the mountains, I said, pointing at a distant rise.

—Make a stand? said Enos. Two hundred of us against Mahijah's thousands? They'll slaughter us.

—We could have died in the canyon, I said, But we're still alive.

The captains shouted to their companies, Do not falter. Climb!

—I see Enoch and Micah! cried Moriah.

The news sparked an increase of energy. The people quickened their steps and began calling out to Enoch as they raced for the hillside.

—A little farther! I urged some of the slower people.

Then we sensed a low rumble from down in the valley that made the earth feel as though it was vibrating. As I looked toward the sound, I saw the Rahaj marching toward us in long, fast columns. Some of the people stopped and cried out in fright.

—Captains! I shouted. Move your people along!

When Enoch and Micah met up with us, some of the people were overcome with fear and fell on the seer's neck, begging for help. Enoch pulled them away and said, There's no time. Keep moving!

—This would be a good time for the promised destruction of Shum, I said to Enoch, as I ran beside him.

—A very good time.

—How will God protect us?

—I don't know, except that he will.

Astonishment rushed through me, for until that time I had thought that because Enoch was God's messenger, he knew everything and didn't struggle for answers as I did. That he wrestled with questions and was ultimately left to rely on his faith in God was amazing to me.

—Are you afraid to die, Rabunel? he asked.

I paused, then said, No, today is as good as any.

—Are you afraid to live?

—Not anymore.

I shielded my eyes and searched for a place of refuge, but saw none. The hillside was mostly bare. Once on the ridge, we stopped, exhausted, having run as far as we could. Mahijah's forces were upon us, and we turned to face them. The army of Shum had split and advanced on our flanks. The Rahaj, as trained fighters, outpaced the remainder of the army and had hemmed us in against the mountain. Soon, the entire force arrived and encircled us on three sides with the mountain at our backs. From where we stood above them, I could look out into the valley and see the host of them. By their incredible numbers, I guessed that virtually every man of Shum was outfitted as a warrior.

—All of these men have come against us? I asked Enoch.

—It seems we've become a considerable threat to the king, he answered.

—They're maneuvering into position for an attack, said Micah.

Moriah came running to me, saying, Look off in the distance. I can see Shum.

We shaded our eyes and saw the city. Though far, we made out its boundaries and saw a strange haze covering it.

—What do you make of it? asked Micah, gazing into the distance.

—Maybe the women of Shum are preparing a victory feast for our slaughter, said Baruch, with a tone a sarcasm.

—What a nice thought, I replied with equal sarcasm, I always wanted a celebration at my death.

—You may get your wish, said Baruch.

—Yes, I said, Perhaps my grandfather, Simeon, will weep and

speak great things of me. Then Mahijah might shed a tear and lament the passing of his dear friend.

—I'll tell you what will happen, said Baruch. Our slain bodies will be paraded as trophies through the streets of Shum. Then they'll be displayed on poles at the borders to cause fear. Mahijah will have his victory, and he'll be able to raise an army large enough to conquer all the lands for which he has lusted.

—Happy Mahijah, I said.

—We're not dead yet, said Micah. The king may be disappointed.

From the body of the army, we saw two horsemen slip away and ease off toward a distant rise behind the forces.

—What do you think they're doing? I asked Micah.

—We should send someone out to follow them, he answered.

I motioned for Enos.

—Sneak behind the army, and follow those men, I said.

—You need me here, he said.

—We need a miracle here. But in case we survive, we need to know all the movements of our enemies.

Enos nodded and slipped away.

—I see Mahijah, said Moriah.

She pointed at the king, clothed in glorious crimson robes, who came to the front of the army, riding a white stallion. The horse carried its head high and reared as Mahijah pulled back on its reins.

Mahijah bared his sword, raised it high so all the army could see it, and cried, Enoch, come forth!

When Enoch stepped to the front, Mahijah laughed. Then he spoke loudly so that his forces could hear, saying, You're a poor commander. Your only escape is up a steep mountain. What will you do now? Do you expect your allies from Sharon to save you?

I was amazed that Mahijah was yet feigning danger from the people of Sharon. At Mahijah's jeer, Enoch stood unflinching, calm and courageous.

—I do not desire your destruction, King of Shum, said Enoch, But your course is one that will bring upon you extinction.

—Will your God come down and fight for you? shouted Mahijah. Who are we to fear your little band of runaways?

The army laughed, and Mahijah again raised his sword.

—Today, Shum will be rid of her enemies, beginning with you, Enoch, and all of your followers!

Micah stepped between Enoch and Mahijah, saying, No matter who dies today, I will not rest until I spill your blood!

Enoch touched Micah's shoulder and drew him back, saying, It is not by the sword that God will deliver us. He has prepared another way.

Micah stood aside, then Enoch cried to Mahijah's army, Come away from the evil influences of Shum, and acknowledge the God of your fathers. Correct your ways before him. Only by this can destruction be avoided.

—I'll tell you how destruction will be avoided, said Mahijah. You and your people must come off that mountain now and swear an oath of allegiance to me, your king. Then I will spare your lives. Otherwise my army will slay you where you stand.

Enoch spoke over the king and again addressed the multitude of his army.

—People of Shum, he said, If you continue to uphold leaders who are liars and murderers, blinding yourselves to the evils among you, only annihilation can be your future. I make this last plea—come away now, and save yourselves.

Silence, the kind that precedes a storm, engulfed the army. Mahijah's face became red, and he shook as though he could not contain his rage. Then he called for the Rahaj to attack. Confusion shot through the army, for Gad could not be found.

—Battle cry! yelled a commander of the Rahaj.

At his signal, the Rahaj began to shout, brandishing their weapons, crying blood oaths, screaming threats.

—Make ready! Mahijah called to the commanders.

Some in Enoch's Camp fell back and wavered. The fear of death swept over us, for we knew we couldn't defend ourselves. Then Enoch went to his knees and offered a prayer, petitioning deliverance. We all knelt and joined him. He prayed with words and power such as I had never heard. When he finished, he stood on his feet, walked to the edge overlooking the army of Shum, and raised his arms to heaven, crying, O God, preserve us!

At that moment, the earth began to shake again, but not from the army of Shum. Those of us standing with Enoch began to stir and cast our eyes about. Some said it was an earthquake. Children held onto their mothers. Mahijah's horse reared, and a great chaos cut through the ranks of his army. The commanders called for order, but as the rumbling grew, so did the looks of anxiety.

—There! cried Micah, pointing toward the horizon.

From the direction of Shum, within the black, billowing smoke, flames shot skyward. Then, black-clad horsemen rushed into the valley with astounding speed, wielding broad swords, shouting terrifying war cries. Their numerous force filled the entire valley, eclipsing the size of Mahijah's army.

—Who are they? I asked Micah.

—The army of Nod.

They overwhelmed the forces of Shum, but seemed uninterested in us. As we ran to higher ground, we watched the invaders cut down the army of Shum with an efficiency I had never thought possible. We stood transfixed on the high ridge, not believing what we were witnessing. The Rahaj fighting on the ground with their unwieldy clubs were no match for the sword-carrying horsemen of Nod. Great warriors of the Rahaj were left to bleed to death, with appendages severed or their bowels cut through. Some of the wounded cried for mercy, begging to be relieved of their suffering, though none would suffer long because of their severe wounds. The ground seemed to bleed red, and still the army of Nod descended on the forces of Shum. Horses trampled upon those who tried to flee. The Watchers were slain, their heads taken as trophies. The warriors of the Rahaj were hewn down as stubble. Mahijah fought with a man of enormous size. The warrior of Nod pulled Mahijah from his horse and wrestled him to the ground.

—Have mercy! cried Mahijah.

—Nod be upon you! shouted the warrior, thrusting a dagger at him.

Mahijah grabbed the man's hand and tried to hold back the point of the dagger. Then the man of Nod shouted and, with one mighty thrust, drove the dagger into Mahijah's heart. An expression of astonishment washed over Mahijah's face. He gazed upon the dagger in his chest, tried to pull it free, then closed his eyes. The warrior fell upon Mahijah's body and slit it from neck to belly, skewering the heart with his dagger, then stood, raising Mahijah's heart in the air and gave a triumphant shout. Chaz charged the man, but before Chaz could avenge his father, he received an arrow through his throat. Eve screamed as Chaz staggered and fell. As he coughed and tried to raise himself, the sharp sword of a warrior severed his head, and his body fell quivering into the dirt. I held Eve in my arms and tried to turn her from the sight, but she stood transfixed and numb, watching the warrior of Nod ride off with Chaz's head.

Like a swarm of locusts can sweep clean a field of grain in moments, the army of Nod overran Mahijah's forces and was riding off toward Shum. To loot it, I supposed. Those of us who were left on the mountain gazed with astonishment upon the bodies that covered the valley. Scavengers gathered for a free feast. Vultures circling overhead would have to wait for lions and wolves to get their share, but there was so much carnage that every scavenger, in time, would be full.

Enoch was the first to walk down to the bodies. As we joined him, we stopped short of moving among the bodies and treading on the red, wet earth.

—Are they all dead? Moriah whispered.

I listened but heard no moans of wounded. I gazed out over the field of bodies and saw no movement.

—Yes, I said.

Shock yielded to soft sobs and low whispers.

—I expected to feel elation at being delivered, said Moriah, But I have a dull feeling.

—I understand, I said. Since the first time I heard Enoch prophesy of the destruction of Shum, I wondered how it could happen. Now, it has come so quickly. I don't even know how to react.

Enoch turned to the people and said, Let's leave this place.

As we walked away from the bloody valley, Enoch's visage was that of profound sorrow. I put my hand on his shoulder.

—It was inevitable, I said.

—But it was no victory, he said, placing his hand over his eyes.

—Most everyone I know is dead on that field, I said.

As we walked, I heard the cries of the people for friends and family slain. Not one of us was without tears. We had been saved from our enemies, but there was no rejoicing.

—For such a long time, I tried to warn and teach this people, said Enoch. I tried to gather them out, but they wouldn't listen. Now Shum burns in the distance. The men are slain, the women and children are dead, and Nod will possess this land.

I stopped and gazed at Shum. The sky above the city seemed to be on fire. At the far rise, the two men who had left Shum's army had been joined by another. The three sat on horses overlooking the valley, then they turned and cantered away.

When Enos returned, we motioned him near.

—Who were they? asked Micah.

—Simeon, Gad, and a man I didn't know.

—Asher, the Watcher of Nod, I said.

—Are you certain? asked Enoch.

—Yes. In the wilderness, I heard Gad and Asher discuss a conspiracy. Later, Danbenihah told me that he had heard men plotting to remove Mahijah from power and deliver up the land of Shum to Nod.

—Why would they do that? asked Enos.

Micah interjected his opinion, saying, Shum is a rich land, but the people were used to their freedom. From Nod's point of view, it was better to kill the people than to waste manpower on trying to subjugate them. I expect the three men have ridden off to report to the king of Nod.

—They wanted the land of Shum, and the people were expendable? I asked.

—Yes.

—And what do Simeon and Gad get out of this slaughter? asked Enos.

—Power and wealth from the new regime is my guess, said Enoch. They knew Mahijah had ambitions to conquer the region, but he lacked the leadership to hold on. Now, with the land of Shum as a hub, the king of Nod can do what Mahijah could not: settle his people there and dominate all the surrounding lands.

—The plan was brilliant, said Micah. With the city left unguarded and Mahijah distracted, Shum was easy to conquer. Mahijah's pride destroyed everything. Now that Simeon, Gad, and Asher have formed an alliance with the king of Nod, the entire world is in danger.

—Including us? I asked.

—Today, Shum was the target, said Micah. Nod wanted the land, not us. We were seen as opposing Mahijah—allies of a sort. But as the City of Enoch grows, we'll be seen as a threat to Nod.

—We'll see the army of Nod again, said Enoch.

Enoch directed us to make camp at a high spot on the mountain. He said we would climb to the City tomorrow. As we hiked to the campsite, the sun burned red in the western sky. Sarah walked beside me.

—We can't go to the City of Enoch without Benjamin, she said.

Her concern became part of a family prayer we offered that night. We prayed that Benjamin would be protected and that our family might soon be reunited. We spoke of our sadness for our slain friends. We expressed our gratitude for our deliverance.

The dark of night brought a spray of stars and a full, orange moon. When the fires faded, Enoch spoke to us.

—Never forget this night. Never forget anything that has transpired during these last few days. For the Lord your God has delivered you and led you to a place where you can keep the covenant you have made with him and with each other. And there are others who desire the freedom you have—people in the lands of Sharon, Omner, Abel, Haner, and Hanannihah. We must go there and invite them to join us, if they will listen.

The dark cool of night brought with it a peace I had not known for days. For the moment, we were not being pursued or threatened. We were free to worship our God. As a camp, we offered our thanks to God, and Micah offered that prayer.

I finally sat to rest against a tree. Moriah came and sat beside me, leaning against my shoulder. For a long while we said nothing as we stared up at the majesty of the heavens. Then Moriah brought me back to earth, saying, There seems to be no end to our blessings.

I turned my head and shot her a questioning look.

—We're going to have a baby! she said.

—We're too old!

—Not *us!* Sarah and Benjamin.

—Oh, I said with relief.

—*Oh?* Is that all you have to say?

—I mean, oh, that's wonderful! We're going to be grandparents again. But how do you know?

—Sarah told me.

Eve came then and said, May I sit with you?

—Of course, we were just talking about...

—Sarah's baby, Eve answered.

—Does everyone know except me?

—You've been too busy, said Eve.

—You two talk, said Moriah. I'm going to sleep.

—You're sure I'm not disturbing you? Eve asked me.

—No, I said, patting a place near my side.

—How is it that we were saved at the very last moment? she asked. Is that the way of God?

—I've wondered about that myself, I said. I've come to think that God rescues us later rather than sooner to let the lesson of the situation burn more deeply into our souls.

—It seems like he's toying with us, she said.

—No. It's not in his character. Unfortunately, we tend to learn our lessons best in adversity.

—It seems a harsh way to learn.

—Perhaps, but I've never known anyone who has been through difficulty and has not come away without profound insight, not to mention the other blessings.

When Eve lay her head on my lap and fell asleep, I gazed up the mountain toward the City of Enoch. The people there knew of our journey and were preparing to gather us in. My longing to be there was exceeded only by my longing to see Benjamin again. Within the camp, all was winding down. Recent days had taken their toll—scaling sharp inclines, carving out trails through foggy vales, running for our lives. Our clothing had become soiled and ragged. The rations Enos had brought provided a supper, but most people were so exhausted that they only nibbled on it, then fell asleep. There was no singing or dancing. We ministered to blistered feet and wept over the destruction of Shum.

I mused over my observations of the day. Baruch doted over Rachel, Miriam's baby. The swelling in his face was receding, and he began to look like the man I had known. During the hike to the campsite, Joshua had walked next to Eve. On steep climbs, she had taken his arm, and they seemed to have plenty to talk about. That night, Nathaniel had taken his first step, and Sarah had wished that Benjamin had been there to see. I was reminded of Jerel's first step. The memory of his death still brought me to the point of tears.

ᴄꙅ

Morning brought the bleating of sheep. I sat up and looked around, but couldn't see through the haze. I called for Sarah.

—Leave Nathaniel with Eve, and come with me, I said. Benjamin has returned!

Sarah didn't wait for me. She handed Nathaniel to Eve and ran down the hillside toward the sounds of the bleating flock that had just entered the valley.

—Benjamin! Oh, Benjamin! she cried.

Sarah fell into her husband's arms, and they embraced and kissed, cried and laughed. When I caught up to them, Dog and Teah intercepted me and knocked me to the ground, licking my face, whining, jumping on me so that I couldn't rise.

—Come here! Benjamin called, offering them chaws of dried beef.

As my son extended a hand and pulled me to my feet, I hugged him and told him how I loved him. Then I stood back and gazed upon him, his sunburned skin, his tied-back hair, his shepherd's staff.

—You've found your life's work, I laughed, pointing at the sheep.

—I think I'd enjoy it, Father, he said.

—Come, you must eat and tell us everything.

—We have so much news, said Sarah, taking his arm.

Just then, the sun came into full view, and the sound of Enos blowing his ram's horn brought the camp to life. Benjamin, Sarah, and I walked into camp to the tears of family and friends.

Soon Enoch stood before the camp and said, Our God has made us a free people. The choice is ours to remain so. Today is a new beginning, for today we go up to the city of our God, even *Zion*.

It was the first time I had heard the word. In future days, the name *Zion* would become to me as common as my own name. At that moment, however, I had no idea what we people would suffer to learn the meaning of the name.

From above us, a sound came, like the rushing of a mighty wind. A trump sounded, and all in the camp looked up. The haze of morning melted before us, and the golden rays of sunlight burst upon the mountain of Zion, making the mount seem to rise from the mist, spire-like, crowned with brightness and glory.

If there is a heaven on earth, this is it, I thought.

The trump again sounded. I lifted my head and beheld an astounding sight. Down the mountain came the people of the City of

Enoch—Zion. They arrived, singing, falling upon our necks, kissing us. They lifted the loads from our backs and shouldered them. Then they took us by the hand and led us up the mountain to the City.

—Are you coming? Moriah asked me.

—Yes.

—Don't be long.

I kissed her, then she hurried off.

In a moment, I was alone. As I stepped to a high point overlooking the valley, I scanned the horizon and let the memories of my long journey to Zion linger in my mind. My heart swelled with deep emotions as I stood there.

I missed Jerel.

And I missed my father.

But I was grateful beyond words for my life, for my family, and for what I had learned: *No matter the difficulty, the journey to Zion is truly a journey home.*

છ

The bleating of a ewe turned my attention to the meadow below. The sounds of Dog and Teah gathering in the straying lambs filled my ears, penetrating my heart with sharp emotion. With not much effort, I could imagine an old shepherd leading his flock lovingly to a place of safety. He would stop when he saw me and beckon me to go with him. I knew I was willing to follow.

afterword

☙

That Zion existed in our world's past, and that Zion will exist in our world's future are verities.[1] Furthermore, the conditions of the world that preceded Enoch's Zion are astoundingly similar to those prophesied to precede the future Zion. Because, even at the outset when we authors first announced this ZION *Series*, there was such a clamoring for more information, we determined to include a brief sampling of some of the ancient and prophetic writings that helped us in writing this book. It should be noted that we made every attempt to use materials that crossed religious and cultures boundaries, seeking truth wherever we could find it. Commonality within the human family is startling, as we think you, the reader, will see.

We'll first look at the conditions our time ("the last days") and see how they're similar to the conditions of Enoch's time. Then we'll look at some of the similarities between the Zion of Enoch's day and the future Zion.

Once we more clearly see our place in history and better understand what the future Zion will be like, it will be easier for us to seek ways to start building Zion in our personal lives, our families, our neighborhoods, and our communities.

OUR PRESENT CONDITION: THE LAST DAYS

St. Paul, the Apostle, made a bold declaration to his companion, Timothy, about the conditions of "the last days"—the time in which we live. He said:

This know also, that *in the last days* perilous times shall come. For men shall be lovers of their own selves, covetous, boasters, proud, blasphemers, disobedient to parents, unthankful, unholy, without natural affection, trucebreakers, false accusers, incontinent, fierce, despisers of those that are good, traitors, heady, highminded, lovers of pleasures more than lovers of God; having a form of godliness, but denying the power thereof: from such turn away. For of this sort are they which creep into houses, and lead captive silly women laden with sins, led away with divers lusts, *ever learning, and never able to come to the knowledge of the truth.*"[2]

In all prophetic writ, is there a better description of the times defined as "the last days"? The conditions of "the last days" are also spoken of in many other ancient sources, including Jewish, Christian, and Hopi Indian prophecies.

One ancient prophet saw our day and described it as a time of "great pollutions upon the face of the earth." The "pollutions" he names are "murders, and robbing, and lying, and deceivings, and whoredoms, and all manner of abominations." These "pollutions" exist because the people of the last days "love [their] money . . . substance . . . and fine apparel more than [they] love the poor. [They] suffer the hungry, and the needy, and the naked, and the sick and the afflicted to pass by . . . and notice them not."[3] We see these "pollutions" all around us today.

Another prophet, Isaiah, tells of the many woes—calamities, suffering, and afflictions—that will come on the people of the last days and gives the reasons why. One woe goes to those who "have cast away the law of the Lord of hosts, and despised the word of the Holy One of Israel" and who presume to be "wise in their own eyes, and prudent in their own sight!" Another woe goes to those who "call evil good, and good evil; that put darkness for light, and light for darkness; that put bitter for sweet, and sweet for bitter!"[4] We see the people of our day exchanging the sweet goodness that God offers them for the bitter evils of our day.

Jesus, himself, spoke considerably of our day, as well, and the evils that would exist. He said that our day would be a time of "distress of nations, with perplexity," a time when "iniquity shall abound."[5]

The Hopi Indians of America were told nearly two thousand years ago by Massau'u, the great white brother from heaven who visited them and foretold what would happen to them to the end of this world, that in our day and time we would see great earthquakes, hot places turning cold and cold places becoming hot, drought and famine, a great hailstorm, storms that would destroy great places, wars and riots, and the government of the white men being mostly destroyed.

Massau'u prophesied to them that time would seem to speed up, fathers and mothers would no longer have time for their children, some men would change themselves to be women and some women change themselves to be men, and all things would be in commotion. But, he told them, after these destructions and changes would occur, which would cleanse the land of the wicked inhabitants, they would participate in the building of a great city of peace to which the peaceful ones of the world would come to join them. Truly a Zion.[6]

We have found numerous other cultures throughout the world who possess very similar prophetic views.

THE CONDITION OF THE PAST: ENOCH'S ERA

The time before Noah was an era marked by great upheavals in nature. It is two thousand years of which we know almost nothing. What we do know is often considered by some to be mystical, fabled, or just plain false—stories to amuse Sunday School children, too miraculous to be taken seriously by scientific thinkers.[7] Much of what we know about this time is compressed into a few chapters of Genesis in the Bible. We "modern" people like to think things change gradually, with only small differences between the earth's conditions from generation to generation. But scripture and other ancient writings speak of catastrophic changes: rivers washing up over the land, terrifying earthquakes, mountains moving, lands coming up out of the sea, the earth's continents dividing, and even a flood of such monumental proportions that it boggles the mind.[8] Clearly, if we have any faith at all in the eyewitnesses who wrote the documents, we must admit that the earth has had a dynamic past, and so have its people.

But, in attempting to understand that era of human history, we often get stuck on things that are beyond our comprehension—people living to extreme ages (969 years in Methuselah's case) and giants of extraordinary height, people who would tower over today's tallest race.

But what if there are plausible explanations?

The pre-Flood world condition actually seems very much like our present-day world. Moses wrote of that time, "The earth also was corrupt before God, and the earth was filled with violence. And God looked upon the earth, and, behold, it was corrupt; for all flesh had corrupted [their] way upon the earth."[9] An earth "filled with violence" is something we can understand today. That "all flesh" was "corrupt" gives us some sense of the widespread evils of the times and gives us an important clue as to why God had to wash that corruption away—a point that we of the last days should take note. (In Abraham's day, a number of generations after the flood, when even "ten righteous" could not be found in a city, God's justice demanded that the wickedness come to a screeching halt, and for Sodom and Gomorrah this was catastrophic.[10]) The writings of Enoch and other prophets show that the only solution to the horrendous wickedness that infested the whole world in the time between Enoch and Noah was to wash it clean and start over. There was no other cure.[11]

What kind of evils could there have been in Enoch's day? All kinds. Every kind.

To the people of his day, Enoch said, "Ye have not remembered the Lord in the days he gave you your riches; ye have gone astray that your riches shall not remain, because **you have done evil in everything.** Cursed are you and cursed are your riches."[12] In Enoch's day, the people were not just seeking riches, they were completely wicked and totally depraved.

It was a time of *misusing wealth and power.* From this we see how early in history we find the curse of the ages—man's craving for riches, wealth, and precious things. This sets the stage for all sorts of pernicious and perverted practices. In Enoch's day, the Watchers—the counterfeits to God's chosen prophets—had great knowledge but used it to establish an order of things in direct contradiction to what was intended by God. They actually attempted to surpass his power and used his name falsely to deceive the people.[13] Enoch's time was also marked by the lust for riches combined with illicit sex. Again, this was perpetrated mainly by the Watchers. An Enoch text reads: "And they brought gold and silver and metals, copper, and iron and all the treasures of the earth, so they married the women and begat the children of darkness; their hearts were closed up, and they became hard by this imitation false spirit."[14]

The merchants of Enoch's day followed a course that made a few rich and plunged the masses into poverty. Dr. Hugh Nibley says, "God recognizes only one justification for seeking wealth, and that is with the express intent of helping the poor. One of the disturbing things about Zion is that its appeal, according to the scriptures, is all to the poor: *'The Lord hath founded Zion, and the poor of his people shall trust in it'.*"[15] "But God has no objection to man's enjoyment of the good things of the earth. What he condemns in the strongest and clearest language is the *unequal* enjoyment of them."[16] Of course, we've heard that "the love of money is the root of all evil" so much that we tend to dismiss it, but isn't it interesting that people have put wealth ahead of God for thousands of years?[17]

Enoch's was a time of *perversions in the social order.* Talking to his son, Methuselah, Enoch said, "In the days of Jared my father, they [the people of the world] transgressed the covenant of heaven; they sinned and betrayed the law of the gospel. They mingled with women and sinned with them. They also married and bore children, *but not according to the spirit, but by the carnal order only.*"[18] Other descriptions of Enoch's day include such things as "Men dressing like women; women like men."[19] Dr. Hugh Nibley, who has researched Enoch and his day extensively, says, "The peculiar evil of the times consisted not so much in the catalog of human viciousness as in the devilish and systematic efficiency with which corruption was being riveted permanently to the social order."[20]

The Apocalypse of Paul says, "They despised the Most High, scorned his laws, and forsook his way. Slavery was not given from above but came by transgression, and *the barrenness of your women does not come by nature but by your willful perversions.*"[21] This is an interesting condition of ancient times—women becoming barren because of "willful perversions." One of these perversions is curtailing the bearing of children, which the Book of Jasher mentions: "For in those days the sons of men began to trespass against God, and to transgress the commandments which he had commanded to Adam, to be fruitful and multiply in the earth. And some of the sons of men caused their wives to drink a draught that would render them barren, in order that they might retain their figures and *whereby* their beautiful appearance might not fade."[22]

It was a time of *violence and murders*. The teachings of the Watchers "fill[ed] all the earth with blood and wickedness as the cries of the slain ascend[ed] to the gates of heaven, their groaning come[s] up and cannot depart because of the crimes being committed upon the face of the earth."[23]

It was a time of *secret oaths and forswearing*. Disavowing God, committing perjury before him, and creating societies based on secret oaths to do evil without getting caught were all great calamities of Enoch's time, and prophecy attests that these same evils will mark the generation of the last days. A "voice from heaven" telling Enoch of the wickedness of his day included these words: "By their oaths, they have foresworn themselves, and, by their oaths, they have brought upon themselves death."[24] One of the leaders of the Watchers, Semiazus, is quoted as saying: "I fear you will not be willing to do this thing." So his followers respond, "Let us swear an oath and bind ourselves all to each other. Then they all swore oaths and bound each other by them."[25] Essentially, they inverted the laws and ordinances of God, while at the same time professing loyalty to God.

It was a time of *secret acts and abominations.* Of other evils, the Psalm of Solomon, says: "The secret places of the earth were doing evil, the son lay with the mother and the father with the daughter, all of them committed adultery with their neighbor's wives, they made solemn covenants among themselves concerning these things."[26] The Watchers led away "myriads and myriads . . . with their Prince Satanel, and defiled the earth by their acts. And the wives of men did a great evil, violating the law . . . a great iniquity."[27] "In secret places underground they wrought confusion; . . . They committed adultery, every man with his neighbor's wife. They concluded covenants with one another with an oath touching these things."[28]

It was a time of *twisted and perverted thinking, words, and actions.* The people of that time employed *rhetoric,* "defined by Plato as the art of making true things seem false and false things seem true by the use of words."[29] By rhetoric, they learned to talk their way out of the inconvenient laws of God and could thereby assume an air of respectability and virtue. They even convinced themselves that they were good, because they were rich—a kind of piety-equals-success kind of thinking.

Contrary to what many people assume, the ancient world enjoyed a high degree of enlightenment and technological sophistication. Numerous ancient writings speak of the people as being skilled in chemistry, the construction of weaponry, jewelry, and cosmetics. "They knew all the arts and all the ruling principles that governed the cosmos."[30] Rabbi Yasah posed this question: "With all that knowledge could they not foresee destruction?" To which Rabbi Isaac answered, "They knew, all right, but they thought they were just smart enough to prevent it, *but what they did not know was that God rules the world.*"[31] They thought they could outsmart God and get beyond his power. They were like Cain, thinking he could kill and not be found out by God. That arrogance and haughty confidence in their own technological and scientific knowledge made them singularly culpable when they used them against God. Dr. Nibley has stated, "In Enoch's time, they had all sorts of engineering projects for controlling and taming nature. The same scientific prowess that led them to reject God led them to insult nature."[32]

In short, the whole world fell into disarray to the point that it could never be set right—it could only become worse. And these evils will always yield the same results—more woes: "Woe unto you who deliberately go astray, who promote yourselves to honor and glory by deceitful practices. . . . Who misapply and misinterpret straightforward statements, who have given a new twist to the everlasting Covenant, and then produce arguments to prove that you are without guilt!"[33] "Their ruin is accomplished because they have learned all the secrets of the angels and all the violence of Satan."[34]

Do we see any parallels in our present-day world and that in which Enoch lived?

ENOCH AND ZION

Today, Enoch is virtually unknown. Unlike Noah, Moses, Christ, Buddha, Allah—each of whom most adults can describe in some detail—few people know anything about the seventh patriarch from Adam. The entire King James version of the Old Testament contains only six verses about Enoch, and five of those verses are about his genealogy, children, and his age. The sixth verse says only: "And Enoch walked with God: and he was not; for God took him."[35]

From many ancient texts, we learn that Enoch was endowed with power to do his work. The records say he had but to speak the word of the Lord and the mountains shook and rivers turned from their courses. He was given power from on high to lead the people of God in their migration, to build their city, and to begin a thousand-year missionary program to call people to repentance and assimilate them into Zion. **As the great-grandfather of Noah, who continued his work, Enoch is the common father to the entire human family as it exists on the earth today.**

Enoch was a builder of temples and taught his people sacred truths within those walls. In the Prayer of Kheriuf, comparing Thoth to Enoch, it says he "established speech and writing, causing the temples to flourish."[36] In the various books of Enoch, we find that he taught his people of the "Messiah," "the Son of Man," "the Elect One." He taught them that they must point their lives to Him to obtain Eternal Life.[37]

In the New Testament, three verses specifically refer to Enoch. However, these few biblical verses provide little insight into such an important character. It's interesting to note, however, that both Paul and Jude refer to Enoch to illustrate a doctrinal point, implying that their listeners were familiar with Enoch:

"And Enoch also, the seventh from Adam, prophesied of these, saying, Behold the Lord cometh with ten thousand of his saints, To execute judgement upon all, and to convince all that are ungodly among them of all their ungodly deeds which they have ungodly committed, and of all their hard speeches which ungodly sinners have spoken against him."[38] "By faith Enoch was translated that he should not see death; and was not found, because God had translated him: for before his translation he had this testimony, that he pleased God."[39] Both Genesis and Hebrews mention an intriguing declaration about Enoch, that of his being "translated," or that "God took him." Now, this goes against everything we see about us. The most learned scientist or medical professional will attest that all life-forms die. But there it is in the Bible: Enoch was translated—taken by God to heaven without experiencing death. (According to other sources, all his people in Zion were taken with him.) Ancient texts tell us that, once Enoch and his people were gone, the saying went abroad, "Zion is fled."[40] That the most notable city in the world was gone made an immeasurable impact. Other texts say that some 600,000 men went with him. Multiply that number by wives and children, and the departure of Enoch's Zion was earth-shaking. And the greatest Zion is yet to come.

THE FUTURE ZION: A PLACE OF REFUGE

Joseph, the son of Jacob, whose story is told in Genesis, as well as in several other writings, was promised that a day would come in the end of times when his posterity would build a mighty city of peace, a "city of refuge." In some texts, it is referred to as the New Jerusalem. Enoch and his translated city are to come down out of heaven and join with the New Jerusalem after the creation of that latter-day Zion.

The Book of Joseph and Aseneth tells the story of Aseneth, Joseph's wife, being visited by an angel of the Lord before she became betrothed to Joseph. He informs Aseneth that she has been chosen of the Lord to be the wife of Joseph, then prophesies to her that from her loins will one day come a mighty city of refuge: "And your name shall no longer be called Aseneth, but your name shall be City of Refuge, because in you many nations will take refuge with the Lord God, the Most High, and under your wings many peoples trusting in the Lord God will be sheltered, and behind your walls will be guarded those who attach themselves to the Most High God in the name of Repentance."[41]

Many Jewish and Christian scholars believe the City of Refuge mentioned here to Aseneth is the same Zion of the future described by Isaiah when he wrote: "Therefore the redeemed of the Lord shall return, and come with singing unto Zion; and everlasting joy shall be upon their head: they shall obtain gladness and joy; and sorrow and mourning shall flee away."[42] Isaiah continues his description saying: "And all thy children shall be taught of the Lord; and great shall be the peace of thy children. In righteousness shalt thou be established: thou shalt be far from oppression; for thou shalt not fear: and from terror; for it shall not come near thee. Whosoever shall gather together against thee shall fall for thy sake."[43]

The Hopi Indians, as well as the Tibetans, believe that this forthcoming utopian society will be a city or society of peace and light, to which all who desire to live in peace, safety, and in harmony with God, their neighbors, as well as nature, shall desire to gather. Christian texts speak of it as a great city of peace and a refuge on a hill, a light unto the world, an ensign of peace to which all the righteous of the nations will flow.

A future Zion has been much anticipated by many cultures and religions. It is often referred to as a city or place of refuge. Many civilizations, both ancient and modern, have been founded upon the proposition that our earthly order should be a faithful reflection of the heavenly. A list of some of these utopians would include Abraham, Moses, Pindar, Plutarch, Solon, Pythagoras, Isaiah, Plato, Virgil, Horace, Petronius, Salvian, Anthony, Pachomius, the people of Qumran, the Essenes, the Gnostics, the Carpocratians, the Montanists, Benedict of Nursia, St. Bernard, the Templars, the Hospitalers, the Knights of St. John, the Knights of Malta, the Franciscans, the Dominicans, the Carmelites, Joachim of Fiore, John Wycliffe, Gerhard Degroot, Savonarola, Martin Luther, Sir Thomas More, Thomas Campanella, Francis Bacon, Joseph Smith, Brigham Young, and the Founding Fathers of the United States. The Founding Fathers placed Virgil's words on the Great Seal, *novus ordo seclorum*— "the new order of the ages," to indicate their belief in such a society.[44]

In fact, Thomas Jefferson, James Madison, John Adams, and Benjamin Franklin studied the Bible in great detail to derive the principles for the foundation of the Constitution. Of the thousands of documents and sources they cited in their research, thirty-four percent were from the Bible.[45] The Founders believed ancient Israel had been given the formula for a utopian society through Moses. But because of wickedness, Israel lost their opportunity and were scattered. However, Moses told them that after being scattered throughout all the world, the day would come in which they would be gathered to build a Zion.[46] It was this mission many of the Founding Fathers saw themselves fulfilling. (See the Appendix that follows about George Washington.) Many believed they were establishing the foundation for that Zion to eventually be realized. John Adams stated: "I always consider the establishment of America with reverence and wonder, as the opening of a grand scene and design in Providence for the illumination of the ignorant, and the emancipation of the slavish part of mankind all over the world."[47] It became commonplace for early Americans to speak of America as the New Israel or new Zion. Some even referred to the Massachusetts Bay Colony as the New Jerusalem.[48]

As can be seen, throughout history, great people have longed for a better world and have tried to do something about it. Yet unsuccessful utopian efforts, failed monastic movements, disbanded communal arrangements, and even half a century of Communism, teach us that a good vision carried out with a bad strategy produces very bad results. Apparently understanding the principles of Zion is as important as recognizing our yearning for Zion. Enoch and his city give us a model to study of a people who succeeded.

An ancient Mandean text offers this description of the forthcoming Zion: "There the saints live without discord or dissension. . . [they are] wise and gentle, without malice or deceit, constantly visiting each other. There is perfect agreement . . . each . . . rejoicing in the glory of the others as all share their treasures of knowledge with each other. . . . They all share a common glorious awareness of each other. . . . Having no law courts, no hunger or thirst, no cold or heat, no hatred or fear, no war, no slavery, no harmful creatures or plants. Magnificent buildings stand beside tranquil seas; flowing springs give life-giving water. Everything vibrates with joy. The wants of the people are few. . . . Their beauty is within them and shines out, as if they were of pure crystal. Force also flows through them from the King as they open themselves to it by persevering in prayer and song. They study and meditate constantly; they exhale the fragrance of divine happiness."[49]

Zion is described as "the pure in heart," those "of one heart and one mind."[50] From these descriptions, we see that Zion is first established in the hearts of individuals, and these hearts are pure. *Pure* means not mixed with anything else, not dirty or filthy in any way, clean and whole. The people with pure hearts unite their efforts to establish a Zion people by covenant. Zion has no poor.[51] The wicked both fear it and call it treasonous, because God protects it and because Zion will not mix with the world. Zion is the heavenly city, the hope of the world.

From the Isle of Patmos, St. John wrote a vision he had of the history of the world with special emphasis on the last days. Of that future event, John writes, "And I John saw the holy city, new Jerusalem [one of the many names for Zion], coming down from God out of heaven, prepared as a bride adorned for her husband. And I heard a great voice out of heaven saying, Behold, the tabernacle of God is with men, and he will dwell with them, and they shall be his people, and God himself shall be with them, and be their God. And God shall wipe away all tears from their eyes; and there shall be no more death, neither sorrow, nor crying, neither shall there be any more pain: for the former things have passed away."[52]

In every description of the future Zion, whether it be from Isaiah, Enoch, John, angelic ministers, Mausau'u, or from God himself, the picture is clearly of a society far surpassing the beauty, peace, intellect, and love of our present world. It is a place where each resident is looking out for his neighbor rather than himself only—a paradise for the poor and meek of the earth.

Much of what we have written has to do with the Christian belief in a utopian future. But our research has uncovered many additional sources from various religions and cultures around the earth that provide significant detail about their belief in the future advent of a Zion-like society, a city of peace and glory. This message is a central tenet and belief of Jews, Christians, the Hopi of America, the Lamaists of Tibet, the Mahayana of China, and the Kukuyu tribe of Africa—to name just a few. The yearnings for the "City of Peace" seems to be nearly universal in the hearts of good people. Of particular interest are the Books of Enoch found among the Dead Sea Scrolls. These writings include portions of nearly eight hundred ancient documents, including books by important biblical prophets such as Isaiah.[53] However, one of the most prominent works in the collection, with over twenty copies—a very high total for any work at Qumran (the area where the scrolls were discovered), is the Book of Enoch.[54] The people of this ancient community were apparently very familiar with Enoch and his teachings of a future-day Zion. Other important texts include the Book of Jasher, the Book of Moses, the Hekhalot, the Ethiopic Book of Enoch the Prophet (Enoch I), the Slavonic Book of Enoch (Enoch II), and the Hebraic Book of Enoch (Enoch III). In writing this story, we incorporated the key ideas found in these and other ancient texts.

OUR PURPOSE: WE YEARN FOR ZION

As we watch the news or read the paper, we are barraged with daily reminders of the violence, abuse, immorality, and other evils that surround us. Even the physical safety of our families has become uncertain. We long for the peace and security of Zion. We are not suggesting that people should abandon society, isolate themselves in the hills, grow beards, and chant. We are suggesting, however, that it is possible to do better.

From our research, we believe Zion begins with the individual living a Zion-like life. Zion then grows as families, one by one, create Zion at home. And, we believe that many individuals and families, working together, transform their communities. By studying a people who succeeded in realizing a Zion society, we may learn principles that will help us transform our own conditions.

We have come to believe that scriptures and other ancient sources, though not well known in our modern society, are very relevant to the problems and challenges we face today. Somehow, in the midst of violence, hatred, widespread war, social decline, and the corruption of every moral principle, an ancient people joined together to form a society of peace, spectacular advancement, a city completely free of crime, pollutions, and contention.

There is a very real commonality that exists among all the peoples of the earth. It is most evident in the discussion of a future Zion society. Perhaps by our seeking to join together with those of the "pure in heart," who desire to see the day when such a Zion will exist, to discuss the steps for obtaining such, we will be able to hasten the day of its arrival.

Why are we researching about Zion and writing the *ZION* series? Simply put, we yearn for Zion. Our deepest desire is that this series of books will further the dialogue of what Zion is and how it can be realized.

So, What's Next?

Four volumes are planned in the *ZION* series. Each will describe how Enoch and his people progressed, failed, and ultimately succeeded. We will attempt to emphasize the principles upon which that Zion was built and how it will be established again. As you read Rabunel's remarkable journey, we challenge you to see the parallels and possibilities in your own life.

Beyond that, we have created a Website to collect prophecies and legends that exist throughout the world concerning Zion.

Visit us at **www.zionpeople.org**. Look through our collections, and add your own thoughts or materials.

You can also email us at **info@zionpeople.org**.

—*Larry, Lance, and Ron*

appendix

CB

An appendix to a work of fiction may seem strange, but we have included this one because of its relevance to events surrounding the coming of Zion and because it was a most remarkable event in the history of the United States of America.

It is widely known that George Washington was a man of prayer. In a most critical era, the winter when his army was at Valley Forge, he retired to a thicket many times to pray. Little publicity has been given to the vision and prophecy he received at that time. The account of this vision was given in 1859 by Anthony Sherman, an old soldier in Washington's army. Wesley Bradshaw recorded and published Sherman's words.

Wesley Bradshaw later wrote, "The last time I ever saw Anthony Sherman was on the fourth of July, 1859, in Independence Square. He was then ninety-nine years old, and becoming very feeble. But though so old, his dimming eyes rekindled as he gazed upon Independence Hall, which he came to visit once more."

Sherman told Bradshaw the story of Washington's vision saying that the nation would soon see the account verified by the "second peril" descending upon the land. In the vision, according to Sherman, an angel sent from God revealed to George Washington that three great perils would come upon the Republic.

To us as authors, the following information is of utmost importance to the subject of Zion: (1) Two perils have passed, and the third may be imminent. Why is that important to the subject of Zion? Because, according to legend and prophecy, an era and place of peace will follow a period of strife such as the world has never known. (2) Washington was told, in our opinion, a way to survive the "third peril."

Except for minor editing and emphasis markings, we include the account as it was reprinted in the December, 1880 *National Tribune*, a U.S. veterans of war publication, which is today called *Stars and Stripes*. The December 21, 1950, issue of *Stars and Stripes* printed this article again.

GEORGE WASHINGTON'S VISION OF AMERICA

"Let us go into the hall (Independence Hall)," he (Sherman) said. "I want to tell you of an incident of Washington's life—one which no one alive knows of except myself; and if you live, you will before long see it verified. Mark the prediction, you will see it verified.

"From the opening of the Revolution we experienced all phases of fortune, now good and now ill, one time victorious and another conquered. The darkest period we had, I think, was when Washington after several reverses, retreated to Valley Forge, where he resolved to pass the winter of 1777. Ah! I have often seen the tears coursing down our dear commander's care-worn cheeks, as he would be conversing with a confidential officer about the condition of his poor soldiers. You have doubtless heard the story of Washington's going to the thicket to pray. Well, it was not only true, but he used often to pray in secret for aid and comfort. And God brought us safely through the darkest days of tribulation.

"One day, I remember it well, the chilly winds whistled through the leafless trees, though the sky was cloudless and the sun shone brightly. He remained in his quarters nearly all the afternoon, alone.

When he came out I noticed that his face was a shade paler than usual, and there seemed to be something on his mind of more than ordinary importance. Returning just after dusk, he dispatched an orderly to the quarters of an officer, who was presently in attendance. After a preliminary conversation of about half an hour, Washington, gazing upon his companion with that strange look of dignity which he alone could command, said to the latter:

'I do not know whether it is owing to the anxiety of my mind, or what, but this afternoon, as I was sitting at this table engaged in preparing a dispatch, something in the apartment seemed to disturb me. Looking up, I beheld standing opposite me a singularly beautiful being. So astonished was I, for I had given strict orders not to be disturbed that it was some moments before I found language to inquire the cause of the visit. A second, a third, and even a fourth time did I repeat my question, but received no answer from my mysterious visitor except a slight raising of the eyes.

'By this time I felt strange sensations spreading through me. I would have risen but the riveted gaze of the being before me rendered volition impossible. I assayed once more to speak, but my tongue had become useless, as if paralyzed. A new influence, mysterious, potent, irresistible, took possession of me. All I could do was to gaze steadily, vacantly at my unknown visitor.

'Gradually the surrounding atmosphere seemed to fill with sensations, and grew luminous. Everything about me seemed to rarefy, the mysterious visitor also becoming more airy and yea more distinct to my sight than before. I began to feel as one dying, or rather to experience the sensations which I have sometimes imagined accompany death. I did not think, I did not reason, I did not move. All were alike impossible. I was only conscious of gazing fixedly, vacantly at my companion.

First Great Peril

'Presently I heard a voice saying, *Son of the Republic, look and learn,* while at the same time my visitor extended an arm eastward. I now beheld a heavy white vapor at some distance rising fold upon fold. This gradually dissipated, and I looked upon a strange scene. Before me lay, spread out in one vast plain, all the countries of the world— Europe, Asia, Africa and America. I saw rolling and tossing between Europe and America the billows of the Atlantic, and between Asia and America lay the Pacific. *Son of the Republic,* said the same mysterious voice as before, *look and learn.*

'At that moment I beheld a dark, shadowy being, like an angel, standing, or rather floating in mid-air, between Europe and America. Dipping water out of the ocean in the hollow of each hand, he sprinkled some upon America with his right hand, while with his left he cast some over Europe. Immediately a cloud arose from these countries, and joined in mid-ocean. For a while it remained stationary, and then it moved slowly westward, until it enveloped America in its murky folds. Sharp flashes of lightning gleamed through it at intervals, and I heard the smothered groans and cries of the American people.

Second Great Peril

'A second time the angel dipped water from the ocean and sprinkled it out as before. The dark cloud was then drawn back to the ocean, in whose heaving billows it sank from view.

'A third time I heard the mysterious voice saying, *Son of the Republic. look and learn.* I cast my eyes upon America and beheld villages and towns and cities springing up one after another until the whole land from the Atlantic to the Pacific was dotted with them. Again, I heard the mysterious voice say, *Son of the Republic, the end of the century cometh, look and learn.*

'And this time the dark shadowy angel turned his face southward. From Africa I saw an ill-omened specter approach our land. It flitted slowly and heavily over every town and city of the latter. The inhabitants presently set themselves in battle array against each other. As I continued looking I saw a bright angel on whose brow rested a crown of light, on which was traced the word UNION. He was bearing the American flag. He placed the flag between the divided nation and said, Remember, ye are brethren. Instantly the inhabitants, casting down their weapons, became friends once more and united around the National Standard.

'Again I heard the mysterious voice saying, Son of the Republic look and learn. At this the dark, shadowy angel placed a trumpet to his mouth, and blew three distinct blasts; and taking water from the ocean, he sprinkled it upon Europe, Asia and Africa.

THIRD AND MOST FEARFUL PERIL

'Then my eyes beheld a fearful scene. From each of these continents arose thick black clouds that were soon joined into one. And throughout this mass there gleamed a dark red light by which I saw hordes of armed men. These men, moving with the cloud, marched by land and sailed by sea to America, which country was enveloped in the volume of the cloud. And I dimly saw these vast armies devastate the whole country and burn the villages, towns, and cities which I had seen springing up.

'As my ears listened to the thundering of the cannon, clashing of the swords, and the shouts and cries of millions in mortal combat, I again heard the mysterious voice saying, Son of the Republic, look and learn. Where the voice had ceased, the dark shadowy angel placed his trumpet once more to his mouth, and blew a long and fearful blast.

Heaven Intervenes

'Instantly a light as of a thousand suns shone down from above me, and pierced and broke into fragments the dark cloud which enveloped America. At the same moment the angel upon whose head still shown the word UNION, and who bore our national flag in one hand, and a sword in the other, descended from the heavens attended by legions of white spirits. These immediately joined the inhabitants of America, who I perceived were well-nigh overcome, but who immediately taking courage again, closed up their broken ranks and renewed the battle.

'Again, amid the fearful noise of the conflict I heard the mysterious voice saying, *Son of the Republic, look and learn.* As the voice ceased the shadowy angel for the last time dipped water from the ocean and sprinkled it upon America. Instantly the dark cloud rolled back, together with the armies it had brought, leaving the inhabitants of the land victorious.

'Then once more, I beheld the villages, towns and cities springing up where I had seen them before, while the bright angel, planting the azure standard he had brought in the midst of them, cried with a loud voice, *While the stars remain and the heaven send down dew upon the earth, so long shall the UNION last.* And taking from his brow the crown on which blazoned the word UNION, he placed it upon the Standard while the people kneeling down said, *Amen.*

'The scene instantly began to fade and dissolve, and I, at last saw nothing but the rising, curling vapor I at first beheld. This also disappeared, and I found myself once more gazing upon the mysterious visitor, who, in the same voice I had heard before, said, *Son of the Republic, what you have seen is thus interpreted, Three great perils will come upon the Republic. The most fearful for her is the third. But the whole world united shall not prevail against her.* **Let every child of the Republic learn to live for his God, his land, and UNION.** With these words the vision vanished, and I started from my seat and felt that I had seen a vision wherein had been shown me the birth, the progress, and destiny of the United States.' "

references

⚭

1. The sources we list here are only a sampling of what will eventually be available at our Website. Visit us at **www.zionpeople.org**. We reproduce here the quotation found at the beginning of this book in order for easier comparison with other versions of the same passage we include here:

For I do know the mysteries of the holy ones; for he, the Lord, has revealed (them) to me and made me know—and I have read (them) in the heavenly tablets. Then I beheld the writing upon them that one generation shall be more wicked than the other, until a generation of righteous ones shall arise, wickedness shall perish, sin shall disappear from upon the earth, and every good thing shall come upon her.

—1 Enoch 106:19–107:1, in James E. Charlesworth, *The Old Testament Pseudepigrapha*, 2 vols. (Garden City, NY: Doubleday & Company, 1983–85), 1:87–88. This quotation from 1 Enoch is a translation from Ethiopic, and the entire book of "1 Enoch is preserved only in Ethiopic" in "more than forty manuscripts." Fragments exist of 1 Enoch in Aramaic, Greek, and Latin. Charlesworth, 1:6. "The full text of [1 Enoch] is preserved only in an Ethiopic translation of a Greek rendering of the Semitic original (written in Hebrew or Aramaic)." James C. VanderKam, *The Dead Sea Scrolls Today* (Grand Rapids, MI: William B. Eerdmans, 1994), 37.

One of the Aramaic fragments of 1 Enoch found in Cave 4 at Qumran contains this same passage:

For I know the mysteries [of the Lord which] the Holy Ones have told me and have shown me [and which] I read in [the tablets] of heaven. In them I saw written that generation after generation will perpetrate evil in this way and there will be wickedness [until there arise] generations of justice and the wickedness and corruption end and violence [vanishes] from the earth, and until [goodness comes to the earth] above them.

—1 Enoch 106:26–29, in Florentino García Martínez, *The Dead Sea Scrolls Translated: The Qumran Texts in English*, 2d ed. (Grand Rapids, MI: William B. Eerdmans, 1996), 254, translated from 4QEnoch[d] (4Q205 [4QEn[d] ar]), frag. 5, col. II. Text in brackets indicates "partially preserved text." (See Martínez, xxvi.) "Among the many fragments found in Cave 4, a relatively large number of manuscripts of Enoch have appeared. All of them are written in the Aramaic language." VanderKam, 37.

Here's the same passage of 1 Enoch translated in 1821 from an Ethiopic manuscript:

For I am acquainted with holy mysteries, which the Lord himself has discovered and explained to me; and which I have read in the tablets of heaven. In them I saw it written, that generation after generation shall transgress, until a righteous race shall arise; until transgression and crime perish from off the earth; until all goodness come upon it.

—1 Enoch 105:16–17, in Richard Laurence, *The Book of Enoch the Prophet* (London: Kegan Paul, 1883), 177.

Another version of the same passage of 1 Enoch:

For I know the mysteries of the holy ones; for He, the Lord, has showed me and informed me, and I have read (them) in the heavenly tablets. And I saw written on them that generation upon generation shall transgress, till a generation of righteousness arises, and transgression is destroyed and sin passes away from the earth, and all manner of good comes upon it.
—Fragment of the Book of Noah 106:19–107:1, in R. H. Charles, *The Apocrypha and Pseudepigrapha of the Old Testament in English*, 2 vols (Oxford: Clarendon Press, 1913), 2:279–80. The Fragment of the Book of Noah is a portion of 1 Enoch that circulated separately but is considered part of 1 Enoch.

A more recent translation from 1 Enoch:
For I know the secrets *of heaven,* for the angels (lit. The holy ones) have shown me and informed me, and I have read them in the heavenly tablets. And I beheld written in them that generation after generation shall wrong them (the descendants of Noah), and wrong shall continue, until there shall arise generations of righteousness; and evil and godlessness shall come to an end, and injustice cease from off the earth, and all blessings shall come on the earth upon them.

—Matthew Black, *The Book of Enoch or I Enoch* (Leiden: E. J. Brill, 1985), 100–101.

A final translation of the same passage from 1 Enoch, this one from Greek:
[. . . . the Lord] has showed them and made them known to me, and I have read [them in] the tablets of heaven. Then I beheld that which was written upon them, that one generation shall be worse than another; and this I saw until there shall arise a generation of righteousness, and wickedness shall perish, and sin shall depart from the earth and blessings shall come to them upon the earth.

—Campbell Bonner, *The Last Chapters of Enoch in Greek* (Darmstadt, Germany: Wissenschaftliche Buchgesellschaft, 1968), 96.

2. 2 Timothy 3:1–7, emphasis added.

3. Mormon 8:31, 37, 39; see also 3 Nephi 16:9, 30:2.

4. Isaiah 5:13, 20–21, 24.

5. Luke 21:25; Matthew 24:12.

6. Personal interviews with Hopi Indian Tribal Council Elders, March 1998. See also Zula C. Brinkerhoff, *God's Chosen People of America* (Salt Lake City: Publisher's Press, 1971), 69–80, 193–200. See also Frank Waters, *Book of the Hopi* (New York: Viking Press, 1963), 334.

7. Hugh Nibley, *Enoch the Prophet* (Salt Lake City: Deseret Book, 1986), 66–67.

8. Ibid., 12–14, 74–75; see also Genesis 6–8, 10:25; Moses 7:13–14.

9. Genesis 6:11–12.

10. Genesis 18:23–19:26.

11. See 1 Enoch 107:13–18; Moses 7–8.

12. Nibley, *Enoch the Prophet,* 8, 71, emphasis added.

13. Ibid., 8–9, 71.

14. Ibid., 9, 71–72.

15. Hugh Nibley, *Approaching Zion* (Salt Lake City: Deseret Book, 1989), 53, emphasis added. See Jacob 2:19, Isaiah 14:32.

16. Hugh Nibley, *An Approach to the Book of Mormon,* 3d ed. (Salt Lake City: Deseret Book, 1988), 53.

17. It's still true, of course, that those who covet after riches "fall into temptation and a snare," and some who do so will apostatize "from the faith, and [pierce] themselves through with many sorrows." See 1 Timothy 6:6–11.

18. Nibley, *Enoch the Prophet,* 11, 73, 181, emphasis added.

19. Ibid., 8, 71.

20. Ibid., 8, 71. We're heavily indebted to Dr. Nibley and thank him for his painstaking efforts.

21. Ibid., 16, 76.

22. *The Book of Jasher* 11:19–20, in *The Book of Jasher* (Muskogee, OK: Artisan Publishers, 1988), 4. This is a reprint of an 1840 translation.

23. Nibley, *Enoch the Prophet,* 10.
24. Moses 6:27, 29.
25. Nibley, *Enoch the Prophet,* 10, 72.
26. Ibid., 11.
27. Ibid., 181.
28. Ibid.
29. Nibley, *Approaching Zion,* 45.
30. Nibley, *Enoch the Prophet,* 17, 78.
31. Ibid.
32. Ibid, 18, 79.
33. Ibid., 181. "Woe to you who pervert the eternal covenant and reckon yourselves sinless." Ibid., 9, 11, 73.
34. Ibid., 10, 73.
35. Genesis 5:24. For Enoch's day, see also Norman L. Heap, *Adam, Enoch, and Noah* (Walnut Creek, CA: Family History Publications, 1992).
36. Nibley, *Enoch the Prophet,* 47.
37. Moses 6–7.
38. Jude 1:14, 15.
39. Hebrews 11:5. By Dr. Nibley's count, Enoch is quoted at least 128 times in the New Testament. See Nibley, *Enoch the Prophet,* 8, and Nibley, *Approaching Zion,* 317.
40. Moses 7:69.
41. Joseph and Aseneth 15:7, in Charlesworth, *The Old Testament Pseudepigrapha,* 2:226–27.
42. Isaiah 51:11.
43. Isaiah 54:13–15.
44. Nibley, *Approaching Zion,* 487–523.
45. Donald S. Lutz, "The relative influence of European writers on late eighteenth-century American political thought," *American Political Science Review* 78 (1984), 189–97. Conrad Cherry, *God's New Israel* (Englewood Cliffs, NJ: Prentice-Hall, 1971), 61–66.
46. Deuteronomy 30:1–2.
47. W. Cleon Skousen, *The Majesty of God's Law* (Salt Lake City: Ensign Publishing, 1996), 19. See also 10–30.

48. Cherry, *God's New Israel*, 1–30. See also Stephen Birmingham, *The Grandees: America's Sephardic Elite* (New York: Harper & Row, 1971).
49. Nibley, *Enoch the Prophet*, 261.
50. Doctrine and Covenants 97:21, Moses 7:18.
51. Moses 7:18.
52. Revelation 21:2–4.
53. Martínez, *The Dead Sea Scrolls Translated*, xxiv.
54. VanderKam, *The Dead Sea Scrolls Today*, 155.